A Testimony

EJV International
Editions NEW YORK, 2022

www:diegoarria.com
twitter@Diego_Arria
Instagram: www.diegoarria.com
www.facebook.com/Arria.Diego/

Ediciones EJV International
Avda. Francisco Solano López, Torre Oasis, P.B.,
Local 4, Sabana Grande,
Apartado 17.598 – Caracas, 1015, Venezuela
Teléfono 762.25.53, 762.38.42. Fax. 763.5239
Email: ejvinternational@gmail.com
http://www.editorialjuridicavenezolana.com.ve

ISBN: 979-8-88680-249-8

Printed by: Lightning Source, an INGRAM Content company
for Editorial Jurídica Venezolana International Inc.
Panamá, República de Panamá

Translation by Carlos Bivero and Diana Volpe
Cover photo: Manuela Arria-Maury
Cover design: Liliana Acosta

Layout, composition and editing by: Mirna Pinto, in print
Palatino Linotype 12, Line spacing 13, Stain 11.5 x 18

To my daughters Karina, Camila and Manuela,
Who grew up hearing me talk about this process,
And have always been my inspiration.

CONTENTS

By Way of Introduction

On the evening of December 25, 1991, Yuli Vorontsov, the Soviet Ambassador to the United Nations Security Council, came into the room and made the announcement: "The Union of Soviet Socialist Republics has ceased to exist!"

The Ambassadors of Colombia, Mexico, Spain and Venezuela were in a meeting with the UN Secretary General Javier Pérez de Cuellar at his official residence, where he had convened us in an effort to give the final push to a peace agreement in El Salvador. For the last three years our governments had been acting as mediators in the negotiations between the government of El Salvador and the guerrilla leaders of the Farabundo Martí National Liberation Front, FMLN, to end a war that was tearing apart that Central American nation since 1981.

With those ten words Vorontsov cut short our meeting. They summarized the surprising and historical event. We welcomed the news with enthusiasm since it meant not only that the Cold War had ended, but also that the FMLN had lost the only ally it still had. On December 31, close to an hour after midnight, the parties signed the Peace Agreement.

War and Genocide in the Heart of Europe is based on my personal experience as Ambassador of Venezuela to the United Nations and as President of the Security Council, the UN organ charged with safeguarding international peace and security, at a time when international politics were set to undergo dramatic changes. I arrived at the United Nations in mid-1990, when the USSR was already in the throes of extinction and the East-West confrontation, which had defined the Security Council almost since its inception, had ceased to dominate its proceedings.

We believed that from that crucial moment on, its effectiveness no longer hampered by a veto by one or the other Cold War contenders, the Council would at last be able to exercise its authority and fully devote itself to strengthening peace and the respect of human rights, ensuring the sovereignty and security of all the nations of the world without discrimination. The invasion of Kuwait by Saddam Hussein's regime in August 1990 would put to the test the new reality. It represented an inflexion point in the history of the United Nations and it was in that context that I had to take charge of my complex responsibilities.

You will find that in many of its pages this book refers to developments that put at risk the world, risks that had not subsided simply because, as many imagined, the Soviet empire collapsed. If indeed many of those turbulent events were linked to the USSR's collapse, others were unforeseen crises. The never-ending sequels to the Gulf War, the growing instability in the Middle East, state-sponsored terrorism in Libya, or failed-state situations, as in Somalia, are just a few. I have chosen to focus my attention on the armed conflicts that once again brought devastation to the Balkans following the disintegration of the Federal Republic of Yugoslavia. Those wars were fueled by the Serbian ultranationalist leadership's territorial ambitions and ethnic hatred. They weighed heavily on the Council's agenda and, beyond their specificities, allowed us to identify new and unfortunate realities: the conflict of interests between the major powers and the rest of the international community, frequently spilling into open wars, into terrorism and genocide, and the inadequacy of the United Nations to play its counterbalancing role. Since the 1990's and up to this day, those imbalances and shortcomings continue to dominate and, at the same time, entangle the UN Security Council's agenda.

The end of the Cold War and the fall of the Berlin Wall left the expectations they created unsatisfied and the Security Council has continued to mirror the serious tensions besieging the world order: disagreements between the Permanent and Non-Permanent members, lack of communication between the major powers and the rest of the membership, exclusion from the major discussion and decision-making processes, and above all, the willful disinformation practices that play such a critical role in how the Council really operates, with the major powers not sharing intelligence available to them and using it to further their own interests. I am proud to have contributed to an improvement of this situation during my tenure as President of the Security Council in 1992. The Arria Formula is a procedure that since then has given the Security Council's proceedings much greater transparency.

In this book, I have endeavored to put forward my thoughts about events in which I participated, experiences I lived through that moved me to raise my voice and take a stand, and the lessons I learned. My intention is to offer insights into international politics by presenting how the UN Security Council, reputed to be the world's foremost forum, dealt with one of the challenges it faced at the time. These pages are also written as testimony of my commitment to uphold those humanity-centered values and beliefs that give meaning to international relations, and of how they served as my guiding principles in the discharge of my duties. They bear witness to my obsessive struggle to make sure crimes against humanity such as genocide and ethnic cleansing, terrorism and the use of force to conquer territory, do not continue to create havoc in the international order. Many other diplomats and high officials of UN member states were engaged at a personal and professional level in the attempt to cope with the many crises the world lived through in those days. Some, like the Yugoslav wars, took on unsuspected dimensions and had unintended consequences such as the upsurge of terrorism.

The turning point for me came when I was entrusted with heading the Security Council's first ever ambassadorial mission to an active theatre of war. It allowed me to witness firsthand events as horrifying as the siege of Sarajevo, the capital of Bosnia and Herzegovina, and the Srebrenica genocide, situations purposely not reported fully nor in a timely manner by the Permanent Members and the UN Secretariat to the Non-Permanent Members of the Council or to the UN General Assembly.

During that mission I was able to observe in horror the results of the ethnic cleansing practiced in the enclave of Srebrenica. And it was from that martyred town that I called the world's attention to the slow-motion genocide taking place there. To no avail. Nothing was done to stop it or to end it. To the contrary, everything was done to cover it up until, in July 1995, little more than two years after the mission's visit, more than eight thousand adults and teenagers were executed in a massacre that went on for two to three days.

This book is also about the efforts made at the time and continued to this day to make sure world powers do not allow themselves to put aside ethical principles in the conduct of international politics. A small number of ambassadors accepted that challenge in the Security Council and never did we fail to stand up against the abuses the Serbian military and civilian authorities committed in Croatia, Bosnia and Kosovo, tolerated by the complicity of some of the Permanent Members, international civil servants and United Nations military personnel. And never did we cease to reject the reprehensible statements made by some European governments alleging that the independence of Bosnia and Herzegovina, a UN member state since May 1992, established an undesirable Islamic state in Europe. Never mind that Bosnia and Herzegovina was not only a European nation but also a beacon of ethnic and cultural diversity!

That argument, full of ethnic and religious undertones, brought to mind the never to be forgotten Holocaust suffered by the Jewish people, victims of the Nazi regime's "Final Solution." It is not a coincidence that before Bosnia was betrayed there were no Islamic terrorist attacks on Western soil, while following it, radical Islamic groups became active all over the world. The West's lack of real concern about what was happening in Bosnia and the nature of a peace agreement that rewarded both Serbian nationalism and its apartheid policies in the Balkans, while sacrificing Bosnia and Herzegovina's sovereignty, has had dangerous consequences still felt all over the world.

Only the determination shown by a few governments and individuals, among which I am proud to be, brought a number of those responsible for crimes against humanity to trial at the International Criminal Court for the Former Yugoslavia, a judicial institution in the creation of which I played a role. I made my contribution and discharged my duty by serving as a witness for the prosecution in the trial against Slobodan Milosevic and as one for the defense in the case against Naser Oric, the Bosnian commander in Srebrenica.

If there is any lesson to be learned from this book, it is the imperative need to ensure the UN does not, in the future, entangle itself as it did in situations like those that took place in Croatia, Bosnia and Kosovo, which allowed for the largest coverup ever attempted by some of the major powers sitting in the Security Council. By resorting to the cynical argument that one cannot put a price on peace, they made a mockery of the very foundations the United Nations is built on, which remain essential to the effective safeguard of peace and international security everywhere in the world.

On my way to the Security Council

Throughout my life, due mostly to the public responsibilities I have had the privilege to hold, I have often received telephone calls of an extraordinary nature. However, none so significant as the one I received in New York at 11 am, on Monday, April 14, 2003.

– Good morning, Ambassador Arria – a woman's voice with a slight Italian accent greeted me in perfect English – This is Carla Del Ponte, Chief Prosecutor of the International Criminal Tribunal for the Former Yugoslavia. As you are certainly aware of, here in The Hague criminal proceedings have been instituted against former president Slobodan Milosevic, on the charge of personal responsibility for the crime of genocide committed in Srebrenica, as well as for other crimes against humanity committed in Croatia, Bosnia, and Kosovo. We have closely reviewed your statements in the Security Council during those years, in particular the report you presented to its members in April 1993, at the end of the fact-finding mission to the theatre of war the Council entrusted you to lead. We are also aware of the denunciation you then made from the very Srebrenica that, as you termed it, a "slow motion genocide" was being committed there in those very days. Considering the situations you directly experienced, and in the belief your testimony would be highly relevant, we would like to consult your availability to join the proceedings as a witness for the Prosecution.

I did not need to think about it twice.

— You may most certainly count on me – was my reply to Del Ponte, who in her prior position as Switzerland's Attorney General, had worked closely with Giovanni Falcone, her Italian counterpart, in his relentless struggle against the Mafia. However, before going any further, I felt obliged to ask if she had made the same request to the Ambassadors who, in those years, had represented the five Permanent Members of the Security Council: Russia, the United States, China, the United Kingdom and France.

— We did – she immediately replied. But all of them were as one in rejecting our invitation under the allegation they did not, at the time, have information about the crimes allegedly committed by Mr. Milosevic and, therefore, could not contribute anything of relevance to the trial.

— They all lie impudently – I then replied. They were all perfectly aware of what was going on in Bosnia.

Ambassador to the United Nations

The story had begun years before. To be exact, on the morning of January 3, 1991, when I became Permanent Representative of Venezuela to the United Nations. On that day, I visited for the first time our Mission's premises, located on New York's 46 th Street, and from there walked over to the imposing glass building that houses the headquarters of the Organization.

In those early days of the year, the Emirate of Kuwait's invasion by Iraqi troops on August 2, 1990, was the focus of the Security Council's attention. The Council had given Saddam Hussein forty-five days to unconditionally withdraw from Kuwait and the ambassadors of its fifteen member states keenly debated the situation. A few days before, Javier Pérez de Cuellar, then Secretary General of the United Nations, had travelled to Baghdad with the aim of meeting Saddam Hussein and to broker a political solution to the conflict. He spent two hours waiting for Saddam to end a meeting with Daniel Ortega, former President of Nicaragua. Hussein wished, no doubt, to send a clear message to the international community:

his government would not waver, not even under the threat posed by the formidable US-led military coalition of thirty-four nations, which had already deployed almost six hundred thousand men along the border between Saudi Arabia and Iraq, thousands of armored vehicles and seven hundred combat aircraft, the biggest military mobilization since the Normandy invasion of June 1944.

The grace period was about to expire and it was generally believed that the code-named Operation Desert Storm would be launched shortly. Consequently, that morning, as I entered the great hall of the Security Council and took a seat in the section reserved for ambassadors of non-Council member countries, I felt privileged to witness the debate then taking place between Abdul Amir Al-Anbari, Representative of Iraq, who in a show of unabashed arrogance and effrontery, insisted on his government's right to intervene in Kuwait - Iraq's "Nineteenth province" as Hussein used to call it in his speeches - and Sir David Hannay, Ambassador of the United Kingdom. Ambassador Hannay was a reputed polemicist whom I hoped never need to challenge but would soon do so in many harsh discussions about the frightful tragedy in Bosnia, and about the less than appropriate behavior of the British and French governments.

The Yugoslav Wars

Every morning and afternoon, during the days that preceded the massive bombardments of Baghdad on the night of January 17, I hurried to the Council. Under no circumstance was I to miss the statements of the world's most powerful governments as they analyzed and took decisions on how to confront a conflict as pressing as this one was. It was also an opportunity for me to closely follow the steps they took in trying to solve the crisis while trying to forestall the use of force. As we all know, such efforts were fruitless. Hussein would not change his stand, not even to avoid the terrible fallout the imminent military intervention would have. Whatever the case, I assumed, not without reason, that the experience gained would serve me well in the coming months and years to understand how best to approach conflicts of similar nature and magnitude.

My initiation to the Bosnian issue would come months later, in September, on occasion of the forty-sixth session of the General Assembly. The Permanent Representative of Yugoslavia, the Croat Darko Silovic, invited the ambassadors of the Non-Aligned Movement to an urgent meeting with his Minister of Foreign Affairs, Budimir Loncar. The purpose of the meeting was to request our support to the appeal Mr. Loncar would make that very afternoon, on behalf of his government, to his European counterparts not to intervene in the armed confrontation that was staining with blood the streets of Yugoslavia since Slovenia and Croatia declared their independence on July 25.

The members of the Non-Aligned Movement shared an idealized vision of Yugoslavia because it had been Josip Broz, the legendary Marshall Tito, architect of modern Yugoslavia, who had defeated the Nazi occupation army in the Balkans and, together with Jawaharlal Nehru from India, the Egyptian Gamal Abdel Nasser, and Ghanaian Kwame Nkrumah had founded the Movement in 1961. On the weight of this historical background and considering the Movement's stand of keeping its distances from the Soviet Union, we agreed to share Loncar's arguments and to support his request, even though we did not know the full extent of the situation in Yugoslavia during those early days of armed confrontation.

My colleague ambassadors had chosen me that morning to accompany Loncar, who insisted on describing what was taking place in the Balkans as "a war of Yugoslavia against itself," meaning that those early armed confrontations were to be understood as a strictly internal affair, a civil war. Therefore, the meeting had been convened to convince European ministers to avoid the temptation of taking a stand in favor or against any of the parties. Although with reservations, I supported Loncar's position given Marshall Tito's legacy as a key figure in the Third World's political arena, confident that it would help to avoid an internationalization of the still incipient Yugoslav crisis.

The meeting also made me aware of an astonishing reality: since the conflict in the Former Yugoslavia did not have a direct impact on Europe's political or economic interests, the appeal made by Loncar fell on deaf ears. During the following years, I would witness how the arguments later employed by European governments to justify their decision not to act in defense of Bosnia's sovereignty and the rights of its Muslim population, based on a distorted understanding of the principle of non-intervention in the internal affairs of other nations, were the very same ones used by Loncar; and how the European members of the Security Council would appeal to them to avoid confronting Serbia's criminal military aggression against Croatia and Bosnia. The way in which the European ministers skirted their responsibilities that day convinced me that whatever path those nations chose to follow, Yugoslavia, as we knew it, had its days numbered.

Europe's comfortable aloofness in relation to the Yugoslav situation would cease towards the end of September, when Helmut Köhl, Prime Minister of Germany, requested parliamentary authorization to recognize the "rebel" republics of Slovenia and Croatia as sovereign independent states. Three months later, on December 23, the authorization was granted and Germany, without consulting her partners in the European Community, nor the United Nations, proceeded to the unilateral recognition of both newly born nations. As was to be expected, the government of Slobodan Milosevic reacted quickly and harshly. From that moment on, the so-called "Yugoslav Wars" became international and would soon constitute a universal, bitter, bone of contention. It all brought to my mind that it was also in a month of June, in 1914, and in those very same streets of Sarajevo, that the assassination of Archduke Francis Ferdinand, heir to the throne of the Austro-Hungarian empire, took place, unleashing the First World War.

Venezuela Becomes a Member of the Security Council

On October 8, 1991, Venezuela was elected to replace Cuba as a non-permanent member of the Security Council for the period 1992-1993. Previously, the two representatives of Latin America and the Caribbean in the Council were Ecuador and Cuba, with the latter's mandate coming to term on December 31. To fill the vacancy to be left open by Cuba, the Latin American and Caribbean Group (GRULAC) had two standing candidates, Bolivia and Mexico. However, in those days, Mexico was engaged in negotiations with the United States and Canada to become a member of the hugely important Free Trade Agreement. Within President Carlos Salinas de Gortari's government it was felt that it was not the most convenient time to be in the Security Council, where differences between Mexico and its northern neighbor would surely be inevitable, putting at risk the magnificent commercial prospects awaiting Mexico if it managed to join the Free Trade Agreement between the United States and Canada.

It was precisely in those days of June when my good friend Jorge Montaño, Ambassador of Mexico to the United Nations, delivered to me a message from Salinas de Gortari: Mexico was willing to give us its support if Venezuela opted to fill the vacancy soon to be left by Cuba. Needless to say, I said yes, and weeks after, proud and happy, I followed the casting of votes one by one, and when its results were read I experienced an emotion comparable only to the one I felt some weeks later, on January 2, 1992, when for the first time I took Venezuela's place in the horseshoe-shaped table in the great hall of the Security Council.

However, the way I would come to see the world since then was to be neither as clear nor as pleasant as I had imagined. In the months following Venezuela's election to replace Cuba in the world's top political body, I had asked myself many times what my role as representative of a Latin American country in a Security Council dominated by the most influential world powers could really be. It was said, not without reason, that only the representatives of those powers took an active part in the international political agenda's decision-making process. Nevertheless, I was determined to prove that to be a representative of a Third World nation did not condemn me to be a mere spectator. On the contrary, I was convinced that, precisely because I represented a country without a prominent role in international affairs, I could take advantage of the greater freedom and independence available to me, and thus offer, based on each situation's merits, an objective perspective, uncontaminated by any national interest and exclusively committed to the task of preserving peace and defending human and political rights for all nations and for all people, as proclaimed in the United Nations Charter. Regrettably, I very soon came to realize that such an illusion had truly little to do with how the United Nations and its Security Council really operate.

The first and probably most revealing aspect of such a contradiction was to realize that the United Nations' most important decisions are not taken in the formal sessions of the Security Council, held in the great hall with the huge horseshoe table, but in other, closed-door meetings, in a smaller and less flamboyant room, not too far from the great hall of the Council, without recordings, stenographers or journalists. It is there, around an ordinary U-shaped table, where the Council's most important decisions are really reached by the Representatives of its fifteen members.

This room, called the "Informal Consultations Room," probably with the intention of hiding its true relevance, has a huge window with a magnificent view on the East River, totally hidden by curtains. In it, the Permanent Five exercise their overwhelming power hidden away from the outside world. In time, I would also conclude that this room's setting is not just about keeping from outside stares the intimacies of the Council, nor about preventing its members from distractions by gazing at a pleasant view, but about keeping the greater and more sanitized distance possible from events taking place in those faraway places where this board of directors of world politics is more or less engaged. That was the reason why I labeled this room "El cuarto sin vista": The room without a view.

When you seat at that table, you have privileged access to the most reserved and sensitive documents and reports on the issues on that day's agenda, even though none of them expose their real nature nor highlight the harshness of the particular situations. In their immaculate white paper printouts, these reports convey in aseptic language the most terrifying developments. This is a feature of the UN Secretariat's work that needs to be highlighted. The Secretary General's reports to the Council tend to be more forensic than analytical. In them the Secretariat usually avoids any thorough analysis of the causes of a given situation, favoring rather a descriptive narration of events. This is the result of a tacit understanding between the Permanent Members and the Secretariat, which would never dare to criticize any of them regardless of their responsibilities, allowing the P5 to skirt any discussion on the role they may have played, by action or omission, in the situation at hand. Thus, the reports submitted to the Council's attention have the detachment of an autopsy of the victim but lack the information needed to assign responsibilities. You may read, for example, that yesterday, at sixteen hundred hours, in Rwanda, hundreds of Tutsis were slaughtered with machetes inside a church, but the screams of the victims will not be heard as the causes of the horrors reported will be muted. A detachment which can only serve the purpose of fostering indifference when the worst of horrors are brought to the attention of the Council.

Another unsavory characteristic of the Council's workings is its rule of ending all its informal meetings at exactly one fifteen post meridiem, no matter how advanced the session might be in its deliberations, simply because at that hour the interpreters' work shift ends. No matter how urgent the issues under consideration or how important any session might be in light of the decisions to be taken, the length and extent of debates is dictated not by the ambassadors, but by the work hours of the support personnel.

The room also serves as a small and very discreet boxing ring, in which contenders solve their differences privately, without much regard to form or polite considerations, in confrontations usually devoid of the rhetorical trappings adorning the debates and the agreements later announced to the world in the great hall of the Council.

Members Only

The most consequential effect of the Security Council's double personality is that UN member states who do not sit on that board of directors' table are denied access to privileged information and participation in the informal sessions of the Council. This is perhaps one of the most remarkable aspects of the Council's inner workings. Every decision it takes and every resolution its fifteen members adopt in public sessions is the result of strictly private, even secret, debates and negotiations. What is more, since such debates and agreements are deemed to be "informal," they are exempted from all public scrutiny. The hermeticism of the Council is thus almost absolute. The closed curtains in the "Room without a view" keep from the outside world the strengths and weaknesses, even the biases, that define the way the United Nations and its Security Council really work. Most governments, observers and media are never in the knowledge of the tortuous and mostly nontransparent paths followed by this UN body to reach its decisions.

It is in the Security Council Chamber, facing microphones and TV cameras, that previously agreed resolutions are adopted and that Council members' statements, previously approved by their governments, are delivered. Both are little more than for-the-record expressions of power game realities. The Security Council's decisions, as we shall see, usually come heavily tainted by the special interests of the five Permanent Members, frequently helped along by the endorsement and cooperation of the Secretary General, whose present and future prospects in his post depend almost exclusively on the will of that quintet.

Such a peculiar reality, obviously not very democratic, made me realize that to be a member of the Council, to have the privilege of participating in its "informal meetings" and to be in the know of all the disagreements, clashes and plots simmering in its executive kitchen, made me a primus inter pares in the eyes of my Latin American and Caribbean colleagues. They, like all other representatives of non-council members, had to rely on whatever privileged information any of us would share in order to convey to their capitals information otherwise impossible to obtain. However, as disconcerting as all of these revelations might have been, I must underline that every time I entered the Council Chamber, or the Informal Consultations Room and took a seat behind the name-banner identifying me as a delegate of Venezuela, I felt a formidable combination of pride and respect for the privilege of representing my country in the foremost forum of international politics. I could not minimize or ignore the importance of such a position.

Very shortly after becoming a member of this extremely selective private club, I became aware of the possibilities open to me, were I to choose to do so, to take part in, and even influence, the game of secret manipulations played within the United Nations by the great world powers. It was equally clear to me that for non-permanent members of the Council it would be simply easier to renounce such a possibility. I cannot forget, for instance, how, as a recently posted Representative to the United Nations, some wise voices suggested that it would be better to avoid opening any Pandora Box when the opportunity came to state my position on any issue under debate. Since then, I have not failed to wonder how many good initiatives may have been lost, cowered by the pull of indifference and the push to oblivion. Precisely to promote keeping such safe distances, the UN is prodigal in providing opportunities. Other fora, also of high importance, are available within the UN to discuss issues such as development, disarmament, the fight against poverty, the environment, the rights of children or of women, among others. They are, however, mostly useful to keep governments and their representatives away from paying closer attention to the great political conflicts and other situations the world powers prefer to manage without interference.

To assist them in ensuring this peculiar division of labor in the exercise of power, the five Permanent Members of the Council and the United Nations Secretary General join efforts to monopolize the information that is to be made available to the General Assembly and, most importantly, to the Security Council. Nations with less resources or lesser capabilities to gather their own intelligence have no alternative but to limit the scope of their activity to those other UN fora, or to simply endorse the positions adopted in the Council by any of the big five, the so-called, P5: The United States, Russia, China, France and the United Kingdom.

In the United Nations, its weaker members suffer the consequences of their condition. Their capacity to adopt independent positions is not strong and they are, consequently, easily influenced by the powerful Permanent Members of the Council. Many hope to find in the Secretary General's reports inputs to sustain the illusion they can resist pressure by any of the world powers. This explains why these powers could not avoid voicing their amazement that a Representative such as myself should actively take part in the consideration of situations of high international importance, such as those in Bosnia, for example, or in Somalia, very distant from what they deemed to be the interests of Venezuela.

The Bosnia Bomb Explodes in the Council

A few months after the meeting between Foreign Affairs Minister Loncar and his European counterparts, on January 2, 1992, Venezuela's first day as a non-permanent member of the Council, the Yugoslav crisis exploded dramatically. A missile fired by a Serbian combat plane had downed a civilian helicopter carrying five Council of Europe observers, four Italians and one French national. As serious as the situation was, the Security Council's reaction went no further than a pro forma statement deploring the "tragic incident." On January 9, barely a week after, new and unsettling information reached me, equally silenced by the United Nations upper management: the Bosnian-Serb leadership, headed by Radovan Karadzic, a deranged psychiatrist born in Montenegro, had announced the establishment of an illegal Serb Republic of Bosnia, the Srpska, with Karadzic as its president, with full military and civilian support from the Government of Serbia.

In this unexpected way, my first steps in the "summit of the world," coincided with the beginning of a new and ferocious stage in the war in the Former Yugoslavia. A war that would radically alter my perception of world politics and its main actors. The Council's main protagonists, with their recurring penchant to look sideways, were giving the Serbian military authorities an absolute free hand to violate at will the territorial integrity of the independent republic of Bosnia. Such impunity implicitly amounted to an authorization to ignore the civilian and human rights of the Muslim population.

It was thus that under the impassive look of a significant part of the international community, the Milosevic government took advantage of this sort of "waiver" to carry out in Bosnia a scorched-earth policy and accelerate, by fire and blood, the creation of an ethnically pure Greater Serbia, to be achieved at the expense of the other republics that had made up the Yugoslav Federation. Soon, such permissiveness would lead to multiple military aggressions against the Bosnian population, all of them "justified" under unacceptable and absolutely illegal racial, political and territorial arguments, to which the powerful members of the Security Council were complicit. Their determination not to abide by their obligation to protect on equal terms all the members of the organization conveyed to the Serbian government the message that the international community would not resort to the use of force to put a stop to its military intervention in neighboring countries.

It was thanks to this accommodating and reprehensible policy that the Serbian aggressors felt they had sufficient support from the international community to continue adding territory to the political geography of Serbia by force of arms. From those crucial weeks on, while Yugoslavia became an absolute hell, European governments and the P5, shielded by a self-serving interpretation of the mandatory respect for sovereignty, chose not to acknowledge the havoc caused by their aloofness regarding the Yugoslav problem. Almost six years had to pass before Kofi Annan, Boutros Boutros-Ghali's successor at the helm of the United Nations, had the courage to admit before the General Assembly the mistake of not having perceived in time "The scope of the evil we were faced with, nor to have fulfilled our duty of protecting cities such as Srebrenica from the Serbian program of mass murder of the Muslim population, mistakes silenced by a pretended policy of neutrality and non-violence, totally inappropriate to the conflict in Bosnia".

The non-permanent members of the Council began to share feelings of alarm and indignation. From one day to the next, the Republic of Bosnia and Herzegovina became, in all official documents prepared by the Secretariat, the "Muslim side" of the conflict, thus framing the war as a mere ethnic and religious struggle, of exclusively Yugoslav concern. This was a particularly malignant distortion of facts since it had been to the Council's very request that the General Assembly had recognized Bosnia as an independent, indivisible, republic. This legitimacy should have reminded the most influential members of the Council of their duty to "see" that two-thirds of Bosnian territory was under occupation by Serbian military and paramilitary forces.

To make it even more reprehensible, the persecution and extermination of the Bosnian Muslims was taking place while, simultaneously, this same and "blind" Council boasted about the honorable and significant role it had played in putting an end to the abhorrent apartheid regime in South Africa. Moreover, the Secretary General himself was cooperating with the Permanent Members of the Council in the task of manipulating the information about what was really taking place in Croatia and Bosnia. All of them, by validating the argument that the Yugoslav wars were the bitter consequence of ancient ethnic and religious animosities in which the international community should not intervene other than to issue calls to peace and send humanitarian aid, chose to simply ignore the multiple and atrocious crimes committed by Serbs in both republics. Even Margaret Thatcher repudiated this policy in a succinct and forceful statement: "Under no circumstances are we to limit ourselves to feed the people, while, on the other hand, we allow them to be massacred."

Such a perverse distortion of reality allowed European governments to fully assume as valid the fiction that only they were able to solve the crisis, as Jacques Poos, Minister of Foreign Affairs of Luxembourg, and then President of the Council of Europe, had stated in June of the previous year. Speaking from his elevated position, Poos had argued that, in view of the urgency with which the conflicts that teared apart the former Yugoslavia must be addressed, it was appropriate to recall that "Europe's time, not that of the Americans, has arrived", thereby implying that one thing is the United Nations, in his mind dominated by the United States, and quite another the European Community. The Serbian aggressors took this to mean that Europe would try to avoid by all means the intervention of non-European actors, particularly the United States, and felt they had been given green light to continue with their ruthless ethnic cleansing war in the very heart of Europe. It was certainly not the time of Europe. The European governments suddenly forgot their "Never again" commitment, made in 1945 as a warning by the war's victors to whomever felt inclined to resort once more to the same execrable practices of the Nazi regime, as the Serbs were now doing.

It should be noted that it was not by chance that the first peace plan for the Former Yugoslavia, put forward on behalf of the European Community by Lord Peter Carrington, of the United Kingdom, and Jose Cutileiro, of Portugal, proposed the division of the Republic of Bosnia and Herzegovina into three territories with borders based on merely ethnic-religious considerations: a Bosnian Muslim territory, the smallest of the three, even though the majority of the Bosnian population was

Muslim; a Croat Catholic territory; and a third, the biggest, for the Christian Orthodox population of Serbian descent. Both mediators argued shamelessly that with this aberrant partition, the Serbs would feel "satisfied." To justify the unjustifiable, they repeated the cowardly reasoning used in 1938 in Munich by the then Prime Ministers of the United Kingdom, Neville Chamberlain, and France, Edouard Daladier, to accept and justify the invasion and occupation of the Sudetenland which held that by recovering that region, lost after World War I, Nazi Germany would be appeased. As is common knowledge, the Sudetenland occupation eventually proved to be the first step towards the invasion of Czechoslovakia and, a year afterwards, of Poland, triggering the Second World War.

In their baleful delirium, the Carrington-Cutileiro duo was on the verge of replaying such a folly to the detriment of the rights of the weaker party in the Yugoslav conflict. Not for nothing, The New York Times and The Washington Post had in those days highlighted the unadorned definition put forth by the Belgian Minister of Foreign Affairs, Viscount Mark Eyskens, stating that "Europe is an economic giant, a political pygmy and a military worm."

To the surprise of many, this extreme Europeanism also clouded the vision of the Bosnian Muslims' political leadership. By March 1992, even though the imminence of the Serbian aggression against Bosnia was no longer a secret, it still defined the republic as European - a definition not shared in the continent's capitals - and stated that only Europe could defend it and prevent the scorched earth war practiced by Serbian troops in Croatia since July of the previous year. This lack of vision by the Bosnian political class prevented them from understanding that Europe cared little about Bosnian rights, because, at the end of the day, as the British representative to the Security Council confessed to me, defending Bosnia's sovereignty amounted to promoting the risky establishment of a Muslim nation in the heart of Europe. Little more than a year afterwards, in Sarajevo, Ejup Ganic, Vice President of Bosnia, admitted to me that because of this misunderstanding of the situation his government made the costly mistake of believing that Europe would not hesitate to come to Bosnia's defense if attacked by a Fascist regime such as that of Milosevic, and that there lied the reason why it did not feel the need to appeal to the United Nations for help from the very beginning of the Serbian aggression. When it finally did, "it was already too late," and the flames of a war of brutal ethnic cleansing were consuming Bosnia, turning it very quickly into a huge cemetery.

The Arms Embargo on the Former Yugoslavia

An arms embargo is one of the preeminent tools the Security Council can resort to ensure peace. It is usually implemented to put the brakes on the further expansion of an armed conflict. On September 25, 1991, the Security Council, meeting at the level of Foreign Affairs Ministers, chaired by the French Minister Roland Dumas, imposed a "total arms and military equipment" embargo on the five nations of the former Federal Socialist Republic of Yugoslavia in the belief that by so doing it was giving the cause of peace in the Balkans a good chance.

The seriousness of such a mistake soon became evident. At the time, however, only the head of US diplomacy, James Baker, called attention to the fact that Serbia had inherited all the arms and equipment bought by the former Yugoslavia from the extinct USSR, leaving Slovenia, Croatia, Macedonia and Bosnia in a situation of clear military inferiority. To Baker, such an imbalance between the parties represented an evident danger since it was no longer a secret that regular troops of the former Yugoslav Popular Army, now of Serbia, had been taking part in combats in Croatia during the previous months, kept a massive and ominous presence on the border of Bosnia, and were abusing human rights in Kosovo. The US Secretary of State had even denounced that "Belgrade has the ambition to create a Greater Serbia at the expense of its neighbors, and this cannot be tolerated." His warnings came to naught, and the Security Council approved by unanimity the arms embargo. The embargo even had the tacit blessing of the government of

Bosnia, which believed that once the dying Yugoslav Federation ceased to exist, the need for the embargo would equally cease. Needless to say, an illusion that never came to be.

On November 27, just a few days after what I had initially believed to be an auspicious decision, the Security Council approved Resolution 271, thereby authorizing the establishment of a peace mission, later to be known as the United Nations Protection Force in Yugoslavia (UNPROFOR). At the time, its mandate centered on Croatia, but with the intent of expanding it later into Bosnia, given the allegations made by its president, the Muslim leader Alijah Izetbegovic, that there were well founded reasons to believe that Serbia was preparing to do in Bosnia what it was already doing in Croatia. It was precisely on that premise that Cyrus Vance, former US Secretary of State and Personal Representative of the Secretary General Pérez de Cuellar in the initial negotiations between Serb and Croat representatives in Geneva at the end of 1992, was ratified in his role by the new Secretary General, Boutros Boutros-Ghali. On January 2, Vance immediately convened a meeting in Sarajevo of the Serbian and Croat military and political leadership, with the intent of reaching for Bosnia an agreement similar to that reached by the parties in Croatia. At the time, we did not realize how different both conflicts were. In the case of Bosnia, the difference between the size of its military forces and those of Serbia were such that we should have anticipated the inevitable failure of the peace initiative proposed by Vance.

Nevertheless, on January 8, the Security Council passed Resolution 727 hoping to foster the approval of a cease fire by both parties. The resolution included no indication whatsoever that the Organization would collectively intervene if Serbia did not abide by the cease fire but chose instead to continue its territorial expansion at the expense of Bosnia. It soon became evident that neither the deployment of Blue Helmets nor Resolution 727 would put a stop to Serbia's military intervention in Bosnia in early 1992, a development defined by some qualified observers as a true "rape of Bosnia". The greedy hands of the Serbian government, a traditional ally of Russia and, since the First World War a French and British ally, fell on Bosnia and on its Muslim population, as the international community did nothing to prevent it.

It should be noted that, as in so many other occasions, neither the Secretariat nor the five permanent members of the Council shared with the rest of the membership that at the beginning of Yugoslavia's brake-up process, Belgrade had transferred one-hundred thousand members of the former Yugoslav Popular Army and a greater part of its equipment and weapons to the illegal Srpska Republic, established by the Bosnian Serbs in the occupied city of Pale, "the other side" of the Bosnian conflict, as the Big Five began to call it. On the other hand, Croatia had a smaller and worse equipped military than Serbia but had harbors and many miles of coastline on the Adriatic along which to contraband weapons, a fact that allowed Serbian aggressors an excuse for their relentless attacks on the Croat cities on the Dalmatian coast, including Dubrovnik, a city declared by UNESCO a World Heritage Site. By contrast, Bosnia, without an army of its own, subject to the arms embargo decreed by the Security Council, with no access to maritime ports for the military supplies it needed to be able to exercise its right to self-defense, was left at the mercy of its Serbian enemies. If Venezuela, as well as other non-permanent members of the Council, had had such information, we would have opposed the arms embargo that condemned Bosnia to death.

In the meantime, and notwithstanding their obligation to monitor compliance with the Geneva agreements, both the European Community and the P5, with the lone exception of the United States, chose to ignore this monumental imbalance and to leave Bosnia, which in May of that year would be admitted as a Member State of the United Nations, as a sacrificial lamb for the Serb military, whose units had unlawfully entered its territory and were conducting ruthless raids. It was all happening with the active support of the Secretariat, responsible for filtering the information and drafting the documents available to the Council. An information monopoly which, in this instance, allowed the

Secretariat to fail to mention the transfer of soldiers, heavy artillery, tanks and combat aircraft from Serbia to the illegal Srpska Republic, led by its President, Radovan Karadzic, and conducted by General Ratko Mladic, its military commander.

Once this Serbian expansion project was set in motion, Bosnian protestations were of no avail. Not even two motions passed by the U.S. Congress in October and November 1991 in favor of an eventual lift of the arms embargo, were able to revert the folly incurred. President Bill Clinton, elected in November, once in the White House vetoed both resolutions in order "not to displease our European allies", thus reneging on the position against the arms embargo he had publicly upheld in a speech given at Georgetown University. To compensate for the damage done by this change of position, the White House put pressure on the new Secretary General, Boutros Boutros-Ghali, to ratify Cyrus Vance as his personal representative for Yugoslavia. No matter, it would soon become evident that Vance's initiatives were also doomed to fail from the start. The military imbalance in Croatia could already be measured in hundreds of dead and thousands of wounded, most of them victims of the relentless three months-long Serbian siege to the border town of Vukobar and the artillery shelling inflicted on Dubrovnik in October. Such destruction and desolation could no longer be hidden from Vance, who was ultimately forced to admit that "The peace agreements and the conditions set for the arms embargo are violated from all the cardinal points."

By that time, it had become clear that the arms embargo had had extremely disappointing results, particularly in relation to Bosnia. By leaving the victims defenseless, the war had been prolonged by almost four catastrophic years, at the end of which more than two-hundred thousand people died, twenty-thousand women were brutally raped, and more than a million people was forced to leave their homes. Notwithstanding this terrible and impossible to hide reality, the numerous resolutions adopted by the Council since September on what was happening in the former Yugoslavia, would continue to be merely rhetorical protestations, since they never included sufficiently strong warnings to dissuade the Serbian government from persisting in its military actions against Bosnia. There can be no doubt that in the history of arms embargoes declared by the Security Council, none has cost more lives nor more misery than that imposed on Bosnia, a nation which, although a member of the United Nations, would suffer in its own territory, in the very heart of the Europe of Maastricht, the devastating effects of a true ethnic cleansing policy. To add insult to injury, the aggression was committed by another member of the United Nations under the most cynical indifference of most of the Security Council.

ON TOP OF THE WORLD

On March 1, 1992, I took over the presidency of the Security Council. The first issue on my agenda was the Somalia crisis. At the time, the country was experiencing the worst famine in its history. On January 1, 1991, after twenty-two years of dictatorship and civil war, its President, General Mohamed Siad Barre, was violently overthrown by war bands fighting among themselves to seize control of Mogadiscio, the capital. One faction was under the command of Ali Mahdi Mohamed – who would soon, and up to 1995, become "interim" president of Somalia - the other, under General Mohamed Farrah Aidid. Mohamed Siad Barre's downfall had worsened the crisis severely, giving way to total social and political anarchy. Not recognizing the existence of a national executive power, the different tribes and clans had fragmented the country into a series of small independent "states." Under such circumstances, many within the military chose to join, with all their equipment and weapons, the militias organized by the leaders of such mini states. By the end of 1991, such developments had turned Somalia into a dangerously impoverished, dangerously armed, and dangerously undernourished country, making it almost impossible to supply aid to the victims.

Somalia's Unfathomable Tragedy

During a Cold War that in those parts of the world had been extremely hot, Somalia's strategic location on the Horn of Africa had for many years made it an important part of Soviet operations. Then, in 1987, the USSR chose to take sides with Ethiopia in the war between both countries. The United States took advantage of the situation to give its support to the

Somalian government and to launch from Somalian territory a failed invasion of Ethiopia. From that day on, abandoned by all, Somalia sunk into an abyss of chaos. By March 1992, with deaths counted by the thousands and violence prevailing everywhere, its situation finally came to the attention of the international community.

The problem was huge since Somalia had practically ceased to exist as a state. It had neither a government nor institutions, nor diplomatic relations with other nations. At this stage of its agony, it had no representation in the United Nations, and therefore we had truly little information about developments in the country. It was such an impossible situation that the only thing I could think of was to ask the United Nations' Department of African Affairs if any Somalian citizen worked in the Secretariat. Luck smiled on me: one of its staff members informed me that, indeed, a Somalian national worked in the Publications Department. He, in turn, told me that a conational, who in the past had been posted at the Somalia Mission to the United Nations, now lived in New York's Borough of Queens. The following day I was able to reach her on the phone. Two days later I had an assistant pick her up and we met in my office.

My very first goal was to convey to her my wish to be of help to Somalia in dealing with its extremely serious problems. I then brought to her attention that, to do so, UN peace operations and humanitarian assistance procedures demanded the interested member state to formally request such international assistance. Without such a request nothing could be done, and since Somalia had no government nor any contact with the United Nations, nobody was able to formally request its assistance. I then proposed to overcome such an obstacle by suggesting she underwrite, as if still a Somali diplomat, a request for UN humanitarian assistance to the civilian population of Somalia addressing it to me as President of the Council.

Her surprise was indeed great.

— I cannot do that – she said. I do not legally represent Somalia.

— It is of no relevance – I replied –. To begin with, the state of Somalia does not exist, and therefore, there is no Somali authority to complain about anything. And then, what we all wish is to assist the Somali people. By signing the request, you would decisively contribute to make it possible for us to do so.

Overcoming her justified fears, she signed, and I then made copies available to all Council members. Even though the initiative was absolutely irregular from all points of view, not a single ambassador objected, and our intervention in Somalia was approved. The Council's decision gave institutional legitimacy to the dispatch of the first military unit to Somalia with a mandate to facilitate the entry and distribution of international humanitarian aid to the most needed segments of the population.

Unfortunately, the Council´s initiative met with continued and furious resistance by the many armed groups fighting among themselves in Somalia. The situation deteriorated to such an extent that a few months afterwards, in December of that year, President George H. W. Bush announced that the United States, together with other twenty-four nations, had decided to send to Somalia a military contingent in order to guarantee the security of those in charge of humanitarian assistance.

We all know the tragic end met by such operation. In June 1993, two dozen volunteers of the Pakistan Army were massacred in Mogadiscio by armed bands, and some months afterwards, in October, Mohamed Farrah Aidid's band took down two Black Hawk helicopters carrying a small US military unit. During the fight, eighteen American soldiers died, and eighty were wounded. Afterwards, the body of one of the fallen was drawn along the city streets by General Aidid's men. The horrible images of this slaughter went viral and President Bush's successor to the White House, Bill Clinton, cancelled the United States' participation in the UN peacekeeping operation in Somalia. Since then, the US government has drawn what in Washington came to be known as "the Mogadiscio Line," a decision by which the United States would cease to take part in peace missions that could put at risk its military.

Libya and State-Sponsored Terrorism

During that month of March, while the Security Council did what it could to give assistance to the tormented Somali population, the Council had to deal with the first consequences of the bombing of two passenger planes: Pan Am flight 103, downed in 1988 over Lockerbie, in Scotland, and a French UTA airline flight downed over Niger in September of the following year. The joint investigation conducted throughout several years by the American, French and British police had established the responsibility of two Libyan citizens in the first attack, one of them a member of Muamar Ghaddafi's security services. Consequently, the Libyan authorities were asked to hand them over to be tried in Scotland. Ghaddafi denied the request under the argument that those responsible for such monstruous crimes, which had taken the lives of more than four-hundred-and-four citizens from thirty-two nations, were already in prison, and that as Libyan citizens they could only be tried by a local tribunal. Ghaddafi's refusal only deepened the suspicion that these attacks might have been acts of terrorism committed under the auspices of his dictatorship. Rejecting Libya´s arguments, the governments of the United States, United Kingdom and France, requested the Security Council to impose stringent sanctions on Colonel Ghaddafi's government. Boutros Boutros-Ghali tried to mediate and suggested Libya hand over the accused in a third country, not directly involved in the events. Ghaddafi, however, would not be swayed.

As President of the Council, I met several times with Ahmed Elhouderi, Libya's Ambassador to the United Nations, as well as with the representatives of the Arab Group of UN member states, the regional block with the highest interest in a diplomatic solution to the situation. I also discussed the case with Andrés Aguilar, my predecessor as head of Venezuela's Mission to the United Nations, who by then was a magistrate at the International Court of Justice. I consulted his opinion on whether the Council could serve as an *ad hoc* tribunal, as was proposed by the United States, France and the United Kingdom, or whether it was possible, as I believed, for the International Court to take up that task as the highest judicial body of the United Nations. However, the International Court of Justice ruled in favor of the first alternative, and therefore the Council, acting under my presidency, had to proceed on its own authority. One day later, for the first time in the history of the United Nations, the Council formally took upon itself the right to put on trial and sentence a member state accused of taking part in acts of terrorism.

Up to the very end, I had insisted on the Court's involvement because I believed any actions we might take to clarify and condemn those despicable acts of terrorism needed to be based on un-biased and legal foundations, thereby avoiding an undue contamination of the Council's proceedings by political prejudices or convictions. At the same time, in keeping with the principles of international criminal justice, I could not accept that a United Nations member state should try to obstruct, as Libya did, the impartial administration of justice. Most and foremost, I was of the firm belief that however the Council chose to act, it should do so guided by the need to both serve justice within the realm of the law and be effective in the discharge of its duty to preserve peace and international security, and not by the United Nations political interests or those of Libya.

Early in that month of March 1992, Libya's Minister of Oil visited Caracas and tried to persuade President Carlos Andres Pérez not to vote against his country in the Council. A few days after, our ambassador in Tripoli was summoned by Ghaddafi, who expressed "His displeasure about Ambassador Arria's declarations, in which he stated that Libya is a terrorism sponsoring state" and reiterated the request his government had made to President Pérez. I must mention here that President Pérez never mentioned to me his meeting with the

Libyan minister. He was perfectly aware of Venezuela's responsibility to confront such acts of terrorism and of the need to stand in solidarity with the universal aim to ensure acts of such nature are not repeated or left unpunished.

I should also mention that in those days an Arab ambassador forewarned me that, whatever sanctions we might impose on Libya, we should not remove Ghaddafi from power, since: "He is the only one able to control the more than one hundred tribes that coexist in Libya." It was a prophetic vision of the reality that country and its people are currently under. Finally, on March 31, 1992, acting under Venezuela's chair, the United Nations Security Council passed Resolution 748. The Resolution imposed on the government of Libya a significant trade embargo and a prohibition to buy weapons until it agreed to stop giving assistance to terrorist groups.

The following day, agents of the Ghaddafi regime set fire to our embassy headquarters in Tripoli. Some leftist Venezuelan politicians, long time beneficiaries of Ghaddafi's generosity with extremist groups, denounced Venezuela's vote in favor of the Resolution, arguing that both countries were partners in OPEC. We paid no attention to such complaints. On the contrary, I immediately addressed a note to the Security Council requesting reparations from the Libyan government for damages suffered from the fire set to our embassy and the two terrorist attacks. Acting in consequence, the Council approved the pertinent reparations, a process that took years, until finally, on August 15, 2002, the Libyan ambassador to the United Nations formally acknowledged his government's responsibility in the bombing of the two airplanes and agreed to pay ten million dollars in compensation to each of the victim's families.

What I could not have imagined then and was overwhelming proof of the dubious ways in which the behavior of international powers belittles the United Nations′ reason-to-be, was that the two countries that had most ardently sponsored the adoption of sanctions against Ghaddafi – France and the United Kingdom – were the very same that not too many years later would act in complete oblivion of the enormous gravity of the two terrorist attacks. In December 2007, the President of France, Nicolas Sarkozy, received with full honors Muamar Ghaddafi, on a five-day state visit. Just months before, several French oil companies had signed with the Libyan government contracts worth more than fifteen billion dollars. Some years later, in March 2011, Tony Blair, Prime Minister of the United Kingdom, met with Ghaddafi in his luxurious Saharan tent and with great satisfaction announced the signature of a five-hundred-and-fifty million pounds contract between the oil company Shell and the Libyan government. It all came to prove that anything, even the worst acts of terrorism, can be forgotten, and even condoned, on the strength of Euros, Dollars, or Pounds Sterling.

Iraq Once More on The Dock

In keeping with its Arab affairs tilt, March ended with the announcement of an imminent visit to New York by Tariq Aziz, Deputy Prime Minister and Minister of Foreign Affairs of Iraq, who for many years had been Saddam Hussein's right hand, to meet with the Security Council's members.

After Iraq's invasion of Kuwait, the Security Council had imposed sanctions on Hussein's government which included an embargo on all its international trade and financial transactions, except for those on food and medicines. Following Iraq's surrender on February 27, 1991, the Security Council held numerous debates that ended with the adoption, on April 3, 1991, of Resolution 682, dubbed by many, paraphrasing Saddam, the "Mother of all Resolutions". Under this Resolution, the Council expanded the sanctions, ordered Iraq's military forces to completely disarm and the repatriation of Kuwaiti prisoners, imposed important economic reparations to Kuwait and the return of property seized during the occupation of the Emirate. It imposed serious restrictions on the production and export of oil, limiting them to the strictly necessary to pay for Iraq's most urgent humanitarian needs. It equally ordered the deployment of a UN Observer Mission along the Iraq-Kuwait border, the demilitarization of a fifteen-kilometer-wide corridor between both countries, the destruction of all chemical and biological weapons, and of all the facilities that might serve Iraq to research, develop, and fabricate such weapons, as well as ballistic missiles with a range of more than one hundred and fifty kilometers. Finally, it put the Saddam Hussein government under the obligation not to acquire in the future nuclear weapons nor the materials and components necessary for their production and requested the International Atomic Energy Agency to verify on the ground Iraq's nuclear development potential. On his visit to the Council, Aziz wished to strongly protest this last and decisive resolution.

No doubt, it was to be a historic meeting, and as it fell on me to chair the proceedings, I took a few precautions to ensure the Iraqi Minister of Foreign Affairs did not turn his visit to the United Nations into an act of political propaganda. To begin with, I met with the former Swedish Minister of Foreign Affairs, Hans Blix, at the time head of the United Nations International Atomic Energy Agency, and with the also Swedish diplomat Rolf Ekeus, who was the Secretary General's Representative for monitoring sanctions on Iraq. Both coincided in pointing out to me that there was no indication that Iraq, while not fully complying with the agreed inspections program, was in possession of nuclear weapons or had the capacity to develop them. Not even an underwater exploration team of divers sent by the French government had found any trace of radioactivity along the Tigris River. I also met with the ambassadors of the Arab countries to sound their governments' positions and brief them on the Security Council's views on the situation in Iraq.

Finally, on March 9, two days before Aziz's participation in the Council's open session, I met him in my office as President of the Council. He came to the meeting accompanied by Iraq's Representative to the United Nations, Abdul Amir al-Anbari. To my surprise, shortly after exchanging the usual courtesies, Aziz asked his ambassador to leave the room. With me was Counselor Victor Manzanares, of Venezuela's Mission to the UN, in charge of taking notes of all my bilateral meetings.

While the ambassador took his leave and we approached our seats, I took a good look at my counterpart. He carried himself with the demeanor of a mature man. He had left in Baghdad his olive-green uniform and his side pistol and was now dressed in an elegant dark blue business suit, held a big *Cohiba* cigar in his hand and moved and talked with the air of a well-fed lord. I could not help but wonder why the Iraqi minister had so abruptly dismissed his ambassador. What was it he wished to tell me that the latter was not privy to hear?

— Excellency – Aziz began - I come as a brother since, as you know, we are brothers, brothers in OPEC, and we have many times in the past acted united in many struggles. I very particularly remember the visit President Pérez paid to us in 1974, when we were both defending OPEC. I understand exactly how you must feel!

— What do you mean, Your Excellency? I replied.

— I mean how you must feel under the pressure of the big powers that rule in the Council, because both our countries are small and the big powers take advantage of us and...

— Excellency – I interrupted him. I do not know if I understood you correctly but allow me to tell you something. The Council is indeed a place where pressures, many pressures, are brought to bear, but in the case at hand they are not applied by the more powerful nations. Believe me when I say, and I must forcefully stress this, that it is we, the smaller nations represented in the Council, who are putting pressure on the big powers. Indeed, we must make sure that more powerful nations do not abuse their power the way your government did with Kuwait.

My harsh and unexpected interjection irked the Iraqi Prime Minister and made him leave his Cohiba unattended on a close-by ashtray. He even blushed, but after a short pause recovered his composure.

"Excellency this and excellency that," he went on, until I once more interrupted him with not very diplomatic abruptness.

— You should not, I warned him, leave this meeting with a false impression. The Security Council is unanimous about the sanctions we have agreed to place on Iraq and about your government's failure to comply with them. The Council is well informed by all the organizations in charge of monitoring compliance, and we have the support of the vast majority of UN members to fully enforce them within the established period. You will tomorrow be able to verify this state of affairs, which I have conveyed to you speaking in my capacity as representative of Venezuela and as president of the Security Council.

There was not much more to talk about, and I walked him to the door where his daughter, whom he very graciously introduced to me, waited for him in the company of Ambassador Al-Anbari. The following day, eve of his meeting with the Security Council, we met again. He had requested a meeting with the ambassadors of the six Non-Aligned members of the Council: Zimbabwe, Cape Verde, Ecuador, Morocco, India and Venezuela.

— Minister – I said to open the meeting since I also coordinated the activities of this group – you have the floor, and in due regard to your request, all the representatives of the Non-Aligned Movement in the Security Council are here to hear what you have to say.

Aziz begun his intervention with the same words he had used during his meeting with me the day before: "I understand how you must feel under pressure from…" Once more, I curtly interrupted him:

— Excellency, allow me to inform my colleagues that yesterday, on the occasion of the private meeting we had, you pronounced those very same words, and I informed you that you should not make the mistake of thinking we are under pressure from the more powerful members of the Council. I take this opportunity to reiterate to you that it is us, the Non-Aligned, who are putting pressure.

Obviously, the meeting did not go on for much longer. The day after, the Iraqi minister of Foreign Affairs presented his country's position in the great hall of the Security Council. I had taken my place at ten o'clock sharp, and after greeting the Secretary General, Boutros-Ghali, who sat at my right, I opened the session and gave the floor to Saddam Hussein's representative, who went on to reiterate Iraq did not deserve the enormous sacrifice brought upon it by the sanctions, and that "Any fair and professional evaluation of the situation would conclude signaling the time had come to lift them."

In that morning's edition, *The Los Angeles Times* reported that not a single member of the Council was inclined to give its support to the government of Iraq's request. Its exact words were: "Diego Arria, the Ambassador of Venezuela who chairs the Council, will today open the session with a statement on behalf of the same, informing Iraq of the grave consequences that would follow if it continued to not comply with its obligations towards the United Nations." It then went on to say: "After meeting in private with Tariq Aziz, Arria made a statement to the press indicating he had been noticeably clear in reminding the visitor that Baghdad must understand the unconditional nature of its obligations towards the United Nations. And that, only after full compliance would the sanctions be lifted"

In my statement that morning, I reiterated that position: "The decision we are about to adopt on the need to keep or remove sanctions is almost completely the sole responsibility of the government of Iraq. We must insist that Iraq's reencounter with itself will only take place when its rulers completely satisfy all its international obligations. It is equally a priority for Iraq to urgently satisfy all due compensations and indemnities, in particular towards Kuwait, and to abide by its obligations in relation to disappeared persons, devolution of property seized during the occupation of Kuwait, and the delimitation of the border separating both territories."

That morning I asked our Press Attaché, Ramuncho Llerandi, to convene a press conference in the UN Correspondents'

Press Room at the end of the meeting. Shortly after he came to tell me that the Secretariat wished to inform me that the presidents of the Council did not give press conferences. "Well, please inform the Secretariat it is welcomed to witness the first one." And that was what we did. We held the press conference, the first ever by a president of the Council, and I took the opportunity to denounce the hegemonic nature of the information policy practiced by the Secretariat and by the countries that are in control of Security Council procedures. With that in mind, when a journalist recalled that Aziz had denounced that "The Council continued to put sanctions on Iraq because its government refused to name the friendly nations that for years had provided it with weapons and chemicals," my reply was clear cut:

— They do not make them public because the sellers happen to be Permanent Members of the Council.

The Shifting Sands of the Council

The more I immersed myself into the ever-shifting world of negotiations and deals within the Council, the more I realized how important the independent media was. For example: in its May 15, 1991 editorial, the Spanish daily *El País* expressed in very few lines and without any of the customary deceit imposed on the Council by the national interests of Russia, France and the United Kingdom, the seriousness of what was clearly a flagrant military invasion of Bosnia by Serbia:

"Yesterday, new Serbian artillery shelling pounded the city of Sarajevo and its outskirts. Combats are ongoing in other parts of Bosnia. Everything that is taking place indicates that Serbia, notwithstanding President Milosevic's pacifist declarations, continues to carry forward its plan to occupy territory belonging to other republics. To do so, it supports irregular groups that murder and terrorize the civilian population while giving its army leeway to occupy cities and rural areas (...) Fighting does not happen because racial hatreds suddenly blow up between people who have lived in the same places for centuries. It is the result of the plan to create a Greater Serbia by taking territories by force of arms..."

This editorial by the Spanish daily was an exact record of what was taking place in Bosnia, and it made no mention of the Security Council. It was as if Serbia enjoyed enough support within the United Nations to allow itself to simply ignore the commitments and obligations entered upon in Sarajevo on January 4 between the Serbian and Bosnian military leadership, which included the cease fire sponsored by Cyrus Vance as an indispensable step towards a durable and effective peace agreement. The cease fire agreement was an extension of an earlier one, equally promoted by Vance, signed in Geneva on November 23 of the previous year by the presidents of Serbia and Croatia to put an end to the war between both countries. That the Milosevic government should openly ignore the agreed-upon unconditional cease fire evidenced how ineffective was the deployment of UNPROFOR's thirteen-thousand peacekeepers in Croatia and later in Bosnia, even though their mandate, established by the Council's Resolution adopted on February 21, was precisely to guarantee that all parties abide by the terms of those agreements. The Resolution also provided for the mandatory demilitarization of the region's more conflictive areas, a stop to ethnic cleansing and a return home of families displaced by force, all with the purpose of facilitating the establishment of "the peace and security conditions necessary for the negotiation of a global arrangement of the Yugoslav crisis." With equal purpose it established a mission of military observers to be deployed along the border between Bosnia and Croatia.

What Was Really Taking Place in Bosnia?

During those early months, developments made it evident that Serbia would not remotely consider the option of modifying its policy of ethnic cleansing. It followed that the Blue Helmets, restricted by the Security Council and the UN Secretariat to play a role of simple observers of the conflict, would not be able to exercise the kind of pressure needed to dissuade the Serbian authorities.

Belgrade´s frontal and reiterated noncompliance with the agreements negotiated by the political and military authorities of both governments pushed the Council to adopt a remarkable string of ineffective Resolutions, all of them perfectly engineered to support the Permanent Five's comfortable position of not intervening in situations that did not have a bearing on their direct interests. The first of this endless series of Resolutions was the one adopted on May 15, 1992, to reiterate the UN´s suggestion to the Serbian, Croat, and Bosnian leaderships "To constructively take part in the talks proposed by Secretary General Boutros-Ghali to approve and implement without delay the arrangements agreed-upon in the negotiations".

It should be noted that by that time the air in the Security Council had become unbreathable. So much so that on November 16 we approved Resolution 787, which, for the first time, denounced the aberrant violations of the UN Charter committed in Bosnia by the Serbian aggressors, including the persecution and extermination of civilians for ethnic and religious reasons, the physical destruction of areas inhabited by Bosnian Muslims, the establishment of concentration camps, the systematic violation of human rights, and the violation of Bosnia´s sovereignty. Those were the very same crimes that had galvanized the world into action and had led to the establishment of the United Nations in 1947. Crimes that we had wrongly come to believe were things of the past, once the Soviet Union ceased to exist and the perils associated with the Cold War ended.

The very same nations that at the end of the Second World War had taken upon themselves the ambitious project of establishing a free and safe world for all, should have been astonished to witness the boundless cruelty with which the Serbian authorities were challenging the will and mettle of the international community. The very same nations that in Nuremberg and Tokyo had sentenced countless war criminals seemed now unwilling to take concrete measures to put a stop to the killing of defenseless civilians in Bosnia. The resolution deplored the situation, prohibited, starting that very day, military flights over the Bosnian airspace and ordered to place under total control of the United Nations the heavy Serbian artillery used every day to bomb that republic's cities and towns. All to no avail. The Serbs continued to act in Bosnia with total impunity. Even worse, instead of stopping the massacre of Bosnian civilians, the resolution, though strongly worded, made plain to the world's public opinion the growing deterioration of the Security Council's credibility, so much so that Radovan Karadzic, President of the illegal Serbian Srpska republic, and leader of that abhorrent "ethnic cleansing", dared the world with an unheard-of challenge: "We have the Muslim Bosnians trapped as rats in a cage".

Karadzic was convinced, and not without reason, that no harm would come to him from the international community. The silence and aloofness of the Council regarding what was happening in the former Yugoslavia were deafening. That was why, with the support of only a few other ambassadors, such as those of Pakistan and Hungary, I took it upon myself to argue that Bosnia was not only being decimated in both human and territorial terms by Serbian regular troops and paramilitaries, but that the Council's demands and recommendations had become totally irrelevant and even counterproductive, since they made Serbia and its henchmen in Bosnia believe they could carry on with their territorial conquests by fire and blood without any major hindrance. It was a fact that shortly afterwards made Milosevic feel empowered to extend his imperialistic war to Kosovo, Vojvodina and Macedonia.

It should also not be forgotten that in that November 16 session of the Council, Cyrus Vance did not even deign to mention the crimes the Security Council had finally denounced and, in a certain way, placed himself on the side of the aggressors by stating that "The international community did not give up on solving the conflict on the basis of a political agreement negotiated among the parties", omitting to condemn the forced displacement of citizens for ethnic reasons, the illegal detentions, or the Serb pretension to modify the demographic composition of the Republic of Bosnia, openly violating its sovereignty and territorial integrity.

My reaction was immediate.

— Your words – I warned Vance that day – even if they are the very same words ambassadors of the Non-Aligned Movement repeat every day in the Council, amount to the Carrington-Cutileiro plan in disguise, a plan that conditions the solution of the conflict to a real and final breakup of Bosnia as an independent republic, tearing it apart demographically. With all due respect to former Secretary of State Vance, it is my duty to point out that by his statement to the Council he is trying to influence international public opinion in favor of a division of Bosnia into cantons, nothing less, without solving the problem at all.

That morning I denounced Vance's attempt to make the international community swallow a more digestible version of the *apartheid* favored by the governments of France and the United Kingdom, with the full support of the Secretary General and the silent consent of the Bush Administration. In a statement I made to the press in those days, I described the situation in Bosnia as a "Chronicle of a death foretold" paraphrasing the title of a short novel by Gabriel García Márquez. Indeed, no matter how one might have wanted to look at it, it was evident that the Serbian government, without bothering with any kind of dissimulation, was carrying out a war of ethnic cleansing of the Bosnian Muslim population, a tragedy that would very soon merit to be recalled as the chronicle of an execution.

My Patience Runs Out

I must confess that I had come to the United Nations driven by the conviction that by its very existence the UN was proof of the commitment by all to make true the universal aspiration to live in peace, and by the belief that no nation could trample with impunity the rights of other nations. It was inadmissible to subject the world to a tragedy similar to the one caused by the Nazi delirium and to horrors similar to those of World War II. It was precisely to avoid the repetition of such despicable events that the United Nations had been created. I couldn't have been more mistaken! As the final days of 1992 approached, a sense of deep disappointment overcame me. With indignation, I witnessed how, in the name of the same ethnic purification policies adopted by Hitler and his lieutenants to justify the monstrosities of the Third Reich, the Serbian people, who had so valiantly fought against the Nazi, now repeated those very same crimes with identical cruelty, while the world, once again, preferred to look the other way.

In other words, the same powers that controlled the United Nations had put aside the Organization's reason to be. They had chosen to ignore that, to a large extent, the prestige the UN had enjoyed until then was a consequence of its successful fight against discrimination and ethnic segregation. It seemed to me inexplicable that, suddenly, the very same United Nations would refuse to acknowledge that the Serbian government's policy of extermination of the Muslim population in the former Yugoslavia was the other side of that same contemptible Nazi coin. Within this context, the UN was completely discredited by its acceptance of Serbia's continued involvement in Bosnia and by not recognizing the right of Bosnian citizens to defend their very own human rights and the preservation of peace, which are the essence of the values the UN is based on.

I believed then, as I still do now, that the General Assembly and the Security Council should have taken up the defense of the Bosnian people decisively. I have not tired of pointing out the passivity with which the United Nations dealt with the whole catalog of atrocities and war crimes committed by the Serbs, including the systematic violation of thousands of women and girls, and the murder of children: "(Because) if we don't kill them now we'll have to do it when they're older". As the Croat writer Slavenka Drakulic states in her shocking book *"They Would Never Hurt a Fly: War Criminals on Trial at The Hague"*, published in 2004, "The world is in debt with the women and children whose lives have been criminally destroyed. The stories of some of the victims and the statements of some Serbian soldiers describe a situation to be ranked only at the same level of the worst Nazi crimes".

The many voices claiming for justice went unheard. Therefore, on November 16, 1992, addressing the Council, I stated that "It should be sufficiently clear to all that it is inadmissible that might be right. No de facto arrangement derived from the use of force is compatible with the principles of the Organization and should not be accepted by any of its members. It is imperative, without any further excuse or delay, to take collective measures to suppress, as the Charter indicates, such acts of aggression". In that context, I reminded the Council that barely six months after the deployment of UNPROFOR, Egyptian General Hussein Abdel-Razek, who commanded its contingent in Sarajevo and was therefore a witness of exception to the cruelty of the Serbian siege of that city, publicly declared his peace mission had failed, and that "Only a military intervention could put a stop to the Serbian aggression".

It is equally worth remembering the answer given to General Razek by the Serbian General Momir Talic, Commander of the units besieging Sarajevo: "Those who might come here on a war path will not leave alive." Furthermore, during those very same days, the Minister of Defense of the illegal Srpska Serbian Republic of Bosnia, Bogdan Subotic, would add with absolute cynicism: "We will not allow the creation of a Muslim republic in the heart of Europe. By our actions we are really assisting Europe and the United States in guaranteeing that goal. There are no reasons for them to want to intervene."

This exchange of declarations, reported by the international media, did not make any impact on the UN Secretariat nor on the Security Council, prey to the political interests of its more powerful members. That was the reason no initiative was taken to put a stop to Serbian crimes in Bosnia. From that moment on, the moral authority of the United Nations was in doubt. As the end of my first year as a member of the Council approached, I had to admit my patience had run out.

The Murder of Hakija Turaljic, Bosnian Deputy Prime Minister

The event that made me lose what was left of my very diminished capacity for diplomatic dissimulation occurred at the very beginning of the new year, exactly on January 8, 1993, when news reached us that Hakija Turaljic, Deputy Prime Minister of Bosnia for Economic Affairs, had been brutally murdered by seven shots fired by a Serbian soldier into the interior of a United Nations armored vehicle, notwithstanding the vehicle was under the custody of UNPROFOR´s French military personnel.

The vehicle was carrying the minister from Sarajevo airport to his office in the Government Palace, a journey of barely twelve kilometers along the city´s main avenue. Around noon that day, Turaljic had accompanied six Turkish officials who the previous day had delivered an important shipment of humanitarian aid to the city. The journey went ahead without incident until about after four p.m., when, on his way back to his office, the armored vehicle in which he was travelling was stopped at an illegal checkpoint manned by forty Serbian paramilitaries supported by a tank unit, at merely three hundred meters from the French battalion´s encampment.

Later it was disclosed that the French crew had agreed to show its identification documents, but the Bosnian Deputy Prime Minister had refused to show his as the procedure was illegal and placed him at personal risk. Soon afterwards, the Bosnian official´s French military escort, contravening UNPROFOR guidelines that forbade it, opened the vehicle´s rear door and allowed a Serbian soldier inside to try to convince the minister. The soldier exited the vehicle after failing in his endeavor and the French escort closed the door. Almost an hour later, at five p.m., the Serb officer acting as liaison with the Blue Helmet command, arrived at the checkpoint. Once again, the security protocol was violated and the rear door of the vehicle was opened to let this individual in. For unknown reasons, Turaljic, who had spent more than an hour locked inside the armored vehicle, submitted his passport for inspection and the Serbian officer came out, passport in hand, to supposedly verify with his superiors the identity of the passenger, but nobody bothered to close the door. Another mistake that would carry tragic consequences.

In the meantime, Colonel Patrice Sartre, commander of the French battalion, had arrived at the checkpoint, almost simultaneously with four armored vehicles of the UN Protection Forces staffed by troops from the United Kingdom and Ukraine. However, the Serbian paramilitaries did not allow them passage. Instead of taking advantage of those unexpected reinforcements to shore up the vulnerable position in which Turajlic's vehicle stood, guarded by only three French soldiers, Colonel Sartre inexplicably chose to merely ask the Serbian command to allow safe passage to the four newly arrived vehicles. Then, according to his declarations, speaking from the vehicle's rear door, kept unexplainably open, he tried to calm the Serbian soldiers, who were, as he would later recall, "visibly agitated and trying to get inside the vehicle". It is truly unjustifiable that Colonel Sartre should have not tried to make those soldiers withdraw, a decision that led one of them to fire seven shots from his AK-47 at the Bosnian Deputy Prime Minister, who died instantly. Why the French government, instead of condemning Sartre's conduct, chose to decorate him, is beyond understanding.

When news of the crime reached Washington, president Alija Izetbegovic was in a meeting with a group of Bill Clinton advisors. Clinton had won the election and was soon to be inaugurated. The meeting had not been easy to set up since both Vance and Owen were of the view Izetbegovic opposed their peace plan and was withholding his decision waiting for the new administration to take an official position, hopefully in favor of a military intervention in Bosnia by the international community.

Obviously, the meeting was suspended. Soon after, the Bosnian Ambassador, Muhamed Sacirbey, called me to request the president of the Council, Ambassador Yoshio

Hatano, convene an emergency meeting to examine the possibility of responding forcefully to the crime, as mandated by the UN Charter in cases such as this. I shared his position and immediately contacted Hatano. The Council, however, only agreed to draft a statement of condemnation and to request the Secretary General to urgently investigate the incident.

I then talked with President Izetbegovic, who was profoundly saddened by the death of one of his closest collaborators. He told me that thanks to Turajlic his government had been able to block the funds of Bosnian companies registered in Mexico's Federal District, Chicago, and other US cities. According to Izetbegovic, it was what had made Milosevic and Karadzic consider Turajlic a dangerous enemy, and a probable cause of his murder.

The reaction by the Bosnian Vice-President, Ejup Ganic, was forceful and clear cut: "Turajlic was murdered inside a UN vehicle, in a road under UN control, and protected by UN military personnel. The UN is consequently responsible for his murder." Even General Philippe Morillon, Commander of the Blue Helmets in Bosnia agreed with Ganic by stating that the crime amounted to "a failure by UNPROFOR that placed peace at risk".

I remember very well the impact these events had in the United Nations, just as I remember that very soon all interest in the issue was lost. Nobody ever gave a satisfactory explanation of how could it be that a Bosnian Deputy Prime Minister for Economic Affairs was murdered inside a vehicle under the protection of a group of French Blue Helmets, only three hundred meters from their camp. Nor was it clarified why not a single French unit moved to assist their comrades in arms, notwithstanding the fact that from their position they could see clearly what was happening at the illegal checkpoint set up by the Serbs. Turajlic's murder might not have been the reenactment of Archduke Francis Ferdinand's assassination in Sarajevo, but I am absolutely sure that the international reaction would have been vastly different if the victim had been a high-ranking European or American official.

As I would state many years after, on the occasion of Slobodan Milosevic´s trial, the Security Council´s passivity led the Serbian government to believe it could get away with anything. I furthermore believe that Turaljic´s murder marked a turning point in the criminal behavior of the Serbs. If the international community did not react to the murder of a Bosnian Deputy Prime Minister while under UN military protection, everything was possible. Nothing would stop the aggressors. Impunity was the law.

The Darkest Night

On December 25, 1992, while all believed the worst was still to come in the Bosnia crisis, Boutros-Ghali made a surprise visit to Sarajevo, the city under bombardment. Months before, speaking from UN Headquarters in New York, he had made a disconcerting statement on the situation: "If we compare what is taking place in Bosnia with the famine suffered by the Somalian population, which receives a minor attention from the media, Bosnia´s situation is a rich man´s war". When he now arrived in Sarajevo, in the middle of an unrelentless siege by irregular Bosnian-Serb troops, he had nothing better to say than to reiterate to a group of journalists the same unfortunate vision of the Bosnian conflict. "I can give you – he said without hesitation – a list of ten places in the world where there are more problems and where life is more difficult than in Sarajevo".

On that Christmas Day morning, in the company of Cyrus Vance, he went directly from the airport to the government palace, where he would be meeting Vice President Ejup Ganic. A host of local citizens were also waiting for him. Openly defying Serb snipers, they met him to the cries of "Ghali, Fascist" and "Ghali, Hitler". In Belgrade, the Secretary General´s truly unfortunate comments reinforced the Serbian belief that the international community would not go beyond rhetorical denunciations and fruitless recommendations.

Prior to Boutros-Ghali´s trip to Sarajevo, on December 20, 1992, Slobodan Milosevic had been re-elected, in a process totally under his government's control. All polls coincided in giving victory to Milan Panic, an independent opposition candidate, but fraud by officialdom weighed more than real votes. Douglas Schoen, Milan Panic's American electoral strategist, and an old personal friend of mine, who had taken part in several electoral events in Venezuela, later told me that with this fraud democracy had lost "an exceptional opportunity". He would later expound this opinion in an article titled "How Milosevic Stole the Election", published by The New York Times on February 14. In its conclusions he highlighted the gravity of the crisis in the Former Yugoslavia by stating that Serbia had not only committed a monumental electoral fraud, but the international community had equally validated it by its silence, "It had given up on putting an end to the most atrocious armed conflict experienced by Europe in the last fifty years."

Bill Clinton Arrives at the White House

A month after that electoral farce, on January 20, Bill Clinton swore the Oath of Office as the new President of the United States. During his electoral campaign he had condemned the Serbian aggression in Bosnia on several occasions. Once president, he declared: "If the horrors of the Nazi Holocaust teach us anything it is the high cost you end up paying if we remain impassive and silent in the face of crimes against humanity". It was his way of denouncing his predecessor, who had not taken any action to put a stop to the expansion of ultranationalist Serbia at the expense of neighboring nations. President Bush had not even done anything to force Milosevic to close his torture and extermination camps in Bosnia, a passivity that he had justified with the false argument of not having sufficient information to confirm the atrocities denounced by media reports such as those by Roy Gutman and other independent journalists.

Not by coincidence, the White House's position was basically in sync with the comfortable policy of "neutrality" adopted by the State Department to explain why it left in European hands the handling of the Bosnian crisis. It was a policy that allowed the US Ambassador to the Security

Council, Thomas Pickering Jr., to support without reservations the position taken by the United Kingdom, France and Russia in all matters concerning Bosnia. It was the same position that, later on, although with some reservations, Madeleine Albright, President Clinton's nominee to that position, would uphold.

In any case, it might be said that in early 1993 the contradictions between these reservations and the position held by now former president Bush to confront the Serbian aggression in Bosnia did not make any easier the negotiations, conducted for months by Cyrus Vance and David Owen on behalf of the UN Security Council and the European Community. Their goal was to present to the parties a modified version of the already rejected peace plan proposed by Carrington and Cutileiro as mediators. Indeed, the revision basically amounted to an reinterpretation of the latter. Instead of insisting on the partition of the newly established republic into three independent ethnic districts, it proposed the creation of ten semi-autonomous communities, coordinated by a central government made up of representatives of the three ethnic groups. Basically, the same dog with a different collar. This would allow Russia to support both Milosevic's Serbia and the Vance-Owen plan, while at the same time forcefully rejecting Washington's reservations about any territorial division along ethnic lines. Needless to say, the United Kingdom and France went along with Russia in its support of the new peace plan, while China, as usual, kept its distance from the negotiations.

After his visit to Sarajevo, Boutros-Ghali, who never tired of publicly expressing his support for the plan, even went as far as to harshly criticize the Bosnian government, accusing it of not taking a position, waiting for the new American president to announce his. In his mind, Izetbegovic held the secret hope Clinton would favor an international military intervention. The Bosnian Croats, the other main protagonists in the crisis, agreed with the plan, but the Bosnian Serbs rejected it arguing that it only gave the illegal Srpska Republic forty percent of the Bosnian territory, following the maps drawn up by cartographers of the Vance-Owen plan, while in reality its troops already controlled seventy percent. Meanwhile, the Bosnian Prime Minister, Haris Silajdzic, announced his government would only sign the Vance-Owen proposal if the Security Council agreed to take full control of the Serbian heavy artillery deployed in Bosnian territory.

Therefore, a highly tense environment prevailed during the days immediately prior to Bill Clinton´s swearing-in as the new president of the United States. Meanwhile, Vance, who had tired of waiting, suddenly announced that if the agreement was not signed shortly, both he and Owen would withdraw and leave the issue in the hands of the Security Council. Owen, in turn, once again requested the Bosnian Muslim authorities not to prolong needlessly a war that, to his mind, made absolutely no sense.

It is time to end the war - the English diplomat stated – We have truly little time left, and it is imperative Izetbegovic and Karadzic learn to negotiate the limits of their territories and their borders.

I presume both, particularly Owen, native son of an empire that had modified many maps and traced the borders of quite a few territories beyond their legitimate confines, believed that for the aggressors and the attacked to agree was truly such a trivial issue that it did not justify the prolongation of a war he deemed futile. It was precisely with the purpose of skirting the land borders issue and of accelerating the approval of their peace plan, that Vance and Owen requested the US State Department to issue a visa to Karadzic, who was under indictment by a New York District Court for a number of war crimes committed in Bosnia, including genocide, so he could travel to New York and take part in a meeting with the Bosnian Muslim Alija Izetbegovic and the Serb Croat, Mate Boban. They hoped this would be the last chapter in the negotiations. The visa was obviously granted, and the meetings between the representatives of the parties soon began. All the meetings were held at closed doors and all in different rooms of the United Nations building, since the parties refused to negotiate directly with each other and demanded to do so through the intermediation of the plan´s proponents. It was in that context that Vance and Owen reached out to me and asked me, as Coordinator of the Non-Aligned Caucus of the Council, to intercede between them and the Bosnian government representatives to be more flexible in their positions and facilitate a final agreement.

I agreed to do so but, as I had been warned by Ambassador Sacirbey, with whom I had developed a close personal and professional relationship during those difficult months, President Izetbegovic categorically refused to meet with Karadzic, arguing that to do so would amount to a recognition of his mandate as president of the illegal Srpska. And because, bottom line, the Bosnian government was absolutely committed to not signing an agreement that would imply a cession of any part of the territory of the republic to Karadzic´s illegal Bosnian Serb government. Just a couple of days before, Vice President Al Gore had approached the room where the Bosnian delegation was meeting and, according to what Sacirbey revealed to me, told President Izetbegovic the US did not blame his government for refusing to sign the agreement: "I wouldn´t do so, either". Later, Sacirbey would confide in me that on hearing Gore´s message, the State Department´s representative in charge of the Bosnia issue almost had a stroke.

Peace at Any Price

On the eve of the swearing-in of Bill Clinton as Forty-Second President of the United States, Boutros-Ghali and the Permanent Members of the Security Council, concerned about the possibility that US public opinion might exert undue influence and become an uncomfortable factor, did all they could to limit the information available to the media on the magnitude and scale of the Bosnia crisis and to minimize the uncompromising nature of the positions held by Izetbegovic, Milosevic and Karadzic. They were even less eager for the press to divulge the arguments that described the partition of Bosnia as a violation of fundamental ethical and political principles. The Vance-Owen duo thoroughly endeavored to minimize the impact the reasons underlying the Bosnian Muslim leaders′ opposition to the division of their nation were starting to have on public opinion.

In the meantime, and even though the peace negotiations went ahead without much progress, the conviction prevailed in the United Nations that an agreement would soon be signed, ending the war. In such an environment of unfounded optimism, I had the opportunity to meet, at a dinner at the Israeli Ambassador′s residence, *The New York Times′* former director, Abraham Rosenthal, author of an influential weekly column. At a certain point in our conversation someone mentioned I was a member of the Security Council, and he then made the comment that in his February 15 column, he had given the Vance-Owen plan his broadest endorsement.

I had not had the opportunity to read the article, so that very evening, upon arriving home, I impatiently looked for it.

"Everybody shouts, but no one hears - the article begun – Seldom have so many analysts and editorialists raised their voices to express their bitter discomfort and their condemnation of Western diplomats for their support to the Cyrus Vance and Lord Owen plan. Both villains because they have proposed a peace plan for Bosnia that implies the creation of a decentralized state (...) Serbs, Croats, Christians, and Muslims, all of the same nationality, pitted against each other by a secular hatred, without taking into consideration that with the plan now under negotiation each ethnic group would be a majority in some districts, and would all take part in the nation′s government".

This position, so lacking in nuances, expressed by such a prestigious and influential media personality, made me understand how such opinions, presumably in favor of a peace arrangement in Bosnia no matter the price, hid the true intentions of its promoters and the consequences its implementation would have on the harassed Muslim population of Bosnia. Within this context, it is worth recalling another article published by the same daily and following the same absurd reasoning, although much more controversial, titled "To Save Bosnia, Make it Smaller", signed by John Mearsheimer, a professor at the University of Chicago and a very reputed specialist in international political and security issues.

"There is no alternative to a peace settlement in Bosnia – it pointed out – not because such a negotiated peace would save the parties from the terrible consequences of a prolongation in time of what already is a long and bloody war without any winners in sight, but to bring back to life, without frills or artifice, the establishment of a new Bosnian state that, as proposed by Carrington and Cutileiro months ago, would be "a third of its current size, where all the Muslim population would concentrate... and (would leave) the rest of the territory in the hands of the Serbian and Croat populations". Following Mearsheimer's calculations, the adoption of this plan would imply the peaceful resettlement of some six-hundred thousand Bosnian Muslims, three-hundred thousand Serbs and a hundred thousand Croats, who would need to recognize the legitimate existence of a Greater Serbia and commit themselves to help it consolidate its new borders."

Mearsheimer, as a faithful advocate of the so-called "Offensive Realism", a theory that considers the main goal of a state is to strive for or maximize unrestrained power, gave legitimacy to the policies carried out by Serbia in Bosnia, which included ethnic purification, conquest of new territory by force of arms, and the recognition of the Greater Serbia Milosevic dreamed of.

From the Commission of Experts to the International Criminal Court

The issues behind the controversy were tremendously complex, as I stated in my first intervention as member of the Security Council, on January 21, 1992. At the time, I had pointed out that ever since 1948, the United Nations had been prompting the creation of an international criminal tribunal to investigate, put to trial and punish those responsible for any crime against humanity. "But – I added – after forty-two years of deliberations and debates on the issue no substantial results have been reached, and it is high time we do so since we cannot continue to deal with these crimes against humanity with mere academic discussions. Appropriate measures must be taken to punish such crimes, which have a bearing on international security and weigh heavily on the immediate future. Impunity – I concluded - is a menace we cannot tolerate".

I took the floor during the open session of the Council held on October 6, 1992, to denounce that in Bosnia, "The powerful do as they will, and the weak suffer what they must", Thucydides′ words in his monumental History of the Peloponnesian Wars. A barbaric policy the Serbians had been applying without pity or remorse in Bosnia for almost a year, in flagrant defiance of the values that are the foundations of the United Nations and its Security Council. There was not much more we could do – I then said – beyond placing our trust on the establishment and operation of a Commission charged with investigating, putting on trial and sentencing those responsible for crimes against humanity. An approach similar to that which condemned to the scaffold and to long prison sentences many Second World War criminals. I also pointed out that: "The only crime not committed in Bosnia is that Bertrand Russell called "the crime of silence", because, thanks to the extraordinary job done by the media, the world has been able to witness the most terrible devastation brought upon a sovereign nation by another, condemning thousands of innocent citizens to death, hunger, fear and despair".

The international media had begun to disclose information showing the scope of the unfolding tragedy. In the United Nations, nobody opposed any longer drawing the curtains open on such a pitiful reality. Prompted by the Security Council, which could no longer ignore the existence of concentration camps operated by the Serbian authorities in militarily occupied Bosnian areas, Boutros-Ghali had no other option but to address the issue and clarify whether or not in those "detention centers" brutal torture was applied to prisoners, whether some had been murdered and whether the systematic rape of Muslim women had taken place.

On the other hand, those keen on imposing the division of Bosnia into cantons according to the Vance-Owen plan, were spreading news about the high cost a continuation of war would entail. Confronted by the growing scandal brought about by the monstrosities committed by Serbian troops in occupied Bosnia, they took advantage of this apparent contradiction to quell the outrage of some, and dampen the guilt of others, like the Security Council itself, which was not doing its duty to defend the sovereign rights of an independent nation such as Bosnia, nor the human rights of its civilian population.

For all these reasons, during the last weeks of 1992 and the early part of the new year, the number of countries accusing the Council of applying a double standard according to the interests and political, ethnic and religious prejudices of its more powerful members, had grown considerably. The case was made that the decision to organize an exceptional political and military alliance of more than thirty countries to neutralize by force of arms Iraq's invasion of Kuwait was reached with remarkable celerity, while no direct intervention was deemed necessary when confronted with a Christian Serbian aggression which was on the verge of wiping Bosnia out of the map just for being a Muslim-majority nation. In this case, action was limited to the parsimonious delivery of humanitarian aid, and the approval of a never-ending series of resolutions which in no way addressed the magnitude of what clearly amounted to crimes against humanity.

On numerous occasions I had echoed these complaints in the Security Council and expressed my concern for the grave consequences such double standards could have. I believed that they would, indeed, end up fostering solidarity among radical Muslim groups, given that the international community left their Muslim brothers to their own devices. I did not believe it then to be a simple coincidence, nor do I now, that the terrorist menace that lingered for many years over

Europe began immediately after all the details of the abominable tragedy Bosnia had to endure came to be known. I believe that the West's decision not to put a stop to Bosnia's destruction, among other reasons, significantly contributed to foster the terrorist acts committed by Muslim radicals in so many countries. And I never tired of saying so in the Council: "You will be responsible for the consequences of rendering Bosnia helpless". I do not have the slightest doubt that the irresponsible and sectarian conduct of the international community fostered the since then unrelentless expansion of Muslim fundamentalism throughout the world.

All these troublesome circumstances imposed on the Council the need to take decisions that went beyond its comfort zone. In this regard I must highlight the unexpected role played by France. First, it supported the creation of the Commission of Experts in October 1992, initially presided over by Frits Kalshoven, a highly reputed Dutch jurist, and soon after by Cherif Bassiouni, then it entrusted a group of noted French specialists who had been engaged for some years in a serious study of the issue of crimes against humanity with the task of giving advice and support to the Commission. This support proved to be decisive in the process leading to the creation of the Tribunal for the Former Yugoslavia.

It was a complex undertaking and since the representatives of the Non-Aligned countries in the Council had close links to the Commission of Experts, we were able to gain firsthand knowledge of their investigators' findings regarding violations of political and human rights in Bosnia. This, in turn, assisted us in working out a more precise definition of what a "Safe Area" under the protection of the United Nations in Bosnia should be, the initial one being Srebrenica and its surroundings, and to finetune a strategy to end the arms embargo on Yugoslavia, which, as we have seen, only served to leave Bosnia unable to defend itself against Serbia's continued aggression.

All these initiatives proved to be highly consequential:

1. Convinced that the proposed tribunal would never bring to justice any of the high-ranking Serbian officials accused of committing crimes against humanity in Bosnia, the Council's Permanent Members did not oppose its creation. Yet, as time would prove, the establishment of this judicial body has been one of the Security Council's most significant achievements.

2. The P5 could not have imagined that the new institution, although placed under UN administrative control, that is to say, depending on it in both material and financial terms, would overcome all the obstacles brought on by the then-under-negotiations Vance-Owen plan, and serve as a steppingstone for the Rome Statute and the creation of the International Criminal Court (ICC), based in The Hague. This judicial institution embodied a change of historical importance. As opposed to the Nuremberg and Tokyo tribunals, which were of a military nature and derived from political decisions taken by the winners of WWII, the ICC was given total independence to investigate crimes against humanity anywhere in the world with absolute freedom and without limitations, and to bring to justice and punish those found guilty of such crimes.

3. Although a creation of the United Nations, since its establishment the ICC has demonstrated its independence. Currently, with the only exceptions of Russia, China and the United States, almost all the UN member states have signed the Rome Statute.

4. A final observation: The International Criminal Court (ICC), should not be mistaken with the International Court of Justice, which is the UN's main judicial body, charged with dealing with disputes of a legal nature between UN member States. As time would prove, the decision we took in the Security Council in March 1992 to function as an *ad hoc* tribunal in charge of condemning and imposing sanctions on Ghaddafi's Libya, broke ground for the future establishment of the International Criminal Tribunal for the Former Yugoslavia and, later, the International Criminal Court. Those decisions were based on article 41 of the UN Charter which

confers on the Security Council ample authority to take such measures as it deems fit to implement its decisions, including measures such as bringing to justice in international tribunals those responsible for crimes of such hideous nature.

The Harsh Winter of 1993

While these developments were taking place in the Security Council, the rigors of the 1993 winter punished Bosnia without mercy. As temperatures fell to unprecedented levels the Serbian aggressors cut off electricity, heating and water in the main cities of the republic, such as Sarajevo and Srebrenica, while blocking access and delivery of food and medical supplies. The situation was made worse by continued Serbian heavy artillery shelling, by sniper fire - killing with absolute impunity civilians who dared wander in the streets - and by the overwhelming sensation that in a scenario of such violence and arbitrariness anything could happen, including the cold-blooded assassination of high-ranking government officials. The scope of such a tragedy was brought back to me, not long ago, by Ejup Ganic, at the time Vice President of Bosnia, when he shared with me the following terrible thought: "The Serbs had the unconditional support of the Russians, and the Croats that of Germany. We, on the other hand, were left to our own devices by an international community that chose to limit itself to be an indifferent observer of our suffering".

It was a reality that by March of that year had become so oppressive that the UN High Commissioner for Refugees, Sadako Ogata, sent Boutros-Ghali several reports on the serious and rapid deterioration of the situation, particularly in places such as Srebrenica and its immediate surroundings. In her most important report, dated March 18, Ms. Ogata warned the Secretary General about the tragedy about to unfold in that city: "I must – she wrote – call your attention to the on-going developments in Srebrenica. All indications are a massive humanitarian tragedy might very soon take place in that area. The UN Member States and the Security Council must be apprised of the magnitude of this danger. The latest reports by my collaborators dress a picture of horror: thousands of refugees enter the city of Srebrenica coming from neighboring towns systematically razed by the Serbians, and between thirty and forty persons die every day in the area, victims of air attacks, hunger and the lack of medical attention. The only way to stop this massacre of civilians would be to strengthen the international presence in high-risk areas ". To conclude, Ogata reiterated to the Secretary General the urgent need to take the matter to the immediate attention of the Security Council.

This message would have profoundly shaken the members of the Council, in particular the lesser powers in its midst, who were after all the least well informed. Its content, however, only came to my knowledge ten years later, during the ICTFY judicial process against Slobodan Milosevic, in which I participated as witness for the prosecution. When the prosecutor, Sir Geoffrey Nice, showed it to me and requested my opinion, I voiced my "unbound indignation" that I should learn of such reports ten years later. How was it possible, I could not stop asking myself, that the Secretary General would keep this information from the Council and not urgently convene it in special session, as suggested by a high-ranking official such as Ms. Ogata? This irresponsible and arbitrary decision by Boutros-Ghali came to prove, even if far too late, his far from innocent policy of deepening the chasm isolating him and the Secretariat's main officials from the Security Council and other bodies of the United Nations. It was a dearth of communication that allowed him to consolidate his personal power over the organization. It also made evident his irregular relationship with the P5, which allowed him to silence the seriousness of the armed conflict unleashed by Serbia in Bosnia. Never mind that the main purpose of the organization should have been to confront and contain the execrable ethnic cleansing perpetrated by Serbian authorities in the militarily occupied areas of Bosnia.

Even if at the time we were not apprised of the Ogata reports, some members of the Council, including myself, came to understand the complicities that made it possible to hide the magnitude of the Bosnian crisis at the time of the international conference convened to deal with it, held in London on August 26 and 27, 1992. In its conclusions, the conference ratified the European Community's interest in the conflict and endorsed, almost to the letter, the positions agreed by consensus in the Security Council and spelled-out in numerous resolutions. Beyond that, the most relevant outcome of the meeting was the offer the European alliance made to take part in an eventual international humanitarian assistance effort for the reconstruction of Bosnia.

It was Cornelio Sommaruga, a Swiss diplomat, at the time President of the International Red Cross Committee (ICRC), who on the occasion of the London Conference proposed, unsuccessfully, the establishment in Bosnia of protected areas and security zones for its inhabitants. These would save them from having to abandon their homes and seek refuge somewhere else. Soon afterwards, Tadeusz Mazowiecki, Special Rapporteur on the situation of Human Rights in the Former Yugoslavia and former Prime Minister of Poland, picked up Sommaruga's proposal, but with the same lack of success. So much so that, after the massacre of thousands of Muslims in Srebrenica in July 1995, Mazowiecki bitterly accused the United Nations of having "allowed the fall of Srebrenica and Zepa, areas already declared safe by the UN".

That same month of March, Boutros-Ghali, finding it impossible to conceal the situation any further, sent us a copy of a statement issued by UNPROFOR, signed by its commanding officer, indicating that the Serbian Airforce continued to violate the Bosnian airspace without hindrance and to bomb towns and villages, including Sarajevo, capital of the republic, without any opposition. From that day on, debates on the situation in Bosnia became much more frequent during the informal consultations of the Council. On March 31, we finally passed Resolution 816, which for the first time authorized "member states as well as national or regional organizations to take all necessary measures to impede all further violations of the Bosnian air space". Notwithstanding this change of course by the Council, the authorization included two conditions which, in practical terms, made it impossible to fulfil the resolution's mandate. First, the need to obtain from the Council and the UN Secretariat prior authorization to act; and second, the need to ensure any response given to any action be proportionate to the seriousness of the violation. These two prior conditions made Resolution 816 nothing more than a farce.

In The Thick of the Night

The safeguards introduced into the resolution made it clear that the Secretary General's intention, as well as that of the Permanent Members, was not to solve the problem but to appease the feelings of those governments who were outraged by the powerful nations' inaction in Bosnia, hidden under "I want but I can't" false pretenses. It was a crude trick, played with the sole purpose of lessening the impact of the denunciations made by highly credible members of the international media regarding the recrudescence of atrocities by the Serbians and the odd passivity shown by the Council in the face of such outrages. It made me, together with the ambassadors of Pakistan and Morocco, take the initiative to hold consultations with representatives of the Arab and African Groups, to sound their positions about what was truly happening in Bosnia and about the Vance-Owen peace plan. Both, Arabs and Africans, shared the view the United Nations had abandoned Bosnia, as denounced by its government, solely because the young republic was a Muslim-majority nation.

I had held that same position both in the Council and in my exchanges with the media. Now, strong in our shared view, we took the initiative to draft a document, which later became a draft resolution, in which we detailed the issues that should be included in a necessary and viable peace plan for Bosnia. It was obviously not an easy task. First, because in order to approve anything in the Security Council the support of at least nine members is needed and, then, the proposal must not be vetoed by any of the five Permanent Members. It was a goal we presumed would be highly difficult to reach, since the P5 and the Secretary General had amply demonstrated their preference for avoiding as much as possible any UN firm position on the war in Bosnia before the Vance-Owen peace plan was signed, a plan that would give recognition to Serbia's occupation of two-thirds of Bosnia's territory and establish the boundaries of the ten proposed ethnic districts.

Confronted by such a difficulty, in my condition as coordinator of the Non-Aligned countries represented in the Council - Cape Verde, Djibouti, Morocco, Pakistan and Venezuela - I addressed myself directly to the President of the Council, at the time, Jamsheed Marker, Ambassador of Pakistan, requesting that a draft resolution prepared by the majority of the United Nations member states be circulated as a Security Council document.

The main purpose of our proposal was to highlight the responsibility all UN members share to stand up in defense of the Charter when it is challenged, as was the case in Serbia's aggression to Bosnia and Herzegovina and its violation of the political and human rights of its people. We therefore held that the international community was under the obligation to stop this aggression by all necessary means. It was urgent to ensure a durable peace in the region, particularly since the Serbs favored deepening the military confrontation. Even if not much to our liking, this left us with no other option but to support the Vance-Owen plan, a plan that, on the other hand, met with the approval of the Bosnian-Muslims and the Bosnian Croats, an issue of capital importance to us.

In other words, we knew that only if the Security Council finally came to accept the use of all available means, including the use of force, could pressure be put to bear on the Serbian authorities to sign the peace plan and thereby avoid the consequences of a possible collective military intervention. While waiting for this outcome, we proposed to apply immediately, as foreseen by the Vance-Owen plan, economic sanctions on Serbia, the total immobilization of its heavy artillery in Bosnian territory, and an urgent lifting of the arms embargo that continued to leave the government and people of Bosnia unable to defend themselves from Serbian aggression.

It should be noted that if the Non-Aligned now fell behind the Vance-Owen plan it was because President Izetbegovic's government had decided to sign on to it, considering it a lesser evil than the territorial disintegration of Bosnia. In the course of all our discussions, we acknowledged that we could not ask for more than did the Bosnian government itself. On the other hand, we did press the Council to give maximum relevance to the Provisional Order dictated by the International Court of Justice (ICJ) on April 3, 1993, exhorting Serbia to "Immediately adopt all measures within its reach to avoid the perpetration of a crime of genocide in Bosnia and Herzegovina". So, when we addressed the Council as we did, we responded to the need to alert all its members, as well as the of rest of the world, to the dangers of not putting a stop immediately to a rapidly deteriorating situation.

International Justice and Bosnia

As Stanley Meisler would later write in his influential column in *The Los Angeles Times*, "On weekends, the United Nations used to stay as inactive as a fat cat after a full meal". That is, until April, Friday 16, and Saturday 17, 1993, when the exact opposite took place. During those days, the fifteen ambassadors accredited to the Council engaged in a harsh debate on whether to immediately impose newer and stronger sanctions on Serbia, and on whether to designate Srebrenica and its surroundings as Safe Areas. We also pushed for an urgent decision on how to follow up on the providence approved by the ICJ and duly conveyed to the attention of the Council, alerting about the risk of a true genocide by Serbian authorities should no action be taken.

The debate on the Court's decision was enough to set the prairie on fire. According to Article 41 of the Statute of the

International Court of Justice, while the Court considers and passes judgment on any issue, it is empowered to request the Council to apply "provisional measures" aimed at ensuring the equal safeguard of the rights of all parties engaged in the litigation. By its decision, the Court was clearly recognizing the urgent need to immediately address the Bosnian appeal about the menace it faced. More significantly for us, there was no way the Security Council could ignore it, coming, as it did, from the highest judicial body of the United Nations. Thus, even those members who opposed hardening the Council´s position were forced to acknowledge the simple fact that introducing the crime of genocide as a possible aggravating circumstance in a case before the Court had no precedent. From that moment on, it became impossible for the Council members to ignore the pressure applied by the Non-Aligned countries with growing support from the international media, which proved to be our most formidable ally in this sorrowful crisis.

The inclusion of the crime of genocide in the UN agenda dramatically raised the profile of the debate over Bosnia and forced the Council to act in consequence. It also allowed me to state, during my intervention in the open session held on April 12, that "If the international community, represented by the Security Council, is unable to react to the International Court of Justice´s unequivocally stated position, the United Nation´s legitimacy and its political and judicial credibility will be seriously and most gravely compromised. A new world order cannot be based on a Security Council unable to rise to the challenge".

Once the ICJ joined the voices that claimed the Bosnian nation´s right to exercise its sovereignty, preserve its territorial integrity and defend against all odds its political independence, our reiterated arguments gained incredible strength, and served as trampoline for two qualitative jumps ahead that, up to that moment, had seemed almost impossible: the approval of sanctions against Serbia, and the designation of Srebrenica and its surroundings as "Safe areas" under United Nations protection. Our draft resolution, even though it admitted the partition proposed by the Vance-Owen plan, reaffirmed the basic rights of the Bosnian republic, and categorically condemned the "ethnic cleansing" carried out by Serbia in the occupied Bosnian territories, the systematic blockade of humanitarian assistance to war-torn areas, and the frequent attacks carried out by Serbian paramilitaries against UNPROFOR personnel. The resolution ended by acknowledging that the brutal actions conducted by Serbian paramilitary units had forced the massive displacement of civilians, including children, women and the elderly.

Of course, to call "displacement" what in reality was ethnic cleansing lessened the strength of the condemnation, and made us recall Resolution 815, which requested "all parties and other interested", to consider Srebrenica and its surroundings as "safe areas, free from armed attacks and hostile acts", as if it were not clear that only one party, the Serbian one, was responsible of such attacks. Now, once more, in a perverse reinterpretation of reality, victims and aggressors were placed on the same footing by skirting the fact that the Bosnian Serbs were the only aggressors and the Bosnian citizens the victims.

The resolution, in its more relevant paragraphs, denied in a straightforward manner the need-for-neutrality thesis as well as the arguments in favor of appeasement, by clearly rejecting "Serbian actions geared towards carrying out an illicit, unacceptable and abominable ethnic cleansing in Bosnia", and by stating that those who ordered or committed crimes of such nature would be held personally responsible by international justice. It was a commitment that, ten years later, would allow the International Tribunal for the Former Yugoslavia to bring to trial presumed war criminals such as Milosevic, Karadzic, Mladic, and others.

Finally, it is worth underlining that the resolution included the Security Council's decision to send to Bosnia as soon as possible a mission of its members with the mandate to evaluate on the ground and report on what was really happening there, a milestone decision that had no precedents in the history of the Council.

The Contentious Security Council Meeting of April 16

The United States, France and the United Kingdom had let it be known they would be in favor of this draft resolution, although they would prefer that it not be put to a vote during the weekend prior to the consultative referendum on Boris Yeltsin's mandate to be held in Russia, on April 25. Russia, fearing it might have an unfavorable impact on the vote and on Yeltsin's stay in power, might be inclined to veto any resolution placing sanctions on Serbia, a traditional ally. To convince us to postpone the vote until after the referendum, the UN ambassadors of those three countries paid us a visit in the small room used by the Non-Aligned, located just next to the "Inner Sanctum", the Informal Consultations Room, where, if we are to believe Meisler, my insistence on the issue had become an irritant for the representatives of Russia, France and the United Kingdom: "They complain, *sotto voce*, Arria allows his emotions to guide his diplomacy". For over a year I had been denouncing the UN's ongoing hesitation regarding the challenges posed by the war in Bosnia. Now, with the support of the African and Arab ambassadors, I urged the Council to approve the resolution during that weekend, without further delays.

Two days before, the French Ambassador, Jean-Bernard Mérimée, paid us a visit. On that afternoon he let us know that, if the votes in favor held, France, the United States and the United Kingdom would not oppose our proposal as long as we found a way to convince the Russian ambassador not to veto the draft resolution. He stressed that such a veto would not only kill the resolution, but very probably take the peace plan down with it.

The April 16 informal meeting lasted well beyond midnight. On that occasion, I pointed out to the Russian Ambassador, Yuli Vorontsov, that the Muslim population of Srebrenica was suffering under the very same terrible conditions experienced by the inhabitants of Leningrad during the Second World War. Vorontsov remained impassive. He reiterated that the vote on the resolution should wait for the results of the April 25 referendum to be announced. He then raised a very relevant question: "What is really happening in Srebrenica for us not to wait another week?"

Thanks to the information channel we had established by way of the Bosnian ambassador's intermediation, I was able to give Vorontsov a detailed description of the desperate situation in which the civilian population of Bosnia lived. Vorontsov, however, did not waver. Finally, no doubt to close a debate that was going no-where, he said that even though the instructions he had from Moscow were to oppose any sanctions on Serbia before April 25, in consideration of our insistence and of the consequences the lack of a peace agreement would have on Bosnia, he would call President Yeltsin and consult him directly. However, he added that since at that moment it was 4 am in Moscow and on the following day Russia would celebrate Easter Sunday, we would have to wait until Monday.

— I am sure – he told us – you do not wish me to wake up President Yeltsin at this late hour and on the eve of Easter Sunday.

— Yuli – I answered back with a smile – that is exactly what we wish you to do.

— And so, I will - he replied, and then went out to call Moscow.

Half an hour later, he came back into the room and informed us that he had spoken with Yeltsin, who continued to believe that voting on a resolution on Serbia that weekend was a dangerously hasty decision. However, his instructions were for Russia not to veto the resolution but to abstain. The other four Permanent Members of the Council, who were all in agreement to immediately vote on the resolution but feared a Russian veto could not believe their ears. How did the ambassadors of the Non-Aligned manage to make Russia change its position?

Be it as it may, that very evening the Council passed Resolution 819, which mandated very harsh economic sanctions on the Milosevic government. On their own, the sanctions would not be enough to put a stop to Serbia's criminal aggression on Bosnia, but they clearly signaled a change in the way the situation would be dealt with, and made the Serbian authorities understand international tolerance was running out. From then on, Belgrade would have to tread lightly to avoid compelling NATO, under intense pressure by the Clinton Administration, deliver on its warning to bomb the positions illegally held by Karadzic's troops in Bosnia if the brutal ethnic cleansing policy did not cease. Moreover, the Non-Aligned Caucus continued to insist on the need to designate Srebrenica as a Safe Area under UN protection with even more urgency. According to the news we had received, the city was on the verge of falling into the hands of Karadzic and Mladic's troops.

In the course of these informal consultations, Ambassador Chinmaya Gharekhan, Counselor for Political Affairs to the Secretary General, and Boutros-Ghali's most trusted advisor, entered the room and informed us of a recent call by the Swedish General Lars-Eric Wahlgren, Commander of UNPROFOR in the area, at that moment in Sarajevo, warning him that, should the Council approve sanctions on Serbia and designate Srebrenica and its surroundings as a Safe Area, "The reaction by the Serbs could be to bring about a true blood bath."

Garekhan's intervention truly outraged me.

— With all due respect, at this point in the debate we cannot accept such an argument.

Notwithstanding the malaise created by the Secretariat's last minute attempt to torpedo the approval of what would become Resolution 819, we received the Council's overwhelming support. As expected, Russia and China abstained. While in New York we saw our efforts crowned by this decisive vote, in Sarajevo, unbeknown to us, Wahlgren negotiated the surrender of Srebrenica, including the unilateral surrender of all weapons by the Bosnian-Muslim civilians who were still defending the city. Such a decision left Srebrenica at the mercy of the Srpska military authorities, instead of becoming the Safe Area it was supposed to be, and exposed the Security Council to ridicule. How could it be that while the Security Council had given its approval to a Resolution as decisive as Resolution 819, the commander of the Protection Forces, on his own, without our consent, could negotiate exactly the opposite in Sarajevo? The Council had been made a fool by the UN's military chiefs in Bosnia, in a maneuver orchestrated by the Secretariat, the United Kingdom, France and Russia, with UNPROFOR acting as the executing arm. It was a misdeed that carried the signatures of the very commander of the UN Blue Helmets, General Wahlgren, and of a war criminal such as Ratko Mladic, General and Military Commander of the illegal Srpska Serbian Republic in Bosnia. To add insult to injury, Generals Wahlgren and Morillon, commenting on Srebrenica's surrender, declared that by giving their support to the "capitulation", they had helped the parties come to a cease fire, which would "save lives". Morillon went even further, adding that he believed Srebrenica's rendition would be a "first step towards compliance with Resolution 819".

An additional and urgent point, added at the last moment to the resolution, was the designation of a delegation of six ambassadors to travel to Bosnia as soon as possible with the express mandate to verify on the ground the real situation of the conflict and to report to the Council. This point was introduced without prior notice by Ambassador Marker, at the time President of the Council, following our decision to present it that very afternoon of April 16. The P5 had no time to maneuver to try to abort it. On the early morning hours of Saturday, April 17, when it was approved, I had the honor to be unanimously named leader of the delegation, which comprised the ambassadors of France, New Zealand, Hungary, Pakistan, and Russia.

War and Genocide in Bosnia

By Resolution 819 the Council had "strongly condemned" the Serbian aggression in Bosnia, as well as Belgrade's political and military assistance to Karadzic's forces. It was the first time the Council had declared "unlawful and unacceptable" Serbia's occupation of Bosnian territory by use of force, as well as the practice of "ethnic cleansing" in that country.

After the hectic weekend following the authorization of our inspection mission to the former Yugoslavia, I invited my colleagues of the Non-Aligned Caucus in the Security Council to a meeting in order to ascertain the real scope and reach of Resolution 819. We all agreed that the adoption of a set of strong sanctions on Serbia's trade, transport and financial system was not in itself enough to put a stop to Slobodan Milosevic's policy of genocide in the independent republic of Bosnia. Among other reasons, because under the influence of its five Permanent Members, the Council had not changed its position on an arms embargo on the Yugoslav republics, thereby dramatically hampering the exercise of the legitimate right of the government and people of Bosnia to defend themselves against a criminal Serbian aggression.

The Days Prior To Our Trip to Bosnia

In the course of the intense discussions held prior to the approval of our mission, some members of the Non-Aligned Caucus in the Council had come to consider the possibility of not giving our approval to the resolution unless it also included lifting the arms embargo. Nonetheless, we finally agreed to support it since failure to do so would also imply not endorsing the agreed sanctions on Serbia. However, though circumstances forced us to support the resolution, they also imposed on us the obligation to insist, with more urgency than ever, on the need to lift the unfair arms embargo, and to place all the Serbian heavy artillery positioned in Bosnia under the direct control of UNPROFOR. To that effect, during the days prior to our departure we met with representatives of other countries, particularly Arab and Muslim nations that shared our commitment to find a just and fair solution to the Bosnian crisis.

Ambassador Nabil Elaraby, who would later become Egypt´s Minister of Foreign Affairs, played a significant role in those consultations. Elaraby used to brief us regularly on what were the thoughts and feelings in the streets of the main cities of the Arab world, providing us with insights denied to us in the Security Council. It was an extremely valuable information that proved to be of vital importance to fine tune our understanding in those days without Internet and social media.

Precisely during one of those days, on the late afternoon of April 20, I was paid a visit by the Ambassador of Bosnia, Muhamed Sacirbey, who shared with me news of great importance he had just received from President Izetbegovic. On the morning of April 17, while we were still engaged in the final debates on Resolution 819, the Commander General of the Bosnian military forces, General Sefer Halilovic, had held a meeting at the Sarajevo airport with the Serbian-Bosnian General Ratko Mladic. The Bosnian president wanted me to know that during the previous two weeks UNPROFOR´s commanders had put pressure on him to sign a cease fire agreement with the Serbian military, an agreement the main point of which was the unilateral disarmament of the few Muslim defenders of Srebrenica. It was a condition Serbia demanded in order to avoid its troops´ immediate occupation of that enclave.

In his message, President Izetbegovic added that, according to the UN Protection Force's commanders, such a condition was in reality an ultimatum. The Bosnian government felt it had to accept it since no one, not even UNPROFOR, would come to its help. Faced with such a dilemma and taking very much into account the desperate situation of the inhabitants of Srebrenica and surroundings, the Bosnian president wanted me to know he had no alternative but to accept the Serbian condition. The news, about which the UN Secretariat had of course kept us in the blind, was alarming, and I immediately conveyed it to the Ambassador of Pakistan, Jamsheed Marker, at the time President of the Council. He in turn immediately convened an emergency session of the Council, to be held on the morning of April 21, to ascertain the veracity of the information and directly ask the Secretariat to explain why UNPROFOR had taken a decision of such consequence without prior consultation with the Council.

Boutros-Ghali, as had by now become his custom, once more did not participate in this very important meeting, and once again sent his Political Counsellor, Ambassador Gharekhan, who skirted the issue and just pointed out that the Blue Helmets had yet not been able to agree with the Serbian and Bosnian authorities the exact limits of the area to be demilitarized in Srebrenica and its surroundings. Once again, we had not been kept up to speed on this. Nor were we aware that, as Gharekhan was now informing us, to discharge the Council's mandate the number of UN troops in the area would need to be increased, something the Serbian authorities simply did not accept. Finally, he added that the commander of UNPROFOR's Canadian battalion deployed in Srebrenica was waiting for Serbian authorization to destroy the weapons and munitions "recovered" from the Bosnian defenders of Srebrenica.

At this highly tense moment I took the floor to express my perplexity, since none of the resolutions approved by the Security Council had authorized the Protection Force commanders to collect and destroy weapons belonging to the Bosnians in Srebrenica. I also pointed out that such an initiative could only be interpreted as an act of unacceptable cooperation with the Serbian aggressors, which, needless to say, went over the Council's decision to designate Srebrenica and surroundings as a Safe Area. The ambassadors of France and the United Kingdom, somewhat unhinged by my comments, proposed that the discussion be postponed until our mission had returned from Bosnia and presented its report on the conflict's real situation. Knowing they were lying, they added that we could rest assured that Srebrenica "had not fallen nor had it surrendered".

Again, needless to say, the P5 representatives were fully aware of all the details of the operation and preferred to put a swift end to the discussion. To round up the unsettling description of what we would come to verify in Bosnia in the coming days, Gharekhan informed us that in the course of the last three months, Srebrenica's population had increased from seven thousand to almost forty thousand; a direct consequence of the Serbian "ethnic cleansing" operations conducted in areas close to the city. This forced exodus into Srebrenica had dangerously lowered life conditions for its inhabitants. Even though the Serbian troops had temporarily halted their attacks, basic services such as power, water and gas remained cut, and UN humanitarian assistance convoys were not allowed to enter the city.

That very same April 21 in the afternoon, once the informal consultations were over, the members of the Council's delegation came together to coordinate criteria for the mission and to agree on its tight agenda. As a first measure, in view of the fact that both Vance and Owen were still in negotiations with Milosevic in Belgrade, we agreed not to interfere with their agenda, even though we were convinced Milosevic's intention was to win time so his men could continue to gain ground in Bosnia and consolidate, by fire and blood, his grand scheme of a Greater Serbia. We did agree to meet Radovan Karadzic, although not in Pale, the "capital" of his imagined Srpska Republic, but in Belgrade, where he used to spend most of his time. As regards Mate Boban, leader of the Croats in Bosnia, we agreed to see him in Split, and not in Mostar, which he considered to be the capital of his illegitimate Bosnian Croat Republic. Finally, we agreed to meet the presidents of Croatia and Bosnia in Zabreb and Sarajevo.

The Going Gets Rough

Throughout the day before our trip, we remained concerned with what seemed to us a very strange situation: not once, during the whole week prior to our mission, had any high-ranking member of the Secretariat approached us to exchange views on the mission's mandate. Not even our good friend Kofi Annan, at the time Under Secretary General for Peacekeeping Operations, and therefore with responsibilities strongly associated with our trip to Bosnia, showed any interest in meeting with us. It made us come to terms with reality: the decision to send a mission to Bosnia had been made due solely to the multiple pressures the ambassadors of the Non-Aligned members of the Council had put to bear on it, and the lack of interest we were witnessing was rooted in the UN's powers-that-be's rejection of our interference in the situation. So, by the time we boarded the Lufthansa flight that would take us to Zagreb via Frankfurt, we had fully understood the term "distancing".

Ambassadors Hervé Ladsous, of France, Vasily Sidorov, of Russia, André Erdos, of Hungary, Terence O'Brien, of New Zealand, Sher Afgan Khan, Alternate Representative of Pakistan, and myself, arrived at Zabreb on the early evening of April 23, 1993. The capital of Croatia was the first scale in our mission to Bosnia, as it headquartered UNPROFOR's general command for the Former Yugoslavia. At Zagreb airport we were met by officials of the Croat Ministry of Foreign Affairs, the UN Secretariat and some Bluc Helmets, who informed us their commander-in-chief, General Lars-Eric Wahlgren, had suffered a road accident on his way to the airport and would meet us at the Hilton Hotel in the city.

I was the first to arrive at the hotel, so I took advantage of the opportunity to be alone with General Wahlgren, who was waiting at the front desk, to clear a doubt that had been troubling me for over a week.

— Why is it – I asked him – that on April 16, past midnight, while we were fully in the middle of a debate about Resolution 819, he had called Ambassador Gharekhan and asked him not to allow Srebrenica to be named a safe area under the argument it would suffer a blood bath if we did?

— I did not call Ambassador Gharekhan! - he answered with astonishment – It was I who received a call by a young Indian official who worked at the department in charge of peace operations directed by Kofi Annan.

Later we learned that he was referring to Shashi Taroor.

By his reply, General Wahlgren confirmed my presumption that the powers-that-be within the United Nations, together with the Secretary General, were bent on creating obstacles to the implementation of the resolution, or at least on substantially modifying its scope. When the general told me that a couple of days before his intelligence services had intercepted a private communication between the US military and General Philippe Morillon, his second-in-command, that in his view represented "an extremely dangerous interference in Srebrenica" my conviction was reaffirmed. Unfortunately, I was unable to learn more as at that very moment my fellow travelers arrived at the hotel and our conversation was cut short.

The news was very important since it clarified the reasons why General Wahlgren, Commander-in-chief of the UN Blue Helmets, a Swedish officer, stayed put in Croatia, where the cease fire had been holding for months, rather than venture into Bosnia, where the political and military crisis continued to worsen. It was an absence that left the command of UN troops deployed in Bosnia in the hands of General Morillon, a French officer, and of his second, General Vere Hayes, a British officer. In other words, the heads of UNPROFOR in Bosnia were French and British officers, which happened to be the countries with the larger number of peacekeeping troops on the ground. They also happened to be the very same countries that were leading within the Council the resistance to our mission's goals. The incident also shed light on why the cold-blooded murder of Bosnia's Deputy Prime Minister, Hakija Turajlic, committed in front of impassive French servicemen at the outskirts of Sarajevo, was not duly investigated by UNPROFOR, nor by the UN Secretariat.

Not long after this conversation with General Wahlgren, we moved to the Protection Forces General Command in Zagreb, where both he and General Morillon made formal presentations on the military and humanitarian situation in Bosnia. During the presentations we received confirmation of unsettling news. On April 6, without prior authorization by the Security Council, they had completed negotiations with the Bosnian and Serb military authorities for the total unilateral disarmament of Srebrenica, which they considered absolutely necessary to ensure a cease fire in the city and in surrounding areas. Wahlgren concluded by adding a disconcerting opinion: "The Serbians act in irrational ways, so it was best not to put too much pressure on them".

The general's words highly alarmed me. Not only did they offer no clarification at all as to why the UN forces had shown such unbelievable passivity in the face of the brutal Serbian aggression, but also pretended to portray as necessary the agreement reached with the Serbian military command to disarm the city's Bosnian defenders. General Morillon, who had remained cautiously quiet, then added that it was precisely thanks to this strategy that it had been possible to contain the troops of the Serbian General Ratko Mladic, the infamous "Butcher of the Balkans", who were set on taking Srebrenica by assault. This evidenced UNPROFOR's disregard for the Security Council's mandate to urgently guarantee Bosnia's sovereignty over Srebrenica.

Confronted by such a serious irregularity, I could not refrain myself, and asked from both Wahlgren and Morillon:

— Generals: How is it possible that you collaborated with the Serbian aggressors in bringing about the unilateral disarmament of the Bosnian defenders, leaving Sarajevo's population completely defenseless, when the Security Council's mandate ordered you to do the exact opposite?

Under whose authority did you embark on an action patently contrary to UN decisions? From now on will UNPROFOR take full responsibility for what might happen in Srebrenica and in the rest of Bosnia?

Wahlgren's reply was even more disconcerting:

— When the Security Council designated Srebrenica as a Safe Area within the terms of the Geneva Convention, it omitted the most critical issue: to clearly define the boundaries of the area to be safeguarded.

General Wahlgren was publicly correcting the Council, something in my opinion akin to insubordination. I therefore asked both of them a second key question:

— Pray tell me, how is it that the Bosnian civilian and military authorities accepted UNPROFOR to disarm them and not disarm the Serbians?

Wahlgren replied without hesitation:

— Because it was the only option they had not to be massacred.

It is worth recalling that on April 14, General Morillon, defying the Serbian siege, had entered Srebrenica at the head of a convoy carrying UN humanitarian assistance. On that occasion, he had rallied a sizable number of the city's inhabitants, as well as media covering the event, and declared: "I will stay with you until the day Serbian attacks cease and a humanitarian corridor is permanently opened". My initial reaction upon hearing about the French general's stand was one of sincere admiration. My enthusiasm did not last long. Barely three days had gone by when, on the night of March 17, shielded by darkness, General Morillon escaped from Srebrenica. Years later, in July 2020, I attended a religious service at the city's cemetery, held in remembrance of the eight thousand men and children murdered in cold blood in July 1995 by Serbian paramilitaries acting under the command of General Mladic. Morillon was also present but was forced to leave by the victims' indignant mothers and widows, who did not forgive his conduct in those days.

During my tense meeting with both generals, the sad episode of General Morillon's furtive departure from Srebrenica during the previous month of March 1993 was very much in my mind. However, I chose to keep silent during the hour and a half both officers took to offer their peculiar understanding of a conflict that in their view was absolutely under UN forces' control, minding two exceptions: the relentless siege of Srebrenica, and the mass killing of the Bosnian Muslim residents of Ahmici, a city in Central Bosnia, on April 16.

That was the true and pitiless reality with which we were to be confronted from the next day on.

My First Time in Sarajevo

On April 24, at 8 am, a paratrooper unit of UNPROFOR picked us up at the Hilton Hotel to take us to the airport. Half joking, its commanding officer advised us to have a good breakfast since it would be the last full meal we would be having before our return from our mission to Bosnia. We took his advice very seriously and had a copious breakfast. We then headed towards Zagreb's airport in the company of a group of prominent international journalists: Paul Lewis, of *The New York Times*; Harry Smith, CBS's international affairs analyst; Anthony Goodman, from *Reuters*; Allan Ferguson, from *The Toronto Globe & Mail*; John Lyons, from the *BBC*, and Luis Torres, from *France Press*. A quarter of an hour later, we reached the airport's military ramp and, as programmed, left for Sarajevo in time for our first scheduled meeting of the day, with President Alija Izetbegovic.

Once on board the huge aircraft that would take us to the Bosnian inferno, the Swedish paratroopers urged us to put on the bulletproof vests we had been handed the night before at the end of our meeting with generals Wahlgren and Morillon, and to keep handy at all times our helmets, blue- colored as those of UN peacekeepers. I was struck by the airplane's cabin arrangements. Designed for the transport of military personnel, it had no windows, and instead of the regular seats found in commercial aircrafts, it was fitted only with long metal benches, stretching all along both sides of the cabin. I had never travelled in such austere conditions, but this was not a pleasure trip. I was seated between the American Harry Smith and the Spaniard José María Mendiluce, the UN Agency for Refugees (ACNUR) Representative. We were practically unable to talk, so thunderous was the engines′ noise. At one point, we were instructed to remove our bulletproof vests and sit on them should Serbian soldiers fire at the passing airplanes′ belly for shooting practice. The final proof that we were not taking a stroll in the park came as we approached Sarajevo airport, when the pilot suddenly, without warning, nosedived the plane towards the landing track to minimize the time it would be within firing range.

The plane landed abruptly, its fuselage shaking heavily, but without any mishap. The experience became ever more unforgettable when the paratroopers urged us to exit the plane running as fast as possible and led us inside the airport building through a sandbag tunnel. We went rapidly through the empty lounges and, upon exiting, were shoved into a dozen UN armored vehicles.

The trip between the airport and the Presidential Palace lasted barely fifteen minutes, but I will never forget it. With me in the car were the British General Vere Hayes and Ramuncho Llerandi, our UN Mission′s Press Attaché. I took the front seat, beside the driver, which allowed me to take a good look at the overwhelming views of a city under siege for over a year and subject to unrelenting shelling by Serbian heavy artillery, posted on the hills surrounding Sarajevo. Empty streets littered with the remains of vehicles, trucks, even tramways, some still smoldering; ruined buildings, fires here and there, columns of a thick, black smoke rising towards the blue, bright sky of a Central-European Spring. As we crossed the city, my attention was powerfully drawn to the Holiday Inn Hotel, standing strangely intact; and just a few meters away, by a street that General Hayes told me carried the nickname ¨Sniper Alley¨, as it did not provide any shelter from sharpshooters posted on the side of a hill that sloped down towards it.

We finally arrived at the Government Palace. It was a magnificent building; clearly Austro-Hungarian in its architecture, in Sarajevo's city center, next to Titova Street, the city's main artery. Barely nine years before, Sarajevo had hosted the Winter Olympics, and for many it was the European Jerusalem, since for centuries Muslims, Christian Orthodox, Catholics and Jews had lived together in holy peace. Now, it had become the devastated shell-shocked scenario of a fight to the death.

To my surprise, a small group of children, displaying signs with the names of our countries was waiting for us, standing before the building's splendid stone façade. It was a welcome so emotionally charged that I approached them to say hello. Immediately, for security reasons, two paratroopers ran to my side and made me turn around and join the rest of the ambassadors, who by then were entering the palace. In its vestibule, we were greeted by Vice President Ejup Ganic, members of the Executive Cabinet, and by General Sefer Halilovic, Commander-General of the Bosnian Army.

The very first news Ganic shared with us was that the day before the Serbs had cut the palace's water supply.

— No doubt – he added with a mocking smile – to bid you the welcome you deserve for coming to visit us.

On behalf of the delegation, I then briefed him on the goals of our mission, the considerations that had led the Security Council to send us to Bosnia and the reasons for our special interest in Srebrenica, the siege of which was turning the city into a tragedy of biblical proportions.

The Meeting with President Alija Izetbegovic

After our quick exchange of greetings, Ganic guided us to the palace's ceremonial room, where President Izetbegovic waited for us, seating at a long ornate wooden table with very worn leather upholstered chairs. The room was poorly lighted, with windows boarded for security reasons and half concealed by dull red curtains. The coffee-with-milk color of the walls added to the room´s somber aspect. In our honor, the table had been layed with trays of glasses and refreshments but no water. Even in the palace the consequences of the Serbian siege were felt. Ganic, for example, told me he lived in the basement, and the President in the armored vaults of a nearby bank.

I was the only member of the delegation who knew Izetbegovic personally. We had met two months before in New York, thanks to his Ambassador, Muhamed Sacirbey, and I was aware of his serious and withdrawn but kind character. He was always measured in his conversations, neither raising his voice nor speaking with precipitation, and pondered with care his words, virtues that made one feel one was dealing with a very self-confident individual. I was concerned that the stress caused by an atrocious war might have changed him. I was wrong. Izetbegovic was still the same interlocutor he had been two months before, even though he was visibly thinner. I also feared our meeting might turn out be a much more difficult one because he was well aware of the positions of the more powerful members of the Security Council, the UN Secretariat, and UNPROFOR commanders.

It was a painful situation, and it was becoming even more delicate because the hope once placed on Clinton had vanished as soon as he was inaugurated President and chose to keep the Vance-Owen plan as the only road map to overcome the crisis in Bosnia. In that context, we thought it best to postpone any thoughtful analysis of the conflict until after our visit to Srebrenica and our meetings with Mate Boban in Split, Radovan Karadzic in Belgrade, and Franjo Tudjman, President of Croatia, In Zabreb. Izetbegovic was perfectly aware of the complexities of the situation and that was why he immediately touched upon the issue that concerned him the most.

— You represent a great hope for all of us, but above all, for those in Srebrenica who suffer persistent attacks by Karadzic's troops, and fear that bloodthirsty General Mladic might at any moment deliver on his promise to storm the city with the backing of the heavy weaponry supplied by Belgrade.

Izetbegovic was fully aware that Russia, the United Kingdom and France did not support his country's cause. Nevertheless, he also knew that the members of our group were determined to do the impossible to help put an end to the Serbian invasion and to the ethnic and religious persecution of its Muslim population.

I looked at Izetbegovic and could not stop thinking of Edvard Benes, the President of Czechoslovakia, who fifty-four years before, had been forced, also under pressure from the British and French governments of the time, to relinquish the Sudetenland to Hitler, under the illusion of thereby appeasing the imperial ambitions of the Nazi monster. Hounded by European governments that tolerated, even fostered, Milosevic's plans for Bosnia, Izetbegovic must have felt he was living the same nightmare. Maybe that was why, either in resignation or as a consolation, at the moment of greeting us, he also reiterated his hope that the Serbian government would finally come to abide by the Security Council's resolutions and recognize Srebrenica as a safe area.

Be it as it may, I was fairly sure he did not believe his own words. But he had no other option. President Izetbegovic informed us that he would be travelling to Zagreb on the coming morning to meet with President Tudjman, with whom he shared a difficult relationship. Maybe, in light of the new reality brought about by Resolution 819, Tudjman would be willing to try to convince Milosevic to put a stop to his troops' attacks on Srebrenica. He did not believe Tudjman was a reliable friend of the Muslims but, faced with no other option, he hoped against his better judgment that Germany might convince Tudjman to change his mind and take a more conciliatory position. At this point in the conversation, Ganic, who sat by my side, whispered to me that they did not forget that Tudjman was "a dictator" but, cornered by a violent and aggressive Serbia, they felt the need for tolerance.

Izetbegovic was now describing the brutal murder of one hundred and sixteen Bosnian Muslims in the town of Ahmici. This town had been chosen by the hardliners within the Croat-Bosnian military command because it was a particularly religious community. It had two mosques, served by several imams, and was considered a sacred place by many of the faithful. We already knew about this abhorrent event. Speaking on behalf of our group, I stated that in the course of our meetings with Boban and Karadzic we would address this terrible issue. He thanked us and then added it was "an abhorrent act, motivated by antimuslim fanaticism".

Several members of our delegation then mentioned our bewilderment regarding his government´s acceptance of Srebrenica's unilateral disarmament of its Muslim defenders. Izetbegovic replied he had left that decision in the hands of General Halilovic, who he believed to be in a better position to assess the situation from a military standpoint and evaluate whether or not a unilateral disarmament of the city´s defenders was the only option to avoid an occupation by force and the slaughter of the Muslim population. To his president´s comments Halilovic then added that the UNPROFOR commanders had "recommended" to accept the Serb's conditions, since not even them could provide the necessary assistance to ensure Srebrenica´s military defense.

Terence O´Brien, Ambassador of New Zealand, then asked Izetbegovic whether the slaughter at Ahmici and the forced acceptance of the Muslim disarmament at Srebrenica had any bearing on his position on the Vance-Owen peace plan.

His response was immediate.

— We continue to believe – he held – that the Vance-Owen plan, notwithstanding events, remains viable, and therefore we stand by our commitment to accept it. To a significant extent that is one of the reasons I am travelling tomorrow to Zabreb; to reiterate to Tudjman that the plan is the only formula capable of bringing peace to Bosnia, even if it is not the most desirable one since it implies the division of the republic into pieces. I am convinced that a lasting peace in Bosnia would be unattainable if the Vance-Owen plan, no matter all its undesirable consequences, is not approved. In other words, if we choose to reject it and make it collapse, it will mean we will not have peace in Bosnia until who knows when.

To achieve the goal of a lasting peace in Bosnia – he added – the Bosnian government's support was not enough. The acceptance of the Serbian and Croatian governments was needed and, above all, their commitment to its full implementation.

In this regard - he continued - the Security Council would need to pass a resolution to effectively limit the use of force by all the parties within Bosnia's ten new autonomous districts, or to lift the arms embargo that had brought so much harm and suffering upon Bosnia's civilian population. The Council would have to commit itself to defend minority rights in each of the future districts of Bosnia or allow them to arm and defend themselves.

Ambassador Ladsous, of France, surprised us all by suddenly stating that the dilemma the Bosnian president was highlighting truly put the finger on the crux of the matter. He then asked a question of the utmost relevance: "Do you believe the Security Council has the will and wherewithal to insure this and other resolutions are fully implemented?" In Ladsous' view, harsher sanctions might bring Belgrade to reason, but would not suffice to ensure the safe passage of international humanitarian aid to towns in need, or a minimum level of safety for the civilian and military personnel in charge of its transportation and distribution.

To such a query, Izetbegovic replied that, should we be referring to what UNPROFOR could do in Bosnia, the truth was its mandate was far too limited for it to be able to contain the Serbian aggression. That was why he urged us to fully review its terms of reference if we really wished the Blue Helmets to be something more than mere spectators in his country's unfolding drama. It was an appropriate, albeit pitiless, characterization of the so-called United Nations Protection Force.

Above all – Izetbegovic insisted – because its troop deployment in Bosnia was exceedingly small and its current mandate made it unable to ensure the implementation of that or any other peace plan for Bosnia. He then added: "Believe me when I tell you, the Bosnian people have simply lost all faith on any possible help from the United Nations military forces. It is a situation that compels me to ask how much longer the Security Council will continue to punish us with an arms embargo, the sole result of which is hampering our nation's legitimate right to self-defense".

It had become quite clear that this aspect of the situation was of the highest importance to his government. Presuming he would be interested to know my thoughts on the matter, I told him Venezuela, together with all the other members of the Non-Aligned Movement, supported lifting the arms embargo, and that we would not fail to bring to the UN's attention that it was a just and fundamental decision that needed to be taken urgently. Then, to avoid a debate on this controversial issue among the members of the Council's delegation, I indicated that we would be in a better position to reach a decision by consensus once our mission had provided us with new information.

When the time came to leave, I regretted not having said the many things I would have liked to say, but in my capacity as coordinator, I was under the obligation to conduct and express myself with moderation. Hopefully, in the coming private meeting we would have with the Bosnian president, I would be in a better position to speak frankly.

At the UN Blue Helmets Headquarters

Upon departing the presidential palace, our caravan of armored vehicles headed to the United Nations Forces Headquarters in Bosnia, located at the outskirts of Sarajevo. During the few minutes it took us to cross the city, alongside homes and buildings in ruins, we did not see a single vehicle and, at the most, some ten pedestrians. Not even dogs dared to roam the streets. As we passed the bridge where on June 28, 1914, Archduke Francis Ferdinand, heir to the Austrian throne, and his wife Sophia were murdered by a young Serbian independence activist, I was reminded that the blood spilled over those very same streets had caused the catastrophe of the First World War.

General Vere Hayes rescued me from my gloomy thoughts. A British officer, he was the third in the line of command of the Blue Helmets deployed in Bosnia and was in charge of keeping us company during all our displacements. He told me his forces camped in what had been a family residence. Once we arrived, he led us into a spacious room devoid of windows, with its walls completely covered by military maps of different areas of the country and numerous photos of Serbian weaponry, including their heavy artillery and tanks. It was truly a military operations command post. Ten UNPROFOR staff officers, Victor Andreyev, a Russian national who was a UN international civil servant assigned to this command, and three dozen chairs, aligned as if in a schoolroom, awaited our arrival. Then, Hayes invited us to be seated and, addressing me in a direct and rude manner, said:

— Ambassador Arria, Sir. I watch you frequently on international news programs, mostly on BBC, declaring about the conflict unfolding in this part of the world. But, when I listen as you propose confusing and totally wooly-headed resolutions, I wish to be able to tell you your opinions have nothing to do with reality.

The aggressiveness in his words and the tone of his voice caused me much indignation. I realized that If I allowed that arrogant British officer to address me in such a way on our very first day in Bosnia, the mission I headed would lose all authority and respect. Therefore, I made it plain to him that under no circumstances would I tolerate such brazen tone.

— As Coordinator of this delegation of the Security Council – I replied – I must inform you we are pleased to be here and to spend with you these few days. You carry a very heavy responsibility, and you do so in exceedingly difficult circumstances. So, in the Council's name, I must inform you we respect and highly value the task you are entrusted with in Bosnia. That said, allow me to explain why you should not have greeted me with such words. First of all, I must remind you that you are part of a chain of command that includes Generals Wahlgren and Morillon. They, nor your superiors in

London, would have never authorized you to tell the ambassador of a country member of the United Nations Security Council that the Council was totally in the wrong by approving those resolutions.

General Hayes did not expect this reply and tried a couple of jokes to avoid the confrontation. I continued establishing firmly our authority. I assured him we visited the Force's command post to learn about the current reality of the conflict and its future prospects; in particular, about what was truly happening in Srebrenica. I then reminded him: "All Security Council Resolutions, including of course Resolution 819 of April 16, place all the members of UNPROFOR, without any exceptions, under the obligation to abide by them to the letter. On the other hand, I want you to know I have never considered my opinions to be those of a confused idealist, as you allow yourself to suggest, and to disqualify my thoughts on the war in Bosnia simply shows that you, General Hayes, are the utterly confused one."

I could never have imagined our mission would have such an unpleasant beginning. It was as if, by greeting us the way he did, General Hayes was trying to measure how far he could go in trying to make us abide by his will. Fortunately, I did not know then all that I have come to know since.

The Sins of the United Nations

The very unpleasant encounter with General Hayes had created much tension in our meeting room. The sudden appearance of a group of orderlies bringing coffee and refreshments allowed for a pause and to lighten the atmosphere. However, such a regrettable episode had made it clear to all the ambassadors in the delegation that it would not be possible to rely on UNPROFOR's cooperation in the discharge of our mandate. The implications of this would only come to be revealed in November 1999, when Kofi Annan, Boutros-Ghali's successor as UN Secretary General, presented to the General Assembly two devastating reports, one on the genocide that took place in Rwanda in 1994, and the other on what happened in Srebrenica a year after. In those reports Annan acknowledged both the United Nations' responsibility as an organization and his own personal one, given that when both horrifying crimes against humanity were being committed, he was the head of the UN's Peacekeeping Department. On that occasion, Annan did not shy away from also laying its share of blame on the international community, guilty of indifference when called upon to confront the challenge such massacres represented.

It is worth mentioning that during our mission to Bosnia we were not aware that the Peacekeeping Department had alerted UNPROFOR that Resolution 819 "did not mandate any special military obligations". Had we known about Annan's implementation guidelines, our outrage about Hayes' unbecoming conduct would have been even greater. Particularly so because, after refreshments, several officers from the General Command continued to share with us their vision on the incidents that continued to disturb the peace in several areas of Bosnia and Croatia. In the course of this second round of comments Hayes intervened once again, now to finally admit that ethnic cleansing had not stopped in Srebrenica, and that the effects of this implacable policy had become much more acute in the course of the last few weeks, causing the forced displacement to Srebrenica of thousands of residents from nearby towns to Srebrenica, even though it was in no condition to give them shelter and safe haven. Burdened by such unforeseen developments, Srebrenica had become like the eye of a hurricane, still in calm, but about to explode and wipe out everything at any moment.

Immediately after Hayes' comments, a general staff officer informed us that, as in Srebrenica, in Sarajevo too anything could happen at any moment. The Serbs had around ten thousand troops and hundreds of heavy artillery pieces deployed around Sarajevo, not to mention sharpshooters firing at will on the few civilians who dared go out into the streets. General Hayes interrupted his subordinate to point out that: "In all frankness, our soldiers are not equipped to defend us; our headquarters are within reach of Serbian artillery; and our mandate is strictly humanitarian. The Security Council must consider all these circumstances if it wishes to modify our mandate's terms of reference."

This time, General Hayes' considerations did seem to me to be well founded. The Security Council was not giving the war in Bosnia the importance it deserved and was leaving its own forces defenseless vis-à-vis the powerful Serbian war machine. Those at the helm of the United Nations in New York were responsible for keeping on the ground a military force that could only witness and keep record of the multiple human rights violations.

That is the reason – Hayes went on – we fear the Bosnians might one day dare to attack us and then blame the aggression on the Serbs, provoking a violent reaction by UNPROFOR.

Such a reasoning reminded us of General Lewis MacKenzie's absurd declarations in July 1992, when, as second in command of the UN Protection Forces in Bosnia, he declared that the mortar fire that had killed twenty-two people in Sarajevo might have been coming from the Bosnian side, with the malign intention of feigning a Serb attack. I then asked General Hayes on what grounds he based his fears of a Bosnian *mise-en-scène* of a false Serbian attack, but he did not offer a convincing explanation. It simply came to prove, once more, the racial prejudices and political biases that distorted the vision of the European commands in Bosnia. Maybe that was the reason Ambassador O'Brien changed the course of the conversation and asked what information the UN Command had on the government of Serbia's direct support of the Bosnian-Serb military forces under Karadzic's orders.

General Hayes entrusted the answer to one of his fellow officers, who categorically stated: "Bosnian authorities and members of our own command have confirmed such support". Then, General Hayes' aide picked up on the issue of the sanctions on Serbia approved by the Security Council and considered that, with luck, these would only have very short-term effects since Sarajevo was of exceptionally high strategic importance to the Serbs given its geographic location bordering with Serbia. In his view, Belgrade would stop at nothing to achieve this goal. Now, the Russian political advisor cut into the conversation to remind us "We should not forget that the agreements reached by the parties in Sarajevo on the morning of April 17 were part of a much larger negotiation, the fundamental purpose of which was to put an end to the war and save many lives."

My reply came on behalf of the mission: "Our position on the designation of Srebrenica and surroundings as a safe area by the Security Council points, precisely, in the same direction: to reach a durable cease fire and save uncountable lives". I then clarified we did not place blame on UNPROFOR for not duly informing us about such negotiations since it was not up to it, but to the Secretariat, to do so. Finally, and to bring the meeting to a close, I inquired "What measures will you take as a UN Protection Force to implement the Council Resolution which orders the protection of Srebrenica and of its undefended, unarmed inhabitants?" It goes without saying, my query received no answer.

The Brutal Massacre at Ahmici

At 2 pm we left for Ahmici, a town in Central Bosnia where the cold-blooded killing of a hundred and sixteen Bosnians had taken place. The armored vehicle in which I was travelling was the second in the caravan. When I was about to board it, Paul Lewis, the journalist from *The New York Times* who travelled with us, approached me to ask whether I had any new information on the situation in Srebrenica. I told him what little I knew. By what I had heard the night before in Zagreb and by what the President of Bosnia had said in the morning, I was under the impression neither UNPROFOR nor any other international force was in a position to protect Srebrenica.

— May I quote you, ambassador? – he asked.

— Of course, you may, I replied.

I then boarded the vehicle, taking the seat beside the driver, the only one with enough space to allow me to not bend my left leg, seriously injured years before in an accident. With me traveled General Hayes, his adjutant, a female Bosnian translator, and Ramuncho Llerandi. When we departed, General Hayes informed me we would be reaching Ahmici in less than an hour and would then continue first to Vitez, and then to Kiseljac, where we would spend the night. A few minutes later, at a sharp bend in the road, our caravan run into a T-55 Russian-made tank and a group of five heavily armed Serbian paramilitaries ordered us to stop with unnecessarily threatening gestures.

General Hayes was quick to give me assurances: "Our escort will deal with the situation." From my seat, I took several pictures of the Serbian paramilitary who, with violent gestures, was ordering us to come out of the vehicle. We ignored him. Our reaction made him furious, so much so that he took aim at us with his Kalashnikov assault rifle. Our translator told us the Serbian was shouting that it was not allowed to take pictures of the Serbian military personnel nor of its weapons, and that he demanded that we exit the vehicle and turn over my camera.

General Hayes and his adjutant surprised us by suddenly, and irresponsibly, opening the vehicle's rear door. The same violation of UNPROFOR's security regulations that last January had cost Hakija Turajlic, Deputy Prime Minister, his life. Why was Hayes incurring in the very same mistake that had allowed a Serbian soldier to kill a Bosnian high official by seven shots at close range? While I could not fail to wonder if we were to be the victims of a crime to be similarly committed in the presence of UN peacekeepers, the Serbian paramilitaries gathered at the vehicle's backdoor, kept unexplainably open, pointing their rifles at us.

In the meantime, the tank had turned its turret around and started pointing its 105 mm cannon directly at us. From where I was, I could not see the maneuver. Later, I was informed the situation did not merit the least reaction from our military escort, which simply conveyed to its General Command in Sarajevo that "a Serb tank was menacing the vehicle in which traveled Ambassador Arria, coordinator of the mission sent by the Security Council to Bosnia". A few minutes later, the Serbian tank was surrounded by three small Danish tankettes from the UN Protection Forces and made to point its cannon elsewhere.

Hayes and his adjutant felt bolstered by the Danish reinforcements. However, the Serbs continued to block our passage. One of them, shrouded as all his comrades in a dark blue jumpsuit with a Serbian flag on the shoulder, placed his foot inside the vehicle and aimed his rifle at Llerandi's head. That night, Llerandi told me in confidence he had felt a cold shiver all along his spine. And with reason! UNPROFOR did not have the material or legal means to militarily intervene, not even to protect the five ambassadors who represented the Security Council.

Almost an hour later, with two Danish tankettes now leading the caravan, we arrived at the outskirts of Ahmici. According to the 1991 census, at the time the town had about one thousand two hundred inhabitants, mostly Bosnians and Croats, with a small minority of Serbs. As we entered deep into Central Bosnia, we were able to witness the degree of devastation suffered by the small villages that dotted the road. Surrounded by the impressive natural beauty of the place, kilometer after kilometer, we witnessed how the Serbs, and in this area also the Bosnian Croats, understood the abhorrent concept of ethnic cleansing: mosques burned to the ground, and buildings with windows, doors, and tile roofs totally smashed to the ground by cannon fire.

About what had happened at Ahmici, we only knew what we had been told at UNPROFOR's General Command in Zagreb, and the comments President Izetbegovic had made that morning: that one hundred and sixteen Bosnian men, women and children had been brutally massacred on April 16 by the self-named Croat Defense Council. Nothing more. In other words, while in New York the final text of Resolution 819 was still under discussion, and while in Sarajevo the Blue Helmets cooperated with the Serbians to put pressure on the Bosnians to surrender Srebrenica, at Ahmici, Bosnian Croat paramilitaries were undertaking one of the war's most execrable crimes. We were aware, however, that these forces, initially allied with the Bosnian Muslims in their fight against the Serb invaders, had recently joined the latter to take part in an authentic orgy of blood.

The British battalion deployed in the area, under the command of Colonel Robert Stewart, waited for us at the town's outskirts. I asked General Hayes what had really happened at Ahmici. He explained that on April 16, Bosnian Croat paramilitaries burned and razed numerous dwellings in both Vitez and Ahmici, acting simultaneously in both places; they also murdered in cold blood whole Muslim families. He then added that he would prefer for Colonel Stewart, who had been there, to report to us in more precise details. I then asked why neither he nor his superiors in Zagreb had informed us of such a repugnant crime. Hayes merely shrugged his shoulders.

As we reached the Ahmici outskirts several gunned vehicles joined us. Colonel Stewart, currently a member of the British parliament, alighted from one of them. After introducing himself, Stewart reported the situation was one of very high risk, so his men would escort us throughout our visit. We continued on foot along the gentle slope of a wooded hill. The clicketing sound of automatic weapons became louder as we approached, although we could not make out where the shots were coming from nor against whom. According to Colonel Stewart, the Bosnian Croat units were trying to intimidate us to make us desist from reaching the place where the slaughter had taken place. At his command, the two tankettes went towards the hill's high ridge, and he then asked us to wait until they came back. Ten minutes later the firing ceased and the tankettes returned. We then renewed our march, at all times surrounded by Stewart's men.

From the top of the hill, we were able to see what remained of the town: a lengthy line of almost completely burned-out houses. All of us, including Colonel Stewart, were profoundly disturbed by what we saw. He then asked us if we felt up to taking a look at the crime scene. We agreed, unaware of what awaited us. We walked towards the houses. Upon entering one, we stumbled upon the charred remains of what must have been a man. Not far away, there were three other carbonized bodies, apparently, of a woman and two children. The walls and the floor were covered in dry blood. Colonel Stewart told us the Croat attackers had first "machined gunned them, and then burned their bodies with flamethrowers."

As I write these lines, I still feel blood freeze in my veins. Never, ever, had I seen anything like it. We went on to inspect other houses. Every single one of them offered the same monstrous spectacle. Stewart told us his explosive experts had combed every house in search of boobytraps hidden in the corpses, a frequent practice used by Bosnian Croat military units, and had found none. What they did find, in the garden at the back of one of the houses, were the remains of a few other Bosnian citizens who had apparently tried to escape the massacre but were murdered by sharpshooters. My feelings were a combination of indignation and sorrow for an act of cruelty such as I could never have imagined. A whole town put to death in cold blood. The only remaining living being was a horse that slowly circled the abandoned houses, all destroyed by Mate Boban´s paramilitaries.

On Our Way to Spend a Night in Kiseljac

At nightfall, we continued on our way to Vitez, in the most somber silence. In one of those houses, called the "Intelligence Cell", we had held a meeting with Colonel Stewart and his General Staff. As they were giving us a detailed report on the situation prevailing in the area, we realized to what extent we lacked information. According to Stewart, the Croat paramilitaries practiced ethnic cleansing with the same intensity and cruelty as their Bosnian Serb partners. To my question as to when he found out about the April 16 massacre, the British colonel replied that in the early hours of that day they had heard many shots being fired. Hours later, as they reached the neighboring town of Zenica, he was informed of the massacre. He witnessed the extent of the tragedy only on April 22, when he finally entered Ahmici.

— I will never forget, he told us, barely withholding his rage.

Later on, he confided the worst had been the realization that it had been the victims' Croat neighbors who had betrayed them. That same day he also found out that Dario Kordic, the Croat commander of the operation, had called upon the families of Ahmici's Croat descent residents to abandon their homes before the Croat irregulars began their murderous ethnic cleansing. According to his information, Kordic had ordered his troops to kill first the men, then their male sons and then the rest of the families. Kordic currently serves a twenty-four-years jail sentence in The Hague.

Before continuing on the road towards General Morillon's command post at Kiseljac, we were served a light dinner and I had the opportunity to look closely at Colonel Stewart. His reaction to the crimes he described had been completely different to that of other UNPROFOR officers we had encountered during our trip. The shock those events had caused him was evident, as he would describe years after, once retired from the army, in his penetrating book of memoires about the months he spent in the Former Yugoslavia: *Broken Lives: Personal View of the Bosnian Conflict.*

We reached Kiseljac around midnight and we took lodgings within the military setting prepared for us: camp beds cramped into a windowless room, with just one sanitation facility at the end of an equally windowless corridor. As Head of the mission, Hayes offered me to stay in the private quarters of General Morillon, who in those days was in Zagreb. I declined his offer and instead suggested to raffle the privilege among the ambassadors. The winner was Ambassador Sidorov, of Russia, who accepted the prize delighted. Lights were turned out and all of us, physically and mentally exhausted, surrendered to sleep with the sounds of intense automatic fire as background.

The shooting went on until 5 am of April 25. We were scheduled to travel on a UN helicopter to Srebrenica, main destination of our mission within Bosnian territory. During breakfast with my fellow ambassadors and the journalists travelling with us, we had the opportunity to share our feelings regarding the horrors that we had witnessed at Ahmici a few hours before.

José María Mendiluce, of ACNUR, who would travel with us to Srebrenica, joined our table. Then, General Hayes made a sudden appearance and informed us our agenda had changed and our trip to Srebrenica had been cancelled. I immediately stood up and emphatically asked him the reasons for the cancellation. Hayes tried to avoid giving a clear answer, but I insisted, and the conversation became increasingly tense. Most of all because I immediately realized the decision to cancel was not Hayes′ own but had come from either the UN Secretariat or from the UK government, as the military serving under the UN answered more to their countries′ interests than to those of the Security Council. From that moment on, I had no doubt that the UN Peacekeeping Operations Department had orchestrated our trip in such a way as to give us the runaround in Bosnia, believing it would be enough to satisfy our expectations. Obviously, the Secretariat had made a huge mistake.

As this new confrontation with the general turned far too harsh, I made an aside with the other ambassadors to examine how best to solve the situation. Our conclusion was to convey to General Hayes that under no circumstances would we accept the cancellation of our visit to Srebrenica. This time, the surprised one was Hayes. I took advantage of his bewilderment to inform him that we would that very evening prepare a report to the Security Council and the UN Secretariat denouncing his refusal to acknowledge Resolution 819.

Hayes weathered the storm in silence. He then asked permission to retire. Half an hour later he returned and, without any explanations, announced we could proceed to board a huge Russian-made helicopter to travel to Srebrenica. But after flying for almost forty-five minutes, instead of reaching our destination, we landed on the football field of a town called Zvornik, where a really unpleasant surprise awaited us. A uniformed Serbian colonel, surnamed Rodic, addressed us in his native tongue and welcomed us to the Srpska Republic.

—And which republic is that? I asked him through our interpreter - I do not recall any nation of such a name as one recognized by the United Nations.

Rodic turned his back on us and, joined by Hayes, went towards a coffee shop located on one side of the football field. For quite a while we watched them have a friendly chat. We surmised it was all to see what our reaction might be to what was plainly an attempt to keep us away from Srebrenica. Concerned about this new delay, a maneuver similar to the one we experienced when we had just left Sarajevo on our way to Ahmici, I decided to approach the coffee shop and to ask Hayes what the problem was.

— The Serbian authorities do not authorize the entry of the mission to Srebrenica, he shamelessly answered with bureaucratic indifference.

The reply was, however, confirmation that Srebrenica and its surrounding areas were under Serbian control. It equally evidenced that UNPROFOR, and General Hayes, instead of assisting us in fulfilling our mandate, were trying to obstruct it. That, precisely, was the reason for the cordiality between him and Colonel Rodic, who, we would soon learn, was the area´s Serbian military commander.

The ambassadors of Russia and France tried to tone down the confrontation, but those of New Zealand, Hungary and Pakistan gave me their full support without hesitation. Hayes and Rodic made a new aside and then the British general notified us we could travel to Srebrenica, but on two conditions. First, journalists could not join us and must stay in Zvornik until our return; second, only I, as group coordinator, could travel in the first of the helicopter's two flights. The second flight would take all the other ambassadors and UN officials present. No one could take pictures, and all must leave behind photo and video cameras. Needless to say, I brought my camera along with me and took as many pictures as I pleased. I gave the pictures I took in Srebrenica to Anthony Goodman, the Reuters reporter who came along with us. That was how we were able to circumvent the Serbian's attempt to hide from the world the images of the city's brutal occupation and the criminal harassment of its Muslim population. I remember well a Blue Helmet officer who stayed with us throughout the visit, a video camera at hand. I only came to see the result of his work in December 2005, at the trial of the Bosnian Muslim commander Naser Oric at The Hague, to which I was a witness for the defense, when the prosecution presented the section of those videos dealing with our arrival at Srebrenica.

Before our departure to Srebrenica, I held a short meeting with the other members of the mission, and then talked to Hayes. First, I informed him we were all going to Srebrenica, or none would go. Second, we insisted the journalists would be coming with us. The discussion with the Serbian colonel on these two issues lasted a good fifteen minutes, until Ambassador O'Brien of New Zealand reminded us that time was running short and that in the early evening we had to travel to Split, in neighboring Croatia, to meet Mate Boban. His suggestion was that I should accept travelling in the first plane, but with guarantees that they would follow together with the journalists. Hayes took it upon himself to ensure our two conditions were respected and asked the French colonel in charge of UNPROFOR's aerial operations to prepare the helicopter for immediate departure. When I was finally able to board the device, I received another unpleasant surprise: Colonel Rodic was already seated in the cabin. Fifteen minutes later, my undesirable fellow traveler and I arrived in Srebrenica.

A SLOW-MOTION GENOCIDE

On the afternoon of April 16, just as I was about to enter the room without a view" where the Security Council holds its informal consultations, I noticed a group of officials gathered in the waiting room around a TV set. A report from Srebrenica by independent journalist Tony Birtley was airing on CNN. It showed crude images of severely undernourished women, old people and children, terror in their eyes, keeping warm in the middle of the street around makeshift fires, lit with garbage and rubbish. Like ghostly beings, they all wandered aimlessly in the city's ravaged streets, many without shoes, none with winter clothing, mothers hugging their small ones to their chest to keep them warm.

Under shock, profoundly moved, I kept staring at the TV set, unable to turn my attention away from what I saw. Birtley's report brought home the monstrosities committed in the very heart of Europe during a brutal foreign aggression against an independent nation. Birtley had sneaked into Srebrenica by foot, evading notice by the Serbian soldiers that had been keeping the city under siege for eleven months. Thanks to his prowess the world was able to witness the horrifying tragedy its inhabitants were suffering day after day. General Morillon, on the eve of his visit to Srebrenica, confronted by the seriousness of the situation, could not avoid recognizing it as "infinitely worse than what I had anticipated".

I must admit that the memory of those terrible images has been haunting me ever since. I would even venture that, had it not been for the overwhelming coverage all over the world of

Birtley's reportage, Srebrenica's designation as a Safe Area by the Security Council might not have taken place; and maybe the Non-Aligned Caucus in the Council might not have pushed for approval, the very morning after, of the particularly important Resolution 819. It is important to underline underline that this critically important decision did not come about following a report to the Council by the Secretary General, nor was it an initiative of the members of the P5, two of which, France and the United Kingdom, commanded the UN peacekeeping forces deployed in Bosnia, but was rather the result of the work of independent journalists such as Birtley. Little had it mattered that the UN Secretariat and those governments were well informed by UNPROFOR itself, as well as by high-ranking officials of the UN Agency for Refugees, of the conditions under which the civilian population of the area, and the refugees in particular, barely survived. Their indifference and mutual complicities explain, to a high degree, why the mandate of the UN Protection Force had been restricted to simply keeping developments under observation and to the provision and distribution of such humanitarian assistance as the Serbian authorities would allow.

A few days before, in its April 14 edition, *The New York Times* had published a note by John Burns titled *United Nations Aides Denounce Serbs for Shellings,* relaying statements by ACNUR officials denying the veracity of reports by UNPROFOR and the UN Secretariat; and giving account of the criminal Serbian mortar attack against a school in Srebrenica which caused the death of fifty-six persons, including children killed while in the playground. Larry Hollingworth, a British ACNUR official and head of its operations in Bosnia, confided in Burns that when he received the news, he wished "Whomever had ordered the attack, and those who had carried it out, never to cease hearing the screams of those children and of their mothers, while burning in the hottest corner of hell". John McMillan, also an ACNUR official, blamed the cruelty of the event on the fact that "The Serbians, moved by a pathological ambition to take control of new territories, were willing to kill whomever it took." Thanks to these and other statements we were able to come into the knowledge of other equally execrable situations, such as the famine caused by the Serbian siege to Srebrenica which forced its inhabitants to survive on wild berries and on soup made of hazelnut flour. And, as if these were not sufficient reasons for every alarm to go off, there was only one doctor available, with no medicines, medical equipment, or surgical instruments.

We Reach Srebrenica

As our helicopter continued on its flight towards Srebrenica, I said to myself over and over again that knowledge of all these terrible news would surely give me strength to cope with all the horrors I would yet come to witness. Then, the French colonel in charge of our transportation approached me. Speaking over the engines' noise, he informed me that before landing we would fly at low altitude over Srebrenica and Potocari, a small community where the Canadian Blue Helmet battalion responsible for the area had its headquarters.

— You will be able to see from a short distance – he said - the Serbian artillery located on the hills surrounding Srebrenica.

Earlier, when we landed by surprise in Zvornik, I wondered whether we were being held hostage to UNPROFOR, Colonel Rodic, or both. Now, when instead of landing the helicopter began to fly in circles, witnessing the warm camaraderie between the French colonel and Rodic, I became convinced that their true purpose was to delay as much as possible my arrival in Srebrenica. Their conduct mirrored the previous arbitrary decision of not letting us through when we were reaching Sarajevo, and the improvised stopover at a football field in Zvornik. Who were the real power brokers over the fate of Bosnia? The UN Secretariat? The UN Protection Force commanders? Their overseers in London and Paris? Who was responsible for this murky complicity between the Serbian aggressors and some supposedly allied governments to not abide by the terms of Security Council Resolution 819? Might it be possible that interests as powerful as those were trying to ignore the designation of Srebrenica and surrounding areas as a Safe Area and to obstruct our mission's mandate to ascertain firsthand the situation in Bosnia? Was that why Colonel Rodic acted at all times as if he was the one really in command?

After slowly overflying the city in ruins and UNPROFOR's camp in Potocari, located in a building that had previously served as a car battery fabric, we circled twice again over the Srebrenica football field and, at the third try, finally landed. Several dozen wounded lay in stretchers aligned over the green. About a dozen men, in the white robes of medical orderlies, took care of them, while a few Blue Helmets helped them to move the wounded. A few meters further away, many locals, sitting on a stone wall, watched in silence. I asked the UNPROFOR officer who seemed to be in charge of aiding the wounded if the medical personnel came from *Médecins sans Frontières*. He answered that they were Serbian medical orderlies charged with deciding which of the wounded would be moved by the UN Protection Forces to a hospital in Tuzla, and which would not.

This left me speechless. It was proof that the surrender of the city and its surrounding areas, mediated by the UN Blue Helmets and agreed upon a few days before between Serbian and Bosnian military authorities, had left General Mladic's men in total command of the area. It showed that UNPROFOR was not only helping to carry out a non-authorized disarmament of the city's Muslim defenders, but also helping to deny some Muslim civilians the right to abandon the city without prior Serbian authorization, in flagrant violation of Resolution 819's mandate. It evidenced that the enclave's capitulation was total, and that the Serbian aggressors and the UN military brass refused to acknowledge the importance of such a decisive resolution and of its provisions. In other words, the UN Protection Forces, instead of guaranteeing the Muslim population's security cooperated with its aggressors in the illegal control of the citizenry of Srebrenica.

Needless to say, I was not going to condone such a state of affairs. But I could not even begin to imagine what was to come next. Up to that moment, I believed that however twisted the Council and the UN Secretariat's intentions might be, we had succeeded in having our mission approved, with the mandate to collect, directly on the ground, information unavailable to the members of the Council or the UN Secretary General Boutros-Ghali. I now realized the true purpose of our mission was to distract international public opinion. It suddenly became evident to me that the decision to send us to Bosnia was a ploy designed to hide the surrender of Srebrenica to its Serbian invaders while faking ignorance about an ethnic cleansing process Europe had not witnessed since the days of the Holocaust and the Second World War. It finally dawned on me that the Security Council, instead of taking firm action as was expected of it, was in reality drawing a veil over the process of ethnic extermination taking place in the Former Yugoslavia.

All these concerns were troubling my mind after my landing at the Srebrenica football field. The other ambassadors arrived shortly after. When they told me UNPROFOR had yielded to Serbian demands and had not allowed the journalists, who were part of our party, to travel to Srebrenica, all my fears came true. It was evident that the UN Forces were complicit in the task of precluding international media from reporting about the tragedy unfolding before our eyes. However, they would not get away with it, as our presence in Bosnia was meant to ensure. No matter the obstacles, we would bring to light what was truly happening in Bosnia.

Our First Sighting of a Serbian Massacre

Travelling again in an armed vehicle caravan, we left behind the football field and headed towards the hills where the Serbian heavy artillery was located. From there, we headed on foot towards the Srebrenica city center, almost completely destroyed by heavy shelling. We made it to the main mosque, totally in ruins, before boarding some UNPROFOR tankettes.

Standing in the middle of the city's ruins, surrounded by overwhelming proof of Serbian firepower, we felt firsthand the fear of an attack by a hidden and bloodthirsty enemy. Waiting to welcome us in the city center was a group of civilians, mostly women, carrying hand-painted posters with the name of our countries, just as the group of children had the day before at the presidential palace doorstep. I alighted the armored vehicle and went towards them to reciprocate the greetings, carefully as they were standing behind a barbed wire fence. I never understood, nor was it ever explained to me, why the Blue Helmets placed these Muslim women behind barbed wire, as if in a concentration camp.

Once back in the tankette, José María Mendiluce, who was my travelling companion in that segment of our itinerary, suggested I should talk to General Hayes and ask to be taken to the school hit by Serbian mortar fire two days before. I did so through the military vehicle's radio, but Hayes, as was to be expected, refused my request under the pretense we did not have time to deviate from our schedule. We still had to visit the UNPROFOR Canadian command post before continuing, that same afternoon, towards Split. I insisted, rather doggedly, and in the end, he had no other option but to take us there.

What we saw once we reached the school was terrifying! Upon crossing the door, the first thing we laid eyes on upon were the bloody remains of children scattered in the garden, blown to pieces by mortar fire. It was horrifying proof of the Serbian aggressors' capacity for evildoing, compounded by the shameful fact that the person showing us around the repugnant sight, the very materialization of human cruelty, was no other than Colonel Rodic, personally responsible for the slaughter. A couple of minutes later we passed by a group of about one hundred women who had sought refuge, however precarious, in the school's ruins. Some were the mothers of the murdered children. They stared at us with a mixture of perplexity, sadness and grief, even after our interpreter let them know who we were. When I noticed Rodic standing behind me, I understood the cause of their disdain.

These poor victims of Serbian aggression – ill, hungry, and desperate – could only repudiate us with their silence, while sinking into the deepest and most sorrowful resignation.

From the school we headed towards Potocari. Lieutenant Colonel Thomas Geburt, Commander of the Canadian Battalion, was there, waiting for us. He had arrived only a few days before. Brian Mulroney, Prime Minister of Canada, had paid a visit to the Security Council in New York and had proposed, as an alternative to confronting the Serbian aggression in Bosnia, an immediate armed intervention in the Former Yugoslavia. I was aware of Mulroney's line of thought since at the time of his visit he had complained that some members of the Council completely refused to consider such an option. Mulroney had argued that some principles, such as that of sovereignty, were abused by many to hide the true meaning of self-determination. His reasoning was the seed for what was to become known as Responsibility to Protect (R2P), adopted at the 2005 United Nations Summit: a universal commitment to protect, without need of any validation, any population in the world under threat of ethnic cleansing and crimes against humanity. The Summit equally approved the right to use armed force on such occasions when no other option was possible to ensure that goal.

Lieutenant Colonel Geburt, whom I briefed on my conversation with Mulroney at the Security Council, could hardly imagine that barely a couple of years later, Potocari would become a painfully well-known place throughout the world. In July 1995, eight thousand Bosnian Muslim citizens were brutally murdered on its streets by General Mladic's troops, even though the city was then the headquarters of a Dutch battalion whose commander, instead of resisting the Serbian killers, chose to surrender the defenseless civilians under his protection to General Mladic, who now serves a life sentence in The Hague.

Geburt told us that on April 18 there had been no shots fired in the area thanks to the "agreement" signed in Sarajevo on the 17 th. Consequently, the main problem facing the inhabitants at that time was not so much the war but its consequences, such as the lack of drinking water, an issue not included in the capitulation agreement.

— This is a serious problem, he told us. When the Muslims were in control of the water supply, they did not share it with the Serbians, and now the Serbians think they have the same right and do not facilitate it to the Muslim population.

Ambassador O'Brien took advantage of Geburt's comment to raise a topic we were all genuinely concerned about:

— In your opinion, how long should an UNPROFOR contingent be deployed in Srebrenica?

— Quite some time, I'm afraid – was the very discouraging reply he gave us. – If we retire, I fear the Serbs would immediately murder the whole Muslim population of the city and of its surroundings.

A UN Forces high-ranking officer was thus fully acknowledging the criminal nature of the Serbian aggression while at the same time sharing with us his concern over the helpless situation in which the UN placed his command, no matter the agreement reached with the Serbian authorities and the many Security Council resolutions. He reported that by not allowing international humanitarian assistance to remedy the sufferings of the city's civilian population, the Serbs violated with absolute impunity all Security Council resolutions. The situation was becoming even more desperate – he added – because the Serbian authorities had now also cut the supply of electricity to Srebrenica.

Mendiluce intervened to point out that the continued flow of refugees towards the city, fleeing from the ethnic cleansing taking place in all the surrounding areas, made worse the already unsustainable sanitary conditions in the city dramatically. Since mid-April, when the International Red Cross began activities in Srebrenica, it had been able only to evacuate five-hundred-twenty-six refugees, while their numbers grew exponentially.

When the meeting with Geburt and his general staff was over, we were introduced to three perfectly uniformed officers from General Mladic's army. Hayes identified each one of them by name and rank. On the other hand, the three Bosnian Muslim officers, none of them in uniform, were not similarly introduced. The discrimination was obvious, but Hayes quickly tried to cover it up by telling us they were also his friends. However, it had become patently clear that while relations between the UNPROFOR commanders and the Serb officers was conducted following the usual military protocol, for the UN forces in Srebrenica the Muslim defenders of the enclave did not belong to and had no right to be treated as members of a regular army.

Before leaving for Split, where we would be meeting Mate Boban, leader of the Bosnian Croats, I consulted my colleagues about the possibility of having an informal meeting with the Muslim leaders who were still in Srebrenica, even if only to convey to them words of encouragement on behalf of the Security Council. It was a challenge of sorts since I certainly did not wish for a repeat of the previous month's incident when General Morillon was almost not allowed to leave the city by its inhabitants. Needless to say, I was perfectly aware that my obligation was not to abandon Srebrenica to its fate, and since the members of the mission were in complete agreement with my proposal, we made our way on foot towards the city's Town Hall. There, alerted by UNPROFOR soldiers, many people began to arrive, most of them elderly men. They greeted us as they entered the small room where we would hold our meeting. Colonel Rodic also arrived at the Town Hall in the company of other officers of his army, all in uniform.

As the room began to fill, General Hayes and Colonel Rodic looked at me with a grin on their faces. I sensed they were making fun of me, and I promised myself to take advantage of the opportunity to convey to Srebrenica's overwhelmed citizens that we in the UN Security Council condemned without reservation the criminal activities of Rodic and his followers, and in a very particular way, the inhuman shelling of the school. The Serbian military presence in the room conveyed, however, the opposite impression. It was them, the cruel aggressors of the Muslim people of Srebrenica, who had the city under their total control. One could see in the eyes of the civilians present in the room that they all were absolutely convinced that neither we nor the international community would lay a finger on any of their executioners.

As unpleasant as the circumstances were, I began my intervention, as I usually did on such occasions, introducing the members of the delegation by their name and rank. To my right was the UNPROFOR interpreter, who asked me to speak slowly so she could accurately translate my words and named each of the ambassadors with a brief pause in between. I then proceeded to explain to the audience that we were there representing the UN Security Council, the world's highest political body, and that we had travelled to Bosnia to learn firsthand about the situation in the country. Secondly, I let them know that as soon as we were back in New York we would present to the Council specific recommendations to put an end to the Serbian military aggression, whose commander, I pointed out looking at Rodic directly in the eyes, is over there, "seating among you". I then referred to the murder of the twelve children and more than forty adults in the bombed school, and I assured them that those responsible would be tried by the International Tribunal for the Former Yugoslavia, which would begin its work in a month's time, at the end of May. I had no way to ascertain whether the Serb military present in the room had understood what I had said, but I felt the need to at least try to convey to that group of some eighty men, exhausted, without hope, and visibly discouraged, that I was not Morillon nor Hayes nor any other of UNPROFOR's leaders; and that even if I knew the UN would do nothing for them, I hoped to convince them to take my words as testimony of our true and inalienable commitment to uphold the rights of the Bosnian people.

As was to be expected, my words did not in the least alter their countenance. I knew well that nothing a representative of the international community could say would have any credibility in Srebrenica. Nevertheless, in the face of the atrocities they were subjected to, I insisted on clearly reaffirming my will to relentlessly defend the cause of so many innocent victims. Having been an exceptional witness to so many crimes against humanity, I was absolutely certain I would not rest until those guilty, Milosevic, Karadzic, Mladic, and so many others, received the punishment they deserved. For the very same reason, I would not stop pointing out that the more powerful members of the Security Council had full knowledge of the magnitude of such crimes, that in consequence they too were guilty, and that I would never cease to condemn all of them. As I left the room and saw in the eyes of those present the pain and frustrations of all of Srebrenica, and as I realized that all these events were taking place barely a couple of hours away from London or Paris, I promised myself to never waver in my commitment to have justice done to all the victims of what, without any doubt, amounted to a slow-motion genocide.

With Mate Boban in Split

We headed back to Zvornik that very evening. We travelled in the same huge Russian-made helicopter. We were joined by our journalist friends and continued towards Split. We arrived in this city, located on the Adriatic coast, a little after 8 pm. Not even two hours before, we had witnessed the terrible effects of the Serbian artillery shelling of Srebrenica, the barricades, and the checkpoints manned by Mladic's paramilitaries to stop any humanitarian aid from entering the city. We had seen its exhausted inhabitants, walking among its ruins like zombies, denied access to drinking water and electricity for almost a year. It was all shockingly different from what we now saw as we travelled from the airport to the Park Split Hotel, our meeting place with Mate Boban, leader of the Croat community in Bosnia.

On first sight, the city, dominated by the impressive bulk of Diocletian's Palace, gave us a feeling of peace and normality. Men, women, and children walked around without concern, or sat in the many coffee shop terraces. The contrast with the tragic fate of Srebrenica's Muslim population weighed heavily on our minds because we knew those poor people risked being wiped out from the face of the earth at any moment. And that was exactly what would come to happen in 1995, between June 12 and 14, when the troops led by the infamous General Mladic mass murdered eight thousand men and teenagers.

A few Boban officials, civilian security personnel and UNPROFOR soldiers waited for us at the hotel's reception desk. After greetings and introductions, we crossed the hotel's luxurious lobby with shining marble floors, reached the double staircase, also in marble, and went up to the first floor. In one of its multiple-use rooms Mate Boban was waiting for us. He was the short lived and only president of the imaginary Herzeg Bosnia republic, only recognized at the international level by Franjo Tudjman, President of Croatia and mentor to Boban.

A huge functional table occupied the center of the room. On it rested several trays with water bottles and refreshments, as well as cheese trays. Large photographs of Diocletian's magnificent palace and of the beautiful Dalmatian coast hanged on the walls. A member of the "presidential" entourage, who had taken our names when we arrived, made the formal presentations. As Mission Coordinator I was the first to greet Boban. He was little more than fifty years old, greyish hair, severe expression, neither tall nor heavily built. Then, Boban himself introduced the four members of his government that had joined him for the occasion, amongst them General Tihomir Blaskic, commander of his military forces.

I proceeded to inform Boban that the foremost goal of our mission was to exchange views with the main protagonists of the conflict about how the Security Council could effectively help to end a war that was already in its bloody second year. We had already met in Sarajevo with President Izetbegovic, and we would continue on the coming day to Belgrade, where during the morning we would meet Radovan Karadzic, and then in the afternoon, in Zagreb, with President Tudjman.

— As representatives of the Security Council – I added – we hope to have a frank dialogue with you, Mr. Boban, on the main obstacles we must overcome to reach the inalienable goal of peace, and thereby be in a position to report to the Council on the conflict's situation.

As we flew towards Split, the delegation had agreed that in our meeting with Boban we would convey our position without any restrictions and not fail to ask uncomfortable questions, including regarding his military forces' responsibility in the Ahmici massacre, but would avoid a direct confrontation that could bring the meeting to an early and useless end. It was not going to be easy. For the first time in my life, I was to shake hands and converse amiably with an individual guilty of monstruous and bloody deeds. I would have to resort to the utmost diplomatic prudence to engage in conversation with both Boban and General Blaskic, who would years later be put on trial by the ICTFY and sentenced to forty-five years in jail. Boban told us he was pleased with our presence in Split, adding he would have preferred to welcome and meet with us in Mostar. It was an option we had rejected since Mostar was a city Boban envisioned as the capital of the fictitious Croat republic in Bosnia, which existed only in his imagination. It was the same tactic Karadzic had used in relation to Pale.

We soon realized Boban liked to hear himself talk. His comments went on and on, without any guiding order and always skirting the core issues. Until Ambassador Erdos of Hungary interrupted him with a very concrete question:

— Tell us, Mr. Boban, finally, what is your position on the Vance-Owen plan?

— We agree with the plan, he immediately replied. That was why we were the first to sign it.

Erdos took advantage of the situation to aim straight at the heart.

— I wish you to know, Mr. Boban, that we hold these private meetings in order to be able to talk with absolute clarity. In this context, I must confess that all the members of the mission are absolutely horrified with what happened in Ahmici, where we were able to verify in all its sinister reality the cold-blooded and pitiless murder of whole Muslim families. What is your position on this situation, undoubtedly a crime against humanity? I ask you because according to information at our disposal the massacre was conducted by paramilitaries under your authority, which then displayed an unheard-of cruelty by machinegunning these defenseless families inside their homes and torching their remains with flamethrowers.

When I heard the Hungarian ambassador's denunciation, I feared Boban would react with hostility. However, while the members of his team moved in their seats with noticeable discomfort, Boban showed no such sign, and simply ignored the question.

— Undoubtedly – he went on – the UNPROFOR commanders did not take you to the concentration camps where the Muslims have very many Bosnian Croat citizens in confinement. I also doubt that they have taken you to Zenica, a town where very many of our people fell victim to a ferocious ethnic cleansing. In any case, I can assure you that the soldiers who committed such crimes, no matter their ethnic identity, will be prosecuted and punished with severity. It was for this reason that, in our meeting last night with Izetbegovic, we agreed to establish a commission in charge of liberating prisoners from both sides and with the investigation and prosecution of war crimes.

Boban continued to refuse to debate even the possibility his followers might have engaged, together with the Serbian military, in violations of the most basic human rights of the Bosnian Muslim population. He reiterated his displeasure at our not having accepted to hold this meeting in Mostar since he would have liked to show us how Bosnian Muslims and Croat Catholics lived there in holy and lasting peace.

Sher Afgan Khan, Pakistan's Alternate Ambassador to the Security Council, and a Muslim, reacted to such a manipulation of truth in a rotund manner.

— Mr. Boban. You have told us you are the only legitimate representative of the Croats in Bosnia. If so, you carry a very heavy responsibility in relation to what happened, which places you under the obligation to bring your troops to order and to demand such atrocities simply not be tolerated, even less repeated. I admit it might be difficult to leave behind ancestral ethnic and religious hatreds, but under no circumstances can I accept they be used to justify such monstrosities.

Now Boban did lose his temper. He had not anticipated that any of us would put forward such a complaint and in such direct manner. He paused to think before giving an answer.

— I ratify – he finally sentenced – that the Ahmici massacre was instigated by the Serbian aggressors, enemies, as you know, both of the Bosnian Muslims and of us, Croat Catholics. If it is proven any of our military took part in that crime, they will pay for it. You have my word.

General Blaskic looked at his superior and nodded in agreement. Then, calmly, Boban added that since April 22, when UNPROFOR knew of the Ahmici massacre, he had ordered to execute in situ, immediately and without contemplation, any man caught committing a crime. Boban lied easily. Maybe he believed that giving his support to the Vance-Owen plan was enough to redeem him of any past or future crimes. Maybe that was also why he insisted that the only way for Bosnia to enjoy peace and exist as a sovereign republic was by endorsing the Vance-Owen plan. He was keen to suggest that we should be patient with Milosevic and Karadzic during our coming encounters and give them time to ponder the advantages they would reap if they accepted the plan. He also suggested that the Blue Helmets should be deployed along the corridors used by Belgrade to supply arms, munitions and money to the Serbs in Bosnia since, to his mind, such measures would prompt them to finally accept the plan. To Ambassador O'Brien's question as to whether the agreements reached the previous night with President Izetbegovic meant they both agreed on implementing the peace plan even without Serbian participation, Boban replied: "Yes, absolutely. That would be the way to insure that in the future we have no disagreements with the Bosnian Muslim government."

The meeting could go no further, and we could hardly hide our indignation any longer, so I decided to bring it to a close and did so in a not very diplomatic manner.

— Mr. Boban – I said – everyone knows that the authors of the atrocities, killings and ethnic cleansing committed at Ahmici were soldiers under your command. We also know that for weeks already, your troops have conducted an abhorrent ethnic cleansing operation throughout the Lasva valley, where Ahmici lies. I must then presume, Mr. Boban, that you have not seen the repugnant scenes we have seen, and therefore, your reaction is different from ours. What happened at Ahmici is the worst crime since the start of the war. Since such a crime has been condemned and repudiated at large by an international public opinion that claims for the murderers to be arrested and punished, we cannot be but surprised that you, instead of acknowledging the truth, should choose to put the whole blame on the Serbians. Notwithstanding your efforts to deny it, it is common knowledge that it was the members of the so-called Croat Defense Council who committed the massacre.

Boban and his people looked at me straight in the eyes but did not say a word. In the course of the meeting, Boban had given the impression that he believed his evasions and the probable approval of the Vance-Owen plan would be enough to grant him a sort of license to kill without consequences. It was a serious miscalculation on his part. We left Split with the absolute conviction this self-proclaimed president of a non-existing nation was certainly not a person to be trusted. As we took our leave, I told Boban not to forget the Security Council had already approved the foundations for the establishment of an International Criminal Court, to be in charge of investigating, putting on trial and convicting the authors of crimes against humanity committed in the course of the

Yugoslav wars, no matter their rank or position, and that in just a few days that tribunal would begin to discharge its responsibilities in the Dutch city of The Hague.

I do not know if Boban and his collaborators realized the implicit menace my words carried. Whatever the case, a month after that meeting, the Security Council approved the establishment of the tribunal. Some years later, it would sentence General Blaskic on the charge of war crimes. Boban died shortly before his military commander was put on trial. His death was the only reason he managed to avoid international justice.

In Belgrade, with Radovan Karadzic

Next day, in the early morning, we flew from Split to Belgrade, where we had a meeting scheduled with Radovan Karadzic, President of the illegitimate Srpska Republic. We were very conscious of the hostile environment in which our meeting would take place. The strong economic, financial and transportation sanctions imposed on the Serbian government by Security Council Resolution 820 on April 17 would enter into force on April 26. UNPROFOR had reinforced our military escort for this section of our trip. For the same reasons, the meeting with Karadzic would now take place at Belgrade's airport and not on Serbian government premises.

The flight from Split to Belgrade lasted two hours, and we took advantage of the opportunity to exchange views. All the ambassadors shared the view that Karadzic was the biggest threat to peace in the region and that we needed to be mindful of that fact. The siege of Sarajevo and the infamies inflicted on Srebrenica were reasons enough to put him in jail for life. But just as we had done before our meeting with Boban, we agreed to engage with this ruthless criminal with a certain caution.

Once inside the airport building, we headed to the protocol area, leaving behind the many tax-free shops, all closed now. Karadzic met us at the door, his huge lock of silver hair dangling over his forehead. He greeted us in perfect English, which he had learned years back during his time as a post graduate student at Columbia University. I could hardly refuse his handshake. He told me he knew me well since my frequent statements were broadcasted by international TV news shows, but he made no comment on their tone or content. Then we all took our places at a round table.

On the strength of the experience gained from our encounter with Boban, we agreed I would start the meeting with a brief introduction explaining the reasons for our mission and for this particular meeting, as well as for the sanctions adopted by the Council. Then, I would seek his position on the Vance - Owen plan, and touch upon the situation in Srebrenica.

I must assume - I said – there is nothing new to be said about the tragedy in Srebrenica since you know it better than us. For almost two years your troops have besieged and terrorized its inhabitants and have not allowed the humanitarian aid sent by the international community to reach them. In the few occasions some aid is allowed in Srebrenica, your men take for themselves most of the food and medicines. For example, when we were there, we witnessed how Colonel Rodic and his men seized fifty tents meant for the many Muslim refugees arriving in the city. We also verified that drinking water and electric power are cut off, a crime against humanity, as you know. Worse still, Serbian mortar fire destroyed a school and killed children while they were playing in the school yard. As a medical doctor, Doctor Karadzic, do you condone, or do you condemn an atrocity that has shocked the international community?

Karadzic remained silent. He did not even seem disturbed by my words. I went ahead with my accusations.

— How is it possible that your soldiers do nothing to prevent the danger of a deadly epidemic as a consequence of so much misery, or the unavailability of medicines and the total lack of vaccines for children? Are you aware that not even *Médecins-sans-Frontières* is allowed into Srebrenica to help? I cannot understand how you can ignore the city´s dramatic situation nor how you can assume the Security Council would not react when you do not even acknowledge that it has designated Srebrenica and surrounding areas as a Safe Area under UN protection. I well remember the letter you sent to the Council a day before Resolution 819 was adopted, stating that you would not occupy the city even if you had the means to do so. Indeed, Srebrenica has not been invaded, but you keep it under a severe siege, and you totally control whatever goes in or out, in flagrant violation of Council resolutions. I ask you all of this because, as you know, one of our main goals is to get to know your position as fully as possible. I invite you to speak frankly, as I believe I have done while speaking on behalf of my colleagues. That is why this is a closed meeting.

Karadzic had kept absolutely silent all along my intervention, with an undecipherable smile. Was that his way of minimizing the importance of my accusations? Was he simply trying to impress upon us that he felt so sure in his position that neither our presence nor our words had any relevance? As he still kept silence, I went on to refer to the economic and financial sanctions adopted by the Security Council to isolate Serbia. That too did not make any impression on him. He only broke his heavy silence when Ambassador O'Brien asked his opinion on the fact that both Boban and President Izetbegovic had given their support to the Vance-Owen Peace Plan.

He replied that he had recommended approval of the plan to his legislators in Pale, but that notwithstanding his efforts, he could not make them change their position. The more radical members of the Assembly, former members of the Yugoslav Communist Party, had unanimously voted against and had imposed on his government the obligation to convene a referendum on the issue for the coming month of May. To his understanding, based on information provided to him by the International Committee of the Red Cross, there were more Serbian refugees in Bosnia than Croats and Muslims together, and that, beyond what that organization reported on what was happening in Srebrenica, the truth was that "in Srebrenica six thousand Bosnian Serbs had disappeared, and ten common graves, dug by Muslim Bosnians, had been found close to the city".

We could of course not give any credibility to the "news" this smiling psychiatrist was giving us. They were as fake and absurd as we were certain the May referendum's results would be. Among other reasons, because we were fully aware that the overwhelming number of refugees entering Srebrenica was the result precisely of the ethnic cleansing Karadzic and Mladic were conducting in the city's surrounding villages.

When Karadzic invited us to "go back to Srebrenica and visit its surrounding areas to see the common graves full of the remains of Serbs," we could only be amazed by his words. He well knew, anyway, that on the next day, after meeting with Tudjman in Zagreb, we would be travelling back to New York.

— As to whether or not we will storm Srebrenica – Karadzic told us again – I must insist on what I have said many times before. We will not invade. Unless the Muslim population attacks us. That is also our commitment in relation to Zepa and Goradze. And that is why we have asked UNPROFOR's Canadian battalion command to send some of its units to our battle lines in the outskirts of Srebrenica, or to wherever they choose, so they can verify what the real situation is.

He then let out his last lie for the day. "We have made this request because we have information that the Muslims are planning to bomb Srebrenica and to blame it on us."

Karadzic did not seem to mind that such an operation was impossible, no matter how you looked at it. Not only because it was the Serbian forces that had the city sieged and blockaded, but also because they were the only ones with the heavy artillery needed to shell it. Then, in response to Ambassador O'Brien's question about Srebrenica as a Safe Area, Karadzic said that they did not want areas of Bosnia to be Serb, "but neither can we leave without protection our identity and our culture."

The Ambassador of Hungary then said that we could not go back to the past to solve today's problems. "Europe has many nationalities and does not accept an ignominious apartheid in a Bosnia divided by walls such as that of Berlin."

Once more, Karadzic ignored the comment and denied either Milosevic or himself had started a war with that goal.

— Our goal has nothing to do with what the ambassador of Hungary has said. It is more akin to what happened in India, Nagorno/Karabagh, Lebanon, Cyprus, and, of course, Switzerland. We simply cannot understand why we are being forced to live together as cats and dogs in the same cage, instead of each in its own home as good neighbors.

That was his reasoning to reject the cultural and ethnic integration of the nation, central tenet of the Vance-Owen plan. However, we knew the character well and what his true intentions were, so Ambassador Sidorov insisted in our denunciations of serious violations of the more fundamental human rights in Srebrenica, such as cutting the supply of running water and power to its civilian population.

— It is the first time I hear about that – Karadzic immediately replied – and you may rest assured tomorrow I will order an investigation to see if it is true, and in that case, it will be immediately taken care of, and we will ask UNPROFOR to guarantee it.

It was a commitment that, obviously, was never fulfilled. Later, on our way to the airport in his company, Karadzic reiterated he had requested the international community to investigate the ten common graves he had mentioned, and the situation of the Serb prisoners of war, locked in "terrible detention camps" run by the Muslim paramilitary authorities in Srebrenica. It was his last lie before our departure towards Zagreb to meet with President Tudjman, final stage of our trip.

Our Meeting with Franjo Tudjman in Zagreb

I knew little about President Tudjman except that he had entered politics after his service in the Yugoslav Armed Forces. With Marshall Tito he had fought against the Nazi invasion and distinguished himself so highly that at twenty-three years of age he had become Croatia´s youngest general. He then became a member of the ultra-nationalist Democratic Union of Croatia. When Tito died and his Yugoslav federal project unraveled, he became, as a DUC leader, the main sponsor of the secessionist movement until independence from Serbian domination was achieved. In May 1990, this achievement led to his election by an overwhelming majority as first president of the sovereign Republic of Croatia. He remained president until his death in December 1999.

Tudjman was not in the UN´s eye, mostly because the Milosevic-Izetbegovic confrontation was the main focus of all the information that reached us on the Yugoslav wars. Croatia had, however, played a critical role in the process leading to conflict since, together with Slovenia, it had been at the forefront of breaking away from the Yugoslav Federation, with staunch support from the German government.

The meeting with Tudjman was incredibly important for us since his support to the Vance-Owen peace plan was critical to put pressure on Belgrade to also accept it. After our arrival in Zagreb, we met with UNPROFOR´s command in Croatia. There we decided to bring to Tudjman's attention what had happened in Ahmici, before addressing the peace plan. We did not want the analysis of the overall situation of the crisis in Bosnia to preclude consideration of the terrible massacre committed by the Croat Bosnian military with its government´s support. On the other hand, we needed to determine whether it was true that in early 1991 Tudjman and Milosevic, at Karadjordjevo, during a boar hunting party, agreed to the partition of Bosnia and Herzegovina between Croatia and Serbia, leaving the Bosnian Muslim community with only a small fraction of the republic. Both leaders denied the existence of such an agreement, but the truth of the matter was that in May 1992 an agreement with exactly the same purpose had been signed between Boban and Karadzic.

With those issues on our agenda for the meeting with Tudjman we arrived at the Croat government palace, built by Tito in 1963 and located in Zagreb's outskirts, in the middle of a beautiful forest. The entry was guarded by twelve guards of honor in their gala uniforms, armed with rifles with bayonets. We were greeted in the palace vestibule by members of the Cabinet, headed by the ministers of Foreign Affairs and Defense, who led us into a spacious meeting room furnished with a big and magnificent round table. In the background, a huge window opened into the woods. While we admired the view a waiter served water and refreshments, as was the custom in all the Balkans. President Tudjman made his entry a few minutes later. He was tall, with white hair and an arrogant expression. He bid us welcome and with grandiose gestures invited us to take a seat. The scene and manners were those of a bygone empire, not those of a modern republic, the likes of which I had only seen back in 1975 when, while being governor of Caracas, the Shah of Iran and his large following had visited Venezuela.

As I had done in our prior meetings with Izetbegovic, Boban, and Karadzic, my intention was to begin with a brief presentation on the reasons for our mission. However, President Tudjman took the lead and notified us he wished UNPROFOR's mandate in Croatia to be extended but, similarly, that a time limit for its presence be established by the Security Council. He then stated that he welcomed Boban and Izetbegovic's mutual support to the Vance-Owen peace plan and, in reference to the Bosnian president, added that Izetbegovic had visited him two days before and requested us to ratify our support. You should know – he added – that I have given Boban my full support in his decision to rally all Bosnian Croats in support of the plan. There are still sectors in the South of Bosnia that do not. It is an important endeavor because the Serbians, who are irrational, refuse to do so. Their only interest lies in the creation of a Greater Serbia, an illusion they will continue to pursue until an outside military action takes them on. The referendum Karadzic talks about is just an excuse to win time, since we all know the results will be manipulated to reject the plan.

He then made a brief pause and surprised us with the most radical proposal we had heard so far.

— "I want to tell you, not in my current condition but in that of a former military man – remember I was the youngest general in my country's history – that the fantasy of a Greater Serbia has already taken a very heavy toll in lives, a toll that will only keep growing until a decisive foreign military intervention against Belgrade and Serbian forces operating in Bosnia takes place. I will say even more, I do not believe such military intervention would require an invasion by land. An aerial attack campaign would be enough to make Serbia come to reason.

Several of the members of the delegation shared that view, but we all abstained from making any comments, knowing full well that under no circumstances would the Security Council approve it. Tudjman continued to share his vision, the only one that in his opinion would preserve Bosnia's sovereignty, and indicated that in geographic terms it would be "incredibly important for us since it would protect us from an eventual Serbian invasion. That is why we believe it is important to convince the Bosnian Muslim leadership of the need to negotiate an agreement that includes the three parties. Although President Izetbegovic told us, in this same room, that what they wish for is a plural state, we believe that what they really want is a majority Muslim state. Of course, their aim is to feed Milosevic´s and Karadzic's extremist thesis to get most of Bosnia under their control. Even more, as a historian who has written three books on this problem, let me tell you that Izetbegovic´s decision to deploy seven thousand soldiers in areas that under the Vance-Owen plan fall under Bosnian Croat authority, is a serious obstacle to a political solution. During our recent meeting Izetbegovic denied any truth to this, but Boban assures me he is lying. I hope the eventual agreement between Boban and Izetbegovic holds and that is why I have tried to facilitate a commitment by both of them to abide by its terms in full."

My reply was categorical.

— For us – I said – it is extremely important to know your government´s position on this war, and I take the opportunity of this meeting to recall the firm way in which the Council denounced the Serbian government for the ruthless bombing of Dubrovnik at the beginning of its aggression against Croatia. In the same firm manner, I must tell you that we condemn the atrocities committed by Bosnian Croats along Bosnia's central valley, in particular at Ahmici on the 16 th of this month. Whole families were murdered, and their bodies burned with flamethrowers. I must admit we had never seen such atrocities, and we are sure that you, if you had witnessed what we did, would have reacted with the same indignation. When we mentioned this situation to Boban, his reply was that the Serbians had been the instigators and perpetrators of this massacre. This we know to be absolutely false. To ignore and deny this situation damages Mr. Boban's credibility, and that is a cause for alarm.

Tudjman took his time to reply. When he did, he simply skirted the issue arguing they were still rounding up information on what happened. "I requested the agreement between Izetbegovic and Boban should include their mutual commitment to punish all human rights violations. And I, in turn, two days ago gave Izetbegovic assurances that all such violations, for which either their side or ours might be responsible, will be punished. You may rest assured that we will do so."

Ambassador Khan, of Pakistan, then intervened to ask Tudjman if the innocent victims of Ahmici did not bring to his mind John Donne's verses warning that "when the bells toll, they toll for you". Somewhat upset by Khan's comment but without looking at him, Tudjman replied that, indeed, the bells of Ahmici tolled for all those involved in this conflict, as all of us were.

Was Tudjman sincere? I was sure that he was aware of what happened at Ahmici but did not wish to disavow or, even less, condemn Boban, who was his protégé and loyal ally. Maybe that was why he did not mention at all the situation at Ahmici, or maybe that was his way of letting us know how he felt about Bosnia's Muslim population, as President Izetbegovic did when we met in Sarajevo. It was difficult to fathom what a head of state who believed himself to be far above Milosevic and Izetbegovic really thought. Be that as it may, our meeting with Tudjman had made evident this was a player who deserved a more relevant role in our efforts to bring the cruel war in Bosnia to an end. Beyond his intellectual and military superiority, he was the single "Yugoslav" leader who truly exercised total control over the territory of the country he governed and over the portion of Bosnia under Boban's control. He was an ultranationalist, just like Milosevic, but he was clearly not willing to put his reputation at risk vis-a-vis the international community, in particular the German government, by participating in a criminal ethnic cleansing policy, as that openly promoted by Milosevic and Karadzic. It might have been a purely tactical position, but it worked in favor of peace.

As we said our goodbyes, Tudjman asked us to join him for a photograph, and then walked us to the palace's main entrance, where he gave us a tie adorned with the Croatian crest as a parting gift. We were then invited to dinner in a typical Croatian food restaurant in Zagreb's town center by Gojko Susak, Croatia's Prime Minister and Minister of Defense until his death in 1998. He wished to further explore some of the issues raised during our meeting with Tudjman. We could have spared ourselves that dinner. It lasted three long hours and Susak did not add anything of relevance, not even by chance referring to the Ahmici massacre. We only managed to elicit a strong criticism of Serbian excesses at Sarajevo and Srebrenica.

After saying our goodbyes to Susak, we all went to the Jelacic Café terrace, in Zagreb's city center. There, all the ambassadors freely exchanged impressions about our shared experience in Bosnia and Croatia. To my great satisfaction there were no differences of opinion among us. Undoubtedly, the monstrosities we had witnessed had bound us together as a group. As I reached the hotel in the early morning hours, two disturbing questions haunted me and did not allow me to fall asleep. Had this mission we had sought to conduct truly been worth the while? And, finally, what had it achieved, if anything?

THE BIGGEST COVER UP IN U.N. HISTORY

I returned to New York excited by the urgent need to get back to normal and report to the Security Council on the results of our mission to Bosnia. Yet, at the same time, I regretted not being able to prolong our visit to the Former Yugoslavia for a few more days, to deepen our knowledge of the scale and scope of conflicts about which I did not have yet reliable information.

Barely two weeks before, at midnight April 16, after months of pressure by the ambassadors of the Non-Aligned Caucus – Pakistan, Morocco, Djibouti, Cape Verde, and Venezuela – the Security Council had had no option but to approve a mission expressly mandated to ascertain on the ground what was really happening in Bosnia, particularly in Sarajevo and Srebrenica. Seven days had passed since we had made our way towards Zagreb, Sarajevo, Kiseljac, Ahmici, Srebrenica, Split and Belgrade. Only after verification of the atrocities committed in Bosnia by Serbian and Croatian regular and irregular troops, including unimaginable crimes against humanity, was I in a position to understand the true meaning and reach of that historic initiative, and the implications of the personal and political commitment I had taken by accepting to lead this mission. It was an exceptional challenge, not least because it engaged my country's international reputation.

I also understood that having seen what I had seen, I was no longer the same man who had travelled to the Balkans. To have personally witnessed the tragedy besieging the civilian population of Bosnia, the most serious one experienced by a

European nation since World War II, made me feel the compelling need to write a thorough rendering of that experience, and to present specific recommendations on what we believed was urgently needed to remedy the systematic violation of Bosnia's political and territorial rights, and of its people's most basic human rights. I had never faced such a challenge. I was particularly conscious that what I had experienced required that I commit myself, inside and outside the Council, to the difficult task of telling the truth about the Bosnian crisis and of denouncing the murky handling by the UN Secretariat and the P5 of the issues under the item "Situation in the Former Yugoslavia" at a time when action was needed.

For the very same reason, I gave extraordinary importance to our report. I blamed the Secretariat's and the P5's misguided conduct for our lack of clear knowledge and understanding of the scope of the Serbian project, which included the destruction of Bosnia and the extermination of its Muslim population as part of its territorial expansion plan, thereby creating what in Belgrade was called Greater Serbia. Naively, we believed this lack of information explained why the P5 was against taking charge of the defense of the political and human rights of the Bosnian Muslims. We believed it was for the same reason that the members of the world's preeminent political body blocked any initiative that, in the case of Bosnia as in so many others, did not conform to their wrongful interpretation of the non-intervention and neutrality principle. And therefore that was the reason we had been sent to the Balkans, to ascertain what was happening in the republics of the Former Yugoslavia.

Be that as it may, upon our return to New York, I had to yield to facts. The problem was not that the P5 were not well informed. It was that we, the non-Permanent members, were ill informed. By such a devious tactic, the P5 and the UN Secretariat were able to exercise absolute control over the Security Council. It all went far beyond the principles the Organization had been built upon, and it risked endangering its standing and credibility.

The Mission to The Balkans Report

My first step on the morning of April 27, the day after our return, was to pay a visit to Ambassador Marker of Pakistan, who as President of the Council had put forth my name to lead the mission. After briefing him on our efforts, I suggested he might propose that the report be presented in an official meeting of the Council. After all, that was how the mission had been approved. Marker agreed, checked his agenda and, considering the urgency of the issue, immediately contacted the Council's secretariat and requested the session be held on the afternoon of Friday, April 30. As it turned out, it could not be. Within a few hours the Secretariat informed the meeting had to take place in the "room without a view", since holding a formal session in the great hall required the prior approval by the Council at the informal meeting level. That meant that, at least for the time being, we would have to agree to a closed-doors presentation, without live transmission by the media. Notwithstanding this setback, Marker made arrangements for the report to be circulated as an official document of the Council, thus ensuring its distribution to every UN Member State delegation.

The following day, all the members of the mission came together to review the draft I had been preparing since we boarded the plane in Zagreb. Although I did not share my fears with Marker, I believed the representatives of France and Russia, with whom before our trip I had had some differences on how to approach the situation in Bosnia, might have objections to my report. To my pleasant surprise, neither made the slightest observation to the text.

Even so, I remained concerned and waited expectantly for the Friday, April 30, informal session. Many times before, I had experienced the false calm and normality prevailing in the UN hallways and meeting rooms, as if on the banks of the East River life went on in a different universe, far away from the real world. Maybe that was why I wasn't really surprised by the total lack of interest the Permanent Five took in the report, a report mandated by the unanimous vote of the Council, to be presented in a session that had only one item on its agenda. However, the nonattendance by the UN Secretary General Boutros Boutros-Ghali, and Kofi Annan, recently named Head of the UN Peacekeeping Department, did worry me. Confronted by this demonstration of total control by Boutros-Ghali over the Secretariat, I could not avoid asking myself some very disturbing questions before the Council session begun. Had it been worthwhile to travel to Bosnia? Was the Council justified in not taking a closer interest and not acting more forcefully in relation to conflicts that endangered international peace and security such as the one in Bosnia? What use had the debates and resolutions adopted by UN organs and agencies if most of its members chose not to see reality and were not willing to act in consequence?

I was convinced the distance kept by the Secretariat was based on its fears that it would find it impossible to ignore the denunciations and recommendations our report made, and that therefore it needed to attempt to bury it no matter what. This did not discourage me. On the contrary, it pushed me to do the impossible to insure they did not have their way, particularly since our presence on the scene had allowed me to have a direct knowledge of the conflict´s true dimension. It was a reality that went against the unfettered manipulation of the crisis by the powers in control of the Secretariat and the Security Council. I then realized that it had been worth the while to travel to Bosnia and to have prepared a report, that had already become a Security Council official document, even if it only served to ruin their party. No matter how many nor how powerful efforts might be made to silence its content, it would put in the hands of the press and international public opinion what those interests strived to hide, acting against the UN´s fundamental principles.

The contradiction between what I had seen in Bosnia and the alternative reality that was being constructed by the Council explained why before our trip not a single high official from the Secretariat had traveled to the region, and why the UN Secretariat had not produced a single report on the dramatic situation in the republics of the Former Yugoslavia.

Even though our report's presentation had to take place in "the room without a view", that afternoon we were able to officially inform the members of the Council about the abhorrent ethnic cleansing policy pursued by the Serbian authorities in Bosnia, a crime I had characterized, speaking to the press in Srebrenica, as a "slow motion genocide". Unfortunately, my warning that day would become reality two years later. The genocide, to which reference was made by UN reports in a mechanical way, tragically came to happen in July 1995. Our report was an irrefutable denunciation of the crimes against humanity committed in Bosnia by Serbian military and paramilitary forces already by April 1993, under the impassive watch of the UN Protection Forces' military commanders. From the day of its presentation, against all odds, our denunciations would not allow the winners of the Second World War to continue to boast "Never again" in reference to the Holocaust, while ignoring it in relation to Bosnia. It was by itself and without any doubt a highly significant achievement.

At this point, it might be useful to note that according to the UN Convention on the Prevention and Sanction of the Crime of Genocide, approved in 1948, the crime of genocide is "A crime under international law, contrary to the spirit and goals of the United Nations, which the civilized world condemns and commits itself to prevent and sanction". A beautiful and straightforward statement of principles that, in practice, did not go beyond words. So much so that in those days the US Department of State informed President Clinton and Warren Christopher, Secretary of State, they could use the term "genocide" - first coined by Raphael Lemkin, a Polish Jew, to address the 1939 Nazi extermination of the Jewish population in occupied Poland - freely, since it was a crime that, although typified by the Convention and by international law, lacked any mechanism to prevent or sanction it.

In August 1992, when Clinton was still a presidential candidate, he had stated in reference to the war in Bosnia, that "You could not ignore what seems to be the systematic extermination of human beings based on their ethnic origin".

Yet, once in the White House, he ignored his own advice and instructed Madeleine Albright, his ambassador to the Security Council, to abstain from participating in debates over that issue. So much so that not too long afterwards, on May 23, 1993, Daniel P. Moynihan, a diplomat and Democrat Senator, felt the need to express his moral and political outrage by stating: "While we say we will never forget the Nazi horrors, by our indifference we give legitimacy to the repetition of those same atrocities in Bosnia."

Such a powerful argument made me realize that no matter the efforts undertaken to silence us, our report would have a stronger resonance than many expected. Indeed, it represented documental proof of crimes against humanity, and the international community could simply not continue to ignore them. However, I could not have imagined that our report would very soon foster a radical reaction by the White House, who would invite the governments of Russia, France, the United Kingdom and Spain, to support an initiative for Bosnia called the Washington Joint Action Plan, as if now it wished the world to know that the "time for the Americans" had arrived.

It would not be until 1999, when UN Secretary General Kofi Annan would publicly acknowledge the Security Council and the UN Secretariat's responsibility, under Boutros Boutros-Ghali, in ignoring the denunciations and warnings voiced since April 1993 and up to July 1995, when Serbian troops under the command of Ratko Mladic murdered in three days and in cold blood more than eight thousand Muslim men and teenagers in Srebrenica. Annan's confession of Boutros-Ghali's responsibility, and of his own as Head of the Peacekeeping Department, had no precedent in the history of the United Nations.

The April 30 Council Session. Boutros-Ghali's Nonattendance

At the end of the corridor leading to the Informal Consultations Room there's an area where journalists, who are not authorized to attend the sessions, can wait for the day's meetings to end and for ambassadors to make statements to the press. No one can enter or exit the Consultations Room without crossing the swarm of lights, TV cameras, cables, and dozens of inquisitive journalists and photographers. So it was on that April 30. As I was about to enter the Room, I was immediately surrounded by press correspondents eager to have access to some news on the contents of our report to the Council. As was the norm, I promised I would gladly answer all their questions after the meeting was over.

Once inside the Informal Consultations Room, I mingled with the ambassadors and other officials of the member countries. Everyone takes advantage of those moments preceding the sessions to greet one another and to chat about this and that. Beyond the usual diplomatic detachment with which events in the real world are treated in the Council, I had the depressing impression that the crisis in Bosnia, only item on our agenda, however complex and important as it might have been, was not going to ruffle any feathers during that afternoon's session. In this professional, business-as-usual, environment, I approached Yuli Vorontsov, the Russian ambassador, with whom I had a good personal relationship, to thank him for his support to our report. I also approached the ambassadors of China and the United Kingdom but neither of them, nor I, went beyond the basic, protocolary, mutual greetings. I then took my place at the U-shaped table, much smaller than the one in the Security Council hall. Here too, seating arrangements follow the alphabetical order, so Venezuela was between the United States, to my right, and Brazil, to my left. There was not much space between attendants, so it was always easy for colleagues to steal a sidelong glance at each other's papers. That afternoon, it was a temptation the UK ambassador could not resist, glancing frequently to his left, trying to read from the corner of his eyes Ambassador Albright's papers.

The informal sessions of the Council do not follow a preestablished protocol nor do they have the ceremonial aura of the official meetings. Its procedures are simple. The contrast is almost like that of a religious act performed in a small parish church compared to the completely different, spectacular ceremonies held in St. Peter's Basilica. The "informal" character of the sessions also refers to their relaxed nature, even if it is precisely there, between the room's four walls, far from cameras and journalists, where the fiercest debates take place. Those dialectic confrontations can sometimes raise the small room's temperature significantly. Anything goes, from subtly insinuated menace to directly confrontational and quarrelsome interventions.

The day before, I had personally delivered to the president of the Council our report, signed by all the mission's members. The case had no precedent for the Council only accepts documents sent by the Secretariat, and this was the first time it received a report signed by ambassadors who were members of a delegation sent by that very same Council to an active theater of war. In his opening statement, Marker referred to this double innovation while at the same time highlighting the role played by the Non-Aligned Caucus in dispatching the ambassadorial mission to Bosnia. He expressed the hope that the report and its recommendations would translate into new and effective initiatives by the United Nations to assist the parties in reaching a ceasefire and, ultimately, in bringing a lasting peace to the region. He commended all the mission's members for their efforts, and me in particular, "for Ambassador Arria has presented a report approved by consensus by all the six ambassadors, members of the mission." He added that I was the only Non-Aligned member of the Council who was not a Muslim, and that fact granted my position and my report undeniable institutional independence.

Marker then read the agenda for the session, which had our report as its only item, and gave me the floor. I started my intervention by recalling that in March, during their visit to New York, President Izetbegovic and other high officials from his government, had thanked me for my support to their cause. I had then answered that "I am a Catholic, not a Muslim, but I assure you that if it were Muslims who were massacring the non-Muslim Bosnians, I would defend them just the same way I now defend you. Venezuela's position does not respond to any ethnic or religious reasons, but to the unrestricted defense of basic human rights."

After that brief introduction, I thanked the Council for trusting me to head the mission and indicated that the report I was presenting that afternoon reflected the views of all the members of the delegation. At the same time, I could not avoid expressing my indignation for having had to witness first-hand the terrible aggression suffered by Bosnia's Muslim population without first having been provided by the UN Secretariat or the P5 with the information they had on what was really taking place in the Former Yugoslavia.

— We arrived in Bosnia – I said – blindfolded by a tortuous disinformation campaign, but the realities we were confronted to soon opened our eyes, allowing us to share with you what is really taking place in that unfortunate republic, and our thoughts on what the Council does, on what it does not do, and on what it should do to try to bring this tragedy to an end.

That afternoon, I made it clear we were the victims of what could only be defined as "malicious disinformation" about the war, and most particularly, about everything related to the Serbian program of systematic extermination of the Muslim population in Bosnia.

In that context, I once again regretted the Secretary General's absence, who had chosen to be once more represented by Ambassador Gharekhan, his Advisor for Political Affairs, who did not have the authority to express an opinion, decide, or act. By his absence, the Secretary General could ignore whatever he chose to ignore, and under false pretenses not fulfill his obligation to take part in a highly relevant debate such as this one, in contrast to his predecessors' practice.

I am equally sorry – I added - to have verified how the Security Council has limited UNPROFOR's mandate to the insignificant role of mere observers, with neither the authority nor the necessary means to protect and guarantee the safety of the civilian population in conflict areas such as Srebrenica and its surroundings, and to have witnessed how it is not even able to give humanitarian assistance to those in need barring prior authorization from the Serbian military commanders in the area.

I then proceeded to describe, in all details, the abominable war crimes that were being committed in Bosnia, and to denounce once again the helpless situation in which the Bosnian Muslim population was placed due to UNPROFOR's mandate, which did not allow it to respond to Serbian aggressions, and to the arms embargo which made Bosnia unable to exercise its legitimate right to self-defense. Srebrenica and its surrounding areas were thus deprived of the protection they were entitled to as UN-designated Safe Areas. Finally, and with barely contained irritation, I stated that such deficiencies in the United Nations' approach to the protection of the civilian population in fact represented a validation of the crimes against humanity that were placing at risk the lives of all the Muslim population of the country.

After my presentation, some ambassadors took the floor. The Russian ambassador was the only one to express his shared concern about the lack of reaction by President Tudjman in relation to the crimes against Muslim families committed by Bosnian Croat troops at Ahmici. All the other comments were so detached from what we had seen and denounced in our report that before leaving the room, I invited the other members of the Non-Aligned Caucus to meet on the following day in order to evaluate the situation. Once again, the indifference with which the report had been received placed us in the need to immediately take action, or resign ourselves to see our report, and the mission itself, quickly filed in the UN archives and nothing more. Therefore, I proposed to discuss the possibility of convening a meeting with the press, to which the ambassadors of all regional groups in the UN would be invited, thereby ensuring the content of the report became as widespread as possible.

Upon leaving the Informal Consultations Room, and in anticipation of the meeting with the press, I approached the journalists, who were eagerly waiting, and declared that the Non-Aligned would be holding a press conference on the following day since the issue warranted a formal meeting with the media and not a statement made on the sidelines, in the middle of a hallway. And we did so two days later, in the big conference room located at the ground floor of the UN building. Ambassador Marker made the initial remarks and then the representatives of Morocco, Cape Verde, Djibouti and myself, intervened. Marker deplored the fact that it had not been possible to present the report in a formal session of the Council, and that it was important to ensure it received as wide a coverage as possible. He added that only fragments of the Bosnian tragedy were known, camouflaged by statements that only partially addressed the prevailing situation, and by resolutions that had served the only purpose of making the Serbian aggressors believe that the United Nations would never use force to stop their criminal ethnic cleansing policy in the Former Yugoslavia. On my turn, I stated that such an alarming distortion of facts was aided by the UN Secretariat and by the Permanent Members of the Council, who intentionally hid truthful and timely information on what was happening in Bosnia.

As I headed home later that night, I felt upbeat. Not everything was lost. The press conference had contributed to make our report's contents widely known, and that would undoubtedly help create favorable conditions to advance towards a solution to the tragedy the Bosnian civilian population was living. I was sure it would make the international community take measures to give back to that young and harassed republic, and specially to its Muslim population, their right to exist. I still held on to an idealistic vision of what the UN was and what the Security Council represented.

Peace at Any Price

Two weeks later, on May 14, the members of the Non-Aligned Caucus in the Security Council drafted a memo of grievances to the attention of the president. Our press conference on Bosnia had made an impact but we knew it would in no significant way move the powerful quintet in control of the Council or the UN Secretariat, bent as they all were on making peace no matter the price. Never before had the Council presidency been addressed in such strong terms by a group of its members. We also decided to send our list of grievances to all the diplomatic Missions accredited to the UN as well as to the press. For us, the most pressing issue was to make known the real situation in Bosnia, and to report on the failings of the UN in the discharge of its duty of preserving peace and security in a country under invasion, where Serbian military and paramilitary forces already occupied two thirds of its territory. We wanted it to be known that it was all happening while the most powerful nations did not even try to curtail the aggression's advance, a first necessary step if peace was to be restored. We also intended to reveal that the prevailing line of thought within the UN was to refuse to directly confront the brutal Serb aggression and to refuse to lift the arms embargo, a measure that would allow the Bosnian government and people to defend themselves. We stated that such contradictory approaches left the civilian population at the mercy of foreign troops, a situation akin to a moral rape of that young nation.

In our document, we pointed out how, ever since the London Conference on Bosnia and up to the Vance-Owen plan, the Serbian authorities had repeatedly misguided the international community and not honored even one of the commitments they had undertaken, using the negotiating process to advance their goals of territorial expansion and political control, at the expense of Bosnia and Herzegovina's sovereignty.

We stated our absolute conviction that, as Alija Izetbegovic had acknowledged during our meeting in Sarajevo, there was no political alternative to the Vance-Owen Peace Plan to solve the Bosnian crisis. Even though the plan entailed the partition of Bosnia into three autonomous districts, we agreed with this position because it also demanded the total withdrawal of Serbian troops, and because it preserved the political unity of the country by establishing a single national government to be shared by the three ethnic communities. To put aside the Vance-Owen Plan without first presenting a viable alternative, as the promoters of the Washington Joint Action Plan had in mind, would only pave the way for Milosevic's imperial project. Consequently, we believed that the Council could not continue to ignore reality and risk becoming an accomplice to the destruction of a country the sovereignty of which it was mandated to protect. We reiterated our position, centered on lifting the arms embargo and authorizing an armed international military intervention to destroy Serbia's heavy weapons in Bosnia, steps we estimated were essential to achieve a lasting cease fire and pave the way to a peace agreement.

We believed it was precisely the lack of coercive measures, including the possibility of an international armed intervention, that had taken the floor out of the Vance-Owen Plan, and that by now the Council should have learnt its lesson regarding the consequences of not even mentioning such a possibility in its resolutions. We insisted on this because the most powerful members of the Council seemed to be in denial of their obligations under the Charter, a failing that led us to demand they declare themselves willing to use all necessary means under the Charter to bring the situation in the Balkans under control. Not to do so, we insisted, would in the future leave militarily weaker nations easy prey to the ambitions of more powerful ones.

Our May 14 document represented a direct challenge to the P5, even though the Non-Aligned members of the Council constituted only a third of its membership, not enough to formally approve or not approve anything. Nevertheless, it allowed us to influence somewhat international public opinion and the international media. If so, the US government's May 22 invitation to France, the UK, Russia and Spain to subscribe the Washington Joint Action Plan was in reality a way to bury the Vance-Owen Plan, the plan that had the support of Bosnia, even if reluctant, and of the Non-Aligned countries.

The Washington Joint Action Plan

To some, President Clinton's decision to play a more central role in solving the Bosnian crisis seemed a reaction to a 1991 statement by Luxembourg's Prime Minister Poos, at the time President of the European Community, in which, referring to the nascent crisis in the former Yugoslavia, he held that it was now the time of Europe and "not of the Americans". President Clinton's unexpected initiative could also very well have been a reaction to our report to the Security Council on our mission to Bosnia and to the list of grievances we had sent on May 14 to Boutros-Ghali. Whatever the case, the significant fact was that the European members of the Council, who since the beginning of the crisis, by action or omission, had opposed Bosnia's right to independence and to exercise its right to self-defense, now gave their support to Washington's peace plan.

However, the Clinton initiative was not really a plan, but rather a declaration of intent, hastily drafted in reaction to strong criticism to his foreign policy in relation to the Balkan wars, perceived as being the same as that of his predecessor. Talking to the press on May 22, Richard Boucher, spokesman for the State Department, basically confirmed this when he acknowledged that the Clinton Administration's initiative did not go beyond the reach and scope of Security Council Resolution 824, of May 6. This Resolution had resulted from an initiative by the Non-Aligned Caucus and followed our report's recommendations to establish five secure areas. Boucher insisted the Clinton plan did include the option of international armed interventions when it provided for a no-fly zone over Bosnia for Serbian combat aircraft, even if it conditioned approval of such military option exclusively to possible threats to the safety of the UN Blue Helmets deployed in those areas. Threats to the safety of the Bosnian civilian population were not included.

For the Security Council and for the UN Secretariat, the purpose of such restrictions was to make sure no international military alliance, such as NATO, would feel compelled to use force to stop Belgrade's ruthless attacks against Bosnia's sovereignty. The Clinton Administration's initiative basically mirrored the mockery of the Security Council resolutions, just as Ejup Ganic, Vice President of Bosnia, had pointed out to me in Sarajevo as we said our goodbyes at the door of the presidential palace while a NATO warplane flew over the city.

—As you may see, Ambassador – he said with a smile, sad and sarcastic at the same time - it's from the sky that they protect us from genocide!

This maneuver by the US government simply pretended to hide the contradiction between Clinton's electoral promises regarding the conflict in Bosnia and the very moderate Vance-Owen peace plan. Instead of fostering a stable peace in the Former Yugoslavia it compounded the confusion created by all the criticism thrown at Washington's passive stance, now coming as well from important American political leaders, both Democrat and Republican. That was the reason the Clinton Administration sought the support of the Council's European members, who very much welcomed the sudden US interest in a more active and decisive role in the debate over the crisis in Bosnia.

In the development of this circumstantial alliance between the United States and Europe in the Security Council, mention must be made of the position taken by Ambassador Madeleine Albright. In private conversations, Ambassador Albright confided that she agreed with our position but needed to follow her instructions from the State Department, even if "her heart was beating in the right direction". Maybe, as she witnessed how Bosnia was dealt with, she remembered all the suffering inflicted on Czechoslovakia, her native country, as a result of the cowardly sacrifice of the Sudetenland to Hitler by the British and French governments.

Years later I understood that the distance the United States had kept from the Yugoslav wars and the countless limitations of the Vance-Owen plan to effectively put a stop to the Serbian aggression were just additional reasons for the Clinton Administration to change course in relation to the crisis in the Former Yugoslavia and involve itself directly in the search for a solution. Nevertheless, I believe that our May 14 report stressing the many irregularities committed by the UN Secretariat and the Permanent Members of the Council, as well as the very documented presentation we made during the informal session of April 30 about the atrocities that were being committed in Bosnia, had something to do with that sudden change in the American position. Could it be just by chance that three weeks after our Bosnia mission report was presented, the Council approved Resolution 824, and that just a week after our May 14 report, the Washington Joint Action Plan was announced and negotiations began around what later, on June 4, became Security Council Resolution 836?

All my doubts and queries ended when, after initially giving the impression of being in favor of international military action to bring the crisis in Bosnia to an end, the Clinton Administration made it clear its position was simply rhetorical, taken in the context of an electoral campaign. As soon as Clinton was sworn President of the United States it became evident his goal with this plan was not simply to show to the American public a more active profile, but to definitely sink the Vance-Owen Peace Plan. This, in turn, raised other puzzling questions. Why did Washington go public with an initiative that in reality gave strength to the European approach centered on slowing down the negotiations and keeping the international community's role to a minimum? Why did it propose an alternative that came down to the same policy of "contention" that gave Serbia the right to keep two-thirds of the Bosnian territory already occupied by its troops?

I then thought, as I still do, that Washington was not acting in reaction to the Serbian aggression, as Clinton had said it would as candidate. Rather, it was rewarding the Serbians by recognizing their pretended sovereignty over occupied territory and by denying Bosnia its right to reclaim it. This perverse strategy included keeping in place the arms embargo and denying authorization for eventual NATO airstrikes against Serbian military emplacements inside Bosnia. Clinton always kept in mind that the United Kingdom and France, America's major allies in Europe and key players in the Bosnian puzzle, would never agree to those two controversial initiatives.

Taking the ruse to extremes, Clinton announced a few days later that he was sending Warren Christopher, his Secretary of State, to London and Paris with the task of bringing both governments on board in relation to his proposal to lift the arms embargo and take military action against the Serbian aggressor if it did not desist from its imperial project. However, as soon as Christopher landed back in Washington, the foreign affairs ministers of both the UK and France stated that never in the course of his visit had the Secretary of State proposed either lifting the arms embargo or the use of international military forces in Bosnia.

In the middle of such a muddle, the United States and its allies then requested the UN Secretary General Boutros-Ghali to prepare, within twenty-four hours, a draft resolution on the situation in Bosnia based on the Washington Plan, and to present it for adoption at the Council's June 4 official session. Our surprise as Non-Aligned members of the Council could not have been greater when the US, France and Britain produced the draft of what eventually became Resolution 836. This Resolution was immediately rejected by Senator Joe Biden, Chairman of the US Senate Foreign Affairs Committee, who expressed the view that "(By this resolution), the West has so pathetically wavered in relation to the Bosnia case that the leaders of a nation that has suffered so much rightly suspect that Washington's new Joint Action Plan, now validated by Security Council Resolution 836, abandons the victims, who continue to fight notwithstanding the UN arms embargo and the defenseless situation in which they find themselves in the face of aggressors whose strength lies, not in their troop's abilities, but in their military superiority. If we do not confront with determination this situation, we will soon see other, ethnic based aggressions both in the Balkans and further afield." The Non-Aligned members of the Council rejected Resolution 836 for exactly the same reasons. We also did so because, although the now almost defunct Vance-Owen plan divided Bosnia into ten autonomous districts, it at least limited the fraudulent Serbian sovereignty to only forty-three percent of the territory.

This dismemberment of Bosnia into cantons was inadmissible, from both a moral and a political standpoint. However, for the legitimate Bosnian Government, cornered by the pressing circumstances of a war it was in no position to win, it represented a necessary lesser evil. The Washington "strategists," on the other hand, gave the Serbian government the "right" to keep all the territory occupied by force of arms in Bosnia. In other words, no matter the many statements by Clinton to the contrary, at that point in time, in complete disregard of the most basic principles of the United Nations, he abandoned the Vance-Owen plan and gave legitimacy to Belgrade's territorial conquests, all of them linked to flagrant acts of ethnic cleansing. Moreover, according to the Washington Plan and Resolution 836, what was taking place in Bosnia was not the illegal territorial expansion of one country at the expense of its neighbors, nor the proven criminal undertaking of a policy of ethnic cleansing to achieve such expansion, but a simple conflict between parties who did not understand each other.

Even though both the Washington Plan and Resolution 836 seemed to guarantee the safety of the Muslim population in the five enclaves designated as Safe Areas, the resolution restricted the military response option to situations that placed in danger UN civilian or military personnel deployed in those safe areas. This conveyed to the Serbian government the message it could continue as usual in Bosnia, provided it did not make the mistake of attacking the UN Blue Helmets present in those areas.

Needless to say, the members of the Non-Aligned Caucus in the Security Council decided not to support Resolution 836. Our position had gained standing within the international community, as George Schultz, former Secretary of State, confirmed: "Secretary General Boutros-Ghali has said we should not use force in Bosnia to allow on-going negotiations to come to a happy end. But it seems this gentleman lives in another planet, because in Bosnia force of arms is used twenty-four hours a day. What is lacking over there, is a counterbalancing force." On the eve of the June 4 Council session, the Non-Aligned Caucus pointed out in a statement that "The joy with which the Serbian aggressors have welcomed the US government's initiative and President Clinton's words is enough to gauge the true intentions and probable consequences of this draft resolution".

Faced with this alarming interpretation of "Safe Areas" by the Permanent Members, the ambassadors of Morocco, Djibouti, Cape Verde, Pakistan and Venezuela decided to propose a new draft resolution based on our May 14 document. In it we stressed the need for UN peacekeeping forces to take under their protection, in the broadest sense, the Muslim population of Sarajevo and of the provinces of Goradze, Bihac, Brcko, Tuzla and Zepa, identified by the Vance-Owen plan as Muslim areas and designated as safe areas by Resolution 824, and requested the immediate withdrawal of Serbian troops still occupying Muslim districts in Bosnia. Our proposal insisted on "the recommendations included in the report of the mission sent to Bosnia." As was to be expected, it did not win support from the other council members. The United States, France, the United Kingdom and Russia wanted their understanding of safe areas to be included in the new draft under the false pretense it would update the April 16 Resolution. What they were really trying to do was to repeat its limitations. That would, in practice, indefinitely prolong the situation of helplessness in which the civilian population remained in all the main cities of the country, including Sarajevo, its capital. It would also send the message that the United Nations would not interfere with the Serbian plans of occupation and extermination. In his book *Quiet Diplomacy*, published after his retirement from the UN, Ambassador Marker gives a concise and well-worded summary of our opposition to Resolution 836. "It was a parody, both to the spirit and to the letter, of the concept of safe areas. If the resolution came to validate it, it would only serve to perpetuate the existence of refugee camps and open-air ghettos, to the sole benefice of the aggressor."

Ethnic Ghettos. A Denunciation at the Security Council

On the morning of June 4, while having breakfast, I read in *The New York Times* news that took away my appetite. According to the note, Warren Christopher, US Secretary of State, had the day before declared during the NBC program *Today* that "(The conflict in Bosnia) concerns us from the humanitarian standpoint, but it does not affect our vital or strategic interests. That is why President Clinton has followed a cautious policy and not engaged the United States in an issue that, however you look at it, is a European problem."

This unadorned statement was in open contradiction to what President Clinton had said during the electoral campaign and had reiterated on May 6, after the Serbian representatives to the International Conference on Bosnia, held in Athens, had refused to sign the Vance-Owen plan, arguing that President Clinton had referred to the conflict in Bosnia "as a war of aggression that the United States has interest in stopping", adding "We have seen enough. Over there, we have fundamental interests and under no circumstances are we to not act as responsible members of the international community."

I was not overly surprised by Christopher's declaration. The United States had not been particularly coherent in its policy towards the Yugoslav wars, and by now I had enough experience on the conduct of the Permanent Members of the Council. Nevertheless, I believed that in a matter of such relevance as the preservation of international peace and security, the "vital or strategic interests" of the Permanent Members would not supersede their obligations under the Charter, as was the case when Christopher openly contradicted Clinton's position, formulated when he was a presidential candidate.

June 4 was the date set for the Council session. It was a beautiful spring day and I decided to take a walk from my official residence on 81 st Street down to the United Nations building. On the eve, I had prepared the statement I would deliver during the consideration of the draft resolution. Joining me was Carlos Bivero, Venezuela's Alternate Ambassador, whose contributions I highly valued. On the way to the UN, I went over my arguments for Venezuela not to vote in favor of the resolution, in absolute rejection of the P5 and the Secretariat's maneuverings. Once in the UN building, I went straight to the Delegate's Lounge, located on the ground floor, and from there to the great hall of the Security Council. Ambassador Juan Antonio Yáñez-Barnuevo, President of the Council, started the session by reading the draft resolution.

As I have already pointed out, this draft resolution gave the designated safe areas the necessary guarantees only in appearance since the Council did not commit itself to enforcing them. Once again, it became evident that the drafters' intentions did not go beyond the customary and rhetorical expressions of good will. Even though the text made a formal reference to the use of force under Chapter VII of the UN Charter, it limited it to situations in which any of the parties might endanger the UN civilian or military officials deployed in those areas. No mention was made of the civilian population living in those conflict areas. Consequently, the draft resolution the Council was ready to pass clearly implied that the presence of Blue Helmets in the designated safe areas did not by itself guarantee "full respect of the safety" of their inhabitants, even if in theory that was precisely the main purpose of the resolution.

The draft resolution also kept in place the arms embargo on the republics of the Former Yugoslavia approved on September 21, 1991, thereby keeping Bosnia in a position of evident inferiority towards Serbia which had at its disposal the huge arsenal of the former Yugoslav Popular Army. Neither did the draft resolution clarify why the areas were defined as "safe" and not as "protected", as the Non-Aligned Caucus had insisted on. The difference was not simply semantic since defining those areas as "protected" implied the Council would take upon itself the obligation to effectively enforce their safety for all their inhabitants, be they civilian or military, while the term "safe" translated for the United Nations to nothing more than a desired status. Finally, the draft resolution reiterated that the international community considered unacceptable any acquisition of territory by use of force and ethnic cleansing. Barely two weeks before, on May 20, the spokesperson for the US Department of State, the very same that had authored the Washington Plan, had unabashedly declared: "We do not for the time being foresee any modification to the status quo in relation to Bosnian territory occupied by Serbian forces". Even if just "for the time being", it was a position that legitimized the Serbian aggression and its acquisition of two-thirds of the territory of Bosnia through an abhorrent policy of ethnic cleansing.

To make matters even worse, Serbian troops continued to harass Srebrenica, an enclave that, two months before, had been designated a "safe area", impeding the delivery of humanitarian assistance and the provision of basic services such as running water and electricity. It had served little to no purpose to have Resolution 824 "demand" the withdrawal of the Serbian military that kept Srebrenica under siege and authorize UNPROFOR to take all the necessary measures to enforce such a demand, including the use of force, if the enclave or any other so-called safe area came under attack "by any of the parties".

All these serious and undeniable circumstances made the draft resolution a cruel mockery. So much so that it praised

Bosnia for having subscribed the Vance-Owen Peace Plan, knowing full well the Washington Joint Action Plan had already made it irrelevant.

Both the Non-Aligned and the Secretariat had pointed out that the "safe areas", as defined by the draft resolution, were simply ethnic ghettos to be indefinitely trusted to UN safeguard. The concept amounted to a political and moral aberration. For Venezuela, the "safe areas" should be permanent solutions to the sufferings of the civilian population of the Bosnian towns under Serbian aggression or threat of aggression. In our concept, the areas ought to be temporary mechanisms to provide their inhabitants with protection and access to a relatively normal life, with total respect for human rights, including unencumbered access to humanitarian assistance, until a real and lasting peace agreement is reached. The proposal on the Council table embodied a different concept. It made us wonder if the Security Council would someday understand how misguided it was, if it would ever be willing to call a spade a spade and come to accept that what the resolution called safe areas were nothing more than permanent refugee camps. The aberration was such that a few weeks after the resolution passed, Lieutenant Colonel Barry Frewer, Spokesperson for UNPROFOR, sardonically announced the placement of a signboard at the entrance of Gorazde, one of the "safe areas", alerting passersby that the town was "a very dangerous" safe area, and asked them to immediately leave.

That morning, just a few minutes before the beginning of the debate on the draft resolution in the Council, Víctor Manzanares, First Secretary in the Mission of Venezuela, told me our Minister of Foreign Affairs, Army General Fernando Ochoa Antich, was on the line and wanted to talk to me. I had been alerted by a good friend in the Ministry that Ochoa Antich wanted to contact me with suspicious insistence, so I asked Manzanares to tell the minister I could not take his call because my turn to speak was about to begin. Ambassador David Hannay, who sat one place away from Ambassador Albright, was at that very same time talking to the British representative in Caracas, and I heard him say: "Arria is not about to speak! He simply does not want to pick up the phone." I immediately understood that my decision not to vote in favor of the resolution would not go by without consequences. Ochoa called me again. This time, Manzanares took the call in one of the cabins located in the foyer. Later, he told me that when he answered the phone Ochoa warned him that he made him "personally responsible for giving Ambassador Arria the message that he was to vote in favor of the resolution." Manzanares came back in a hurry, very worried, and gave Bivero, sitting behind me, the minister's urgent message. After calming Manzanares, who was truly terrified, and who later confided Ochoa had used "a menacing tone of voice," Bivero kept the message to himself and told me nothing at that time. I had already warned him that I would not change my position and that if I came into the knowledge of Ochoa's decision, I would resign immediately after my intervention. I was not, under any circumstance, willing to act under the pressure put on the minister by the British and French ambassadors in Caracas. Should that come to pass, I was fully aware that I would have to resign immediately my position as Permanent Representative of Venezuela to the United Nations.

Arm-Twisting in the Council

As one of the sponsors of the resolution, Jean Bernard Mérimée, the French Ambassador, was the first to take the floor. He stated that in the eyes of the international community the draft proposal was proof that the members of the Council had not kept passive regarding the evolving situation in Bosnia. His assertions confirmed that what was truly important was to placate international public opinion, whose impatience with the UN's passivity and shortcomings kept growing daily, rather than offer a real solution to the crisis in Bosnia. He added that the sponsors of the draft resolution did not resign themselves to what he termed "desperate solutions," simply because the conflict had not ended. As an example, he mentioned the withdrawal of UNPROFOR and leaving the parties to sort the conflict out by themselves. He pointed out that it was precisely to avoid that catastrophe that France refused to lift the arms embargo, one of our main proposals as Non-Aligned Caucus in the Council.

Then came Jamsheed Marker's turn. He reiterated our rejection of a draft resolution that radically altered the nature of the so-called safe areas, as proven by the situation in Srebrenica, turned into a huge refugee camp as a result of the brutal siege and absolute control of the Serbian aggressors. Roble Olhaye, Ambassador of Djibouti, one of the smallest UN member states, dared to point out: "If somewhere within the shady world of diplomacy there is a plan to cover up the Serbian aggression and give legitimacy to its gains, anything we might say and do about it would be farcical. Confronted by such loss of life, destruction of homes, suffering and deaths, we would need to add a new chapter to the UN Charter under the heading "Cynicism and international deception".

To conclude the round of those speakers wishing to take the floor before the vote, Ambassador Albright, my neighbor on the Council table, announced that the United States would be voting in favor of the resolution but that it would do so "without any illusions". She then reminded us that "the Washington Plan's proponents have agreed to keep all options open, so as to be in a position to adopt in the future more stringent measures, none of which has been prejudged nor excluded. My government's position about what such measures should be, has not changed."

Albright acted under instructions, even if half-heartedly. Not long ago, I found in the Clinton Presidential Library a recently declassified interview in which Ambassador Albright, tells her interviewer on October 28, 1996: "(It's important) to know from where our position at that time came from, and the fact that to set our own we had to consider those of the United Kingdom, France, and the Non-Aligned group, which included Muslim countries. In the middle of all the contradictions over the situation, particularly during its initial stages, Ambassador Diego Arria, the Venezuelan Representative in the Security Council, was strongly in favor of the more hardline measures proposed by the Non-Aligned and the Muslim nations, an approach neither our Departments of State and Defense, nor the Intelligence agencies, nor The White House, shared at all". By this, Albright acknowledged that she felt closer to our position in the UN than to that of her government, and that for her it had been "very difficult to reconcile both positions when the Non-Aligned talked of genocide, which was exactly what was happening in Bosnia." This contradiction led her to raise in Washington "the need to review our policy about this conflict, because the view held about it in New York was closer to reality than ours."

My turn to speak finally came and the president gave me the floor. I was very conscious it was an exceptional opportunity since it would allow our position to be presented to the whole UN membership in the formal setting of an official meeting of the Council, in front of TV cameras and in the presence of the most important representatives of American and international media. It was an opportunity we had been denied on April 30, when the presentation of our report on our mission to Bosnia was restricted to the Informal Consultations Room. But it also was an opportunity that required to put aside the conventional diplomatic discourse practiced in the UN to disguise reality and sow confusion, and to speak with absolute clarity. It all made me dangerously responsible for my words. So, I began by referring to a dramatic letter President Izetbegovic had addressed the Council, a copy of which I had received three days before, deploring that a communication by the president of a UN Member State, who could not be present in a session devoted to consider his country's situation because Sarajevo had been under fire by armed criminal groups for over a year and a half, had not received any answer from the Council.

Yes, it moved me – I immediately added – because my visit to Bosnia a month ago allows me to better understand President Izetbegovic's distress as he remains encircled by Serbian forces in Sarajevo. It puts me under the obligation to echo his tribulations and to tell the world he is right when he says we are accomplices to the tragedy his country suffers. The Venezuelan delegation's reply to President Izetbegovic is short and emphatic: Mr. President, you are telling the truth when you denounce that Serbian paramilitary units continue their aggression against Bosnia with direct support from the Yugoslav army, and that the aggressors can do so because the Security Council has your government's hands and feet cuffed, while the Bosnian people are murdered and the country is devastated with impunity. By placing all the Former Yugoslavia under arms embargo the Council ceased to be a neutral party in the conflict. By keeping the arms embargo in place for Bosnia-Herzegovina, the Security Council took a decision that has directly and indirectly served only to help a well-armed aggressor, and to tragically weaken its victims, the people of Bosnia. In his letter, President Izetbegovic reminds us of the grave and undeniable consequences: two-thirds of the country are under occupation, two-hundred thousand civilians have perished, between two and three million are internally displaced, hundreds of towns and villages have been devastated, and thousands of women raped by Serbian troops. That is the price Bosnia and its people have paid since September 1991 for the unfortunate decision to impose an arms embargo and the persistent refusal by the Council to amend that decision.

It was with deep pain that on that occasion I pointed out that the sponsors of the draft resolution then under debate lacked the will to put a stop to the systematic massacre of the Bosnian Muslim population, including the inhabitants of the five safe areas established by Resolution 824, notwithstanding the dramatic appeal made by the president of a UN Member State which stood on the verge of annihilation. There was no longer any acceptable excuse to continue to keep silent about what was happening in Srebrenica since April 16, when, by a Security Council resolution, it was designated a safe area under UN protection. The Non-Aligned have always stood in favor of the creation of such areas as long as UNPROFOR had the required mandate and resources to effectively guarantee the safety of their inhabitants. That was the reason Venezuela,

Cape Verde, Djibouti, Morocco, and Pakistan had played such a prominent role in drafting and ensuring approval of Resolutions 819 and 824, establishing the safe areas of Srebrenica, first, and then of Sarajevo, Gorazde, Tuzla, and Bihac. However, on that June 4 session, we felt compelled to put on record that we had requested the Secretary General and the representatives of Spain, the United States, Russia, France and the United Kingdom, to prepare a report on the UN's capacity to implement the new resolution on safe areas, and that such request remained unheeded.

The truth is – I added - this silence only confirms that out of the five Permanent Members, four only pretend to search for a solution to the conflict. By hurriedly promoting this new draft resolution what they really pretend is to push aside the document that on May 14 the Non-Aligned gave the UN Secretary General which contained a critical evaluation of the situation. Not a single proposal of that document, some already included in the Secretary General's report to the Council of May 18, was considered by the sponsors of this draft resolution. We still ignore, for example, what actions is the Council ready to take if the Serbian aggressors refuse to retire from those areas, as is the case in Srebrenica. Would the Council authorize military action to make the Serbian commanders comply with this provision of the resolution? Or are we to be told once again that it is in no position to satisfy that mandate because it does not have the troops nor sufficient financial resources to ensure this new Resolution 836 does not become just another useless piece of paper? With similar directness, I wish to recall that not too long ago, to repel the illegal invasion of Kuwait, the international community deployed five-hundred thousand troops and an impressive war arsenal, without no major contributor blinking at the cost. On that occasion there were no discussions nor doubts about how to respond appropriately. It was clear to all involved that their strategic interests had been threatened. I do not wish to compare both situations, but I cannot fail to ask myself if what is happening in Bosnia is as deplorable as Iraq's aggression against Kuwait, why does the international community not deal with Serbia as it did with Saddam?

It was impossible for me not to mention the crimes against humanity that were being committed in Bosnia, and the consequences of our passivity, so I asked why the Security Council, the uppermost institution of the international order, preferred to take a distant, indifferent stand towards such tragedy, even as Serbian advances towards the annihilation of that independent country, a member of the UN, continued in total impunity, and why it didn't even react to the atrocities committed in a war of extermination the extent of which the world had not witnessed since the Nazi crimes against the Jewish population.

I did not know how to interpret the silence in the great hall of the Council after my statement. Shortly thereafter, the president put the draft resolution to a vote. The silence was not broken until thirteen of the fifteen members of the Council had raised their hands in favor of Resolution 836, which sealed the fate of Bosnia. Only Pakistan and Venezuela abstained. I then looked straight in the face at my good friend and ally, Ambassador Marker, sitting just in front of me on the other side of the Council table. We were the only ones to have resisted the pressure by the sponsors of this fatal resolution. It openly departed from the UN Charter's basic values and principles and ratified that, above all, the UN found in appeasement the real purpose of its existence.

I felt immensely gratified for not having followed the instructions from the Venezuelan Minister of Foreign Affairs, thereby sparing my country any responsibility in the fatal consequences the resolution would have on the people of Bosnia from that day onwards. As the meeting was raised by the president, Marker and I came together in the middle of the Council room and gave each other a strong embrace, proud to have voted as we did. By our vote we made it clear that what was at stake in Bosnia was a moral cause, and not simply the need to bring an end to another conflict. Cyrus Vance, upon hearing that the resolution had passed, declared that the Security Council had simply given its endorsement to "the Serbian policy of ethnic cleansing and of territorial conquest by force." And, David Owen, in his book *"The Balkan Odyssey,"* states that "Resolution 836 was the most irresponsible decision the Security Council adopted during the years I participated in the negotiations".

The vote on Resolution 836 helps to explain why, when Carla Del Ponte, Prosecutor for the International Criminal Tribunal for the Former Yugoslavia, invited the permanent members of the Council to participate as witnesses in the trial against Slobodan Milosevic, they all declined the invitation alleging, falsely, that at the time it was impossible to know what would later come to pass. As I declared during one of my depositions at that trial, the June 4 vote and the whole UN policy towards Bosnia, were "the greatest coverup in the history of the United Nations."

The Safe Areas

After my return to New York at the end of April, and up until June 4, the Council adopted three decisive resolutions on the war in Bosnia and placed under UN protection as safe areas those where the magnitude of the conflict endangered the civilian population. However, just as I had denounced in my crucial June 4 intervention, in none of them was the root of the problem addressed. On the contrary, none went beyond the rhetoric of good intentions in an effort to calm international public opinion and the international media, increasingly impatient with the notorious incapacity displayed by the UN to solve a crisis that continued to worsen by the day.

It would soon become evident how irrelevant were for the Milosevic-Karadzic duo all the "demands" made by the Security Council. For example, just six days after the designation of Gorazde as a Safe Area, this enclave, where some sixty-thousand people were believed to have fled to escape from the unrelenting Serbian attacks, was shelled by General Mladic's heavy artillery. Forty-four bombshells were fired, leaving four-hundred fatal casualties and uncounted wounded.

Serbia Does Not Recognize the Bosnian Safe Areas

Information on such developments did not reach us through the UN Secretariat. Ever since our mission, it was José María Mendiluce, ACNUR's representative in Bosnia, who had become our most trusted source of information on what was taking place in this battered Former Yugoslavia republic. It was also Mendiluce who told us that, since our visit to

Srebrenica at the end of April, Serbian troops had intensified their attacks on the city and its surrounding areas, that it was almost impossible for UN convoys to deliver food and medicine to the inhabitants, and that running water, electricity and gas had been almost completely cut off. The situation was the same in Sarajevo, where Serbian mortar fire killed fifteen youngsters who were playing football in the street, and again a few days later in the Old City caused many casualties and wounded among mourners at a Muslim funeral.

Attacks such as these on the civilian population of defenseless cities were predictable. UNPROFOR did not have the means to prevent them simply because the P5 held on to their cynical interpretation of neutrality and refused to act appropriately to ensure Serbia respect the people of Bosnia's most basic human rights, and to put a stop to the country's increasing military occupation. It was painfully obvious that the humanitarian situation in Bosnia would only deteriorate if the Council just limited its options to a diplomatic arrangement with aggressors unwilling to stop. A radical change was needed from the policy of contention and appeasement.

That was why General Lars-Eric Wahlgren, UNPROFOR's Commander for Croatia and Bosnia, during the April 26 meeting in Zagreb with the members of the Security Council mission, had to acknowledge the Force's inability to provide logistical support to the UN's delivery of humanitarian aid. And that was why on June 15 he convened an urgent meeting at Sarajevo's airport with the Bosnian, Serb, and Croat commanders, to try to convince all three parties to agree to a cease fire, even if provisional, in order to allow UN observers to reach Gorazde, evaluate the situation in the area after the artillery shelling, and provide humanitarian aid to its civilian population.

It was not the first nor last time an international initiative such as that came and went without success. The moderate optimism displayed by UNPROFOR's spokesman, Canadian Commander Barry Frewer, when he said that "maybe we'll make it this time" proved to be unfounded. Once again, the

Serbs proved to be totally unwilling to undertake any initiative that would jeopardize Milosevic's expansionist project. The situation was such that General Mladic gave notice that unless the Bosnian military who were defending Gorazde and Srebrenica unilaterally surrendered their weapons, he would not recognize either city as a safe area. Until then his troops would reinforce their siege of Gorazde, Srebrenica, and Sarajevo. It was a blunt admission by the Serb military authorities in Bosnia that they would not even consider delaying their violent takeover of Srebrenica, demilitarized by UNPROFOR since April 17, nor of Gorazde, a town with an extremely limited number of defenders.

On June 15, faced with a refusal by the supreme Serbian authority in Bosnia to acknowledge Resolution 836, General Philippe Morillon informed Sadako Ogata, ACNUR's High Commissioner, that both he and his General Staff were considering the need to withdraw the eight-thousand troops deployed in Bosnia under his command. *The New York Times* in its following day's edition confirmed the information, indicating that Morillon "With anger and sadness had to admit he did not have the means to protect humanitarian aid deliveries to the safe areas, nor did he have authorization to do so by force of arms, and was left with no other option but to withdraw from the country". His reasons coincided with the arguments I had raised during my intervention on the June 4 session of the Council when I warned that "instead of safe areas, we are leaving the most vulnerable population at the mercy of the Serbian aggressors, who take advantage of the situation to continue with total impunity their ethnic cleansing policy."

The Non-Aligned Countries Do Not Back Down

In view of such a serious turn of events, the ambassadors of the Non-Aligned Caucus in the Council met on Monday, June 7, at the Venezuelan Mission to the UN, and decided that I should call General Lars-Eric Wahlgren to confirm the information, given that he knew me better. Ambassador

Ahmed Snoussi, of Morocco, would request an urgent meeting of the group with the Secretary General. Although it was already eleven p.m. in Zagreb, I immediately called General Wahlgren, while the Secretary General gave us an appointment for the next morning.

After indicating I called on behalf of the group, I directly asked General Wahlgren his opinion on the future prospects of the safe areas if the terms of Resolution 836 and the resources made available to the UN peacekeeping forces remained unchanged, particularly in view of the rapidly deteriorating situation in Srebrenica, Gorazde, and Sarajevo. As was to be expected, he answered very sparingly. Even so, he reiterated the reservations he had expressed during our visit to his command headquarters in Zagreb and confirmed that after the failed meeting with the military commanders at Sarajevo airport, UNPROFOR had been left with the role of a mere and distant observer of the Serbian attacks on the so-called safe areas, a passive role that would surely give way to the occupation of the greater part of Bosnia by Serbian and Croatian forces. He also acknowledged that the troops under Mladic´s command did not allow UN observers access to neither Gorazde nor Srebrenica and, consequently, he did not have additional, first-hand information on the evolving situation in those areas. I immediately shared with my colleagues the general´s observations and comments. They would come in handy for our meeting the following day with the Secretary General and other UN officials.

The Secretary General received us in his office on the 38 th floor of the UN building. Needless to say, he knew perfectly well what was taking place in Bosnia and why we were there. The air in Boutros´s office soon turned heavy, especially after the ambassador of Morocco, having explained the purpose of our visit, reminded the Secretary General that under the terms of Resolution 836 he was under the obligation to react to the rapidly deteriorating situation in Bosnia, the more so since, at our request, he had specified the basic conditions safe areas had to meet to be considered as such. The deterioration of the situation in Srebrenica and Gorazde proved, if anything, that

Resolution 836 was worthless. The ambassador of Morocco reminded Boutros-Ghali that "The Permanent Members of the Council did not even wait for the Secretary General's report before presenting, in an improvised and hurried manner, the draft resolution to be voted on by the Council."

I then referred, almost word by word, my conversation with General Wahlgren. I did so knowing my initiative would not please the Secretary General, always very keen to preserve his prerogatives unchallenged. He was to be even more displeased because the opinions and the information Wahlgren provided left no doubts about the disastrous future awaiting the so-called safe areas. Ambassador Marker went on to mention General Morillon's statement about UNPROFOR withdrawing from Bosnia. The Secretary General, usually as impassive as an Egyptian mummy, could not help showing his uneasiness at having to admit we were in the right. But he washed his hands and reminded us that it was up to the Security Council to take decisions about UN peacekeeping forces, and that these were not under his direct responsibility, not even under that of General Morillon.

Nevertheless – I replied – the unfettered continuation of Serbian assaults on the safe areas, together with the UN's passive stance on the extermination policy and its failure to ensure the safety of the Muslim population in the Former Yugoslavia, might well be understood by the leaders of the Muslim world as the UN giving Serbia the green light to carry on with all kinds of crimes, solely on the basis of ethnic and religious reasons. "As I pointed out during the debates on all those ineffective resolutions, in particular Resolution 836, it is a hard to avoid such conclusion. The Permanent Members placed the non-Permanent members under intense pressure to adopt their proposals by unanimity, and thereby elude their individual responsibilities, hiding behind the appearance of a unified international front. As the Secretary General is well aware of, they failed, no matter all the pressure exerted, because both the ambassador of Pakistan and I abstained, saving our countries the shame of having taken a part in such a catastrophic decision."

I was still hopeful that, if not all, at least some of our arguments would make the Secretary General or some of his most important collaborators participating in that meeting, such as Marrack Goulding, Under Secretary General for Political Affairs, or Kofi Annan, Under Secretary General in charge of peacekeeping operations, change their positions. They did not. Keeping to the strict discipline Boutros-Ghali demanded from his subordinates, they all kept silent. Once that unproductive meeting was over, the three ambassadors who had participated briefed the absent ones, those of Cape Verde and Djibouti, and conveyed to them our conviction that the UN Secretariat would be of no help in our new efforts to hamper the Serbian aggressions. It was clear, in particular, that Boutros-Ghali was unwilling to jeopardize his relations with the Permanent Members of the Council. After all, his reelection as Secretary General would be in their hands. We were, however, very sure that no matter the obstacles, we would not give up.

Serbia Does not Relent

In the meantime, significant developments were taking place in the political front, as was the meeting held in Geneva on June 24 between Slobodan Milosevic, Franjo Tudjman, and Radovan Karadzic. David Owen organized the mini summit on behalf of the European Union, and Thorwald Stoltenberg on behalf of UN, acting as the Secretary General's new personal representative, replacing Cyrus Vance. President Alija Izetbegovic was invited but declined since the main aim of the meeting was to replace the Vance-Owen Peace Plan with the old plan of dividing Bosnia into three autonomous entities, which, just days before, Tudjman had called "constitutional entities." The goal was to deprive Bosnia of its independence and sovereignty, and to establish with UN and European endorsement something very much resembling a new apartheid.

Indeed, the new "Peace Plan" promoted by the Owen-Stoltenberg duo was intended to cancel the negotiations undertaken under the Vance-Owen plan, which divided Bosnia into ten autonomous districts but preserved under a central trilateral government the country's territorial, political and ethnic unity, thereby making it possible to deny the Serbs sovereignty over the totality of their militarily occupied lands. It was the very reason Izetbegovic had reluctantly agreed to the plan, even though under intense pressure from the UN. In the statement issued to explain his absence, President Izetbegovic indicated that the real purpose of the meeting convened in Geneva by Owen and Stoltenberg was to endorse maps raised by precisely those who were responsible for countless war crimes which had already taken the lives of more than two-hundred-thousand Bosnian Muslims.

The proposal had been drafted by both Tudjman and Milosevic and pretended to enclose the Muslim Bosnian population in two zones, covering not more than one-thousand five-hundred square kilometers out of the total fifty-two thousand square kilometers of the republic, and located, one around Sarajevo, in the middle of the country, and the other in the Northwest, around Bihac. At the time, the Serbs occupied seventy percent of the total Bosnian territory and to sign the Owen-Stoltenberg plan - "the last opportunity to reach a reasonable peace agreement" according to Karadzic – demanded recognition of full Srpska sovereignty over all the territory under occupation by its army. By not attending, Izetbegovic expressed his rejection of the Owen-Stoltenberg proposal.

The new plan aimed at dividing Bosnia on the basis of religion and ethnicity, the opposite of what had been under negotiation for over a year and a half. It excluded the Security Council, allowing Owen and Stoltenberg total freedom to act and decide over Bosnia. In that way, the Council would have no responsibility over an arrangement conceived to wipe out Bosnia as an independent nation from Europe's geography.

International public opinion was not fooled. The French daily *Le Monde* was the first to react against this plot. In relation to the meeting in Geneva, it said that "The international community has surrendered to the law of the jungle, and gives recognition to those who have killed, exiled and raped the people of Bosnia." Morton I. Abramowitz, former US Ambassador to Turkey and a specialist in the history and realities of the area, soon joined in the denunciation of the plan. In declarations to the press, Abramowitz pointed out that "The Bosnian Muslim population, the weakest in the conflict, is given the choice of either submitting to the Serbian imposition, or simply be wiped out from the face of the Earth, since the West only provides them with nothing more than cheap rhetoric." And Vice President Ganic warned that "If the international community indeed abandons Bosnia and allows it to be dismembered, it will not be long before the scorch of terrorism takes over Europe." Exactly the same call to reason I had made in the Council over leaving the Bosnian Muslims at the mercy of their Serbian aggressors.

The Second World Conference on Human Rights

The Second World Conference on Human Rights, convened by the UN, was held in Vienna between the 14 and 25 of June 1993. It brought together representatives of all its member states, more than eight hundred non-governmental organizations and hundreds of journalists. It was the UN conference with the largest ever participation. Curiously, by prior agreement between delegations, no specific cases of human rights violations could be raised. This restriction had been proposed by China to ensure the Dalai Lama's representatives to the Conference would not be able to denounce Beijing for its systematic violation of Human Rights in Tibet. It had a negative impact on the Bosnian cause. It was such an out of order agreement that *The New York Times* in its June 16 edition pointed out that the conference was being held "in an environment mysteriously far from reality".

I kept track of the conference from New York and in an informal session of the Security Council expressed my amazement, questioning why the delegates to a UN conference devoted to Human Rights agreed to keep silent over specific violations of human rights. The UN was evidently complicit. Haris Silajdzic, Bosnia's Minister of Foreign Affairs, who was in attendance, could not avoid breaking the diplomatic tranquility of the June 15, 1993 session of the Conference, with an impassioned intervention. "Thousands of orphaned and mutilated children remind the international community of its criminal complicity with my country's Serbian aggressors. What takes place in Bosnia is not a natural disaster. It is genocide, committed in broad day light, before your eyes, you who pretend to have the power to do justice everywhere in the world. That is why I have come today to demand, in the name of humanity, to take whatever measures you have to take to stop the extermination of my compatriots, who, while we meet in this peaceful city of Vienna to talk about human rights, in at least one city, Gorazde, are the victims of savage assaults by Serbian heavy artillery. I want you to know that we will fight and defend ourselves even if the international community has tied us, hands and feet, while we are murdered, our land taken over with total impunity, our women raped, and our children mutilated."

At this strong, impassioned denunciation by Silajdzic, all delegations stood up and gave him a prolonged round of applause. Then, and notwithstanding protestations by a few, the Conference agreed to put aside the "prohibition" about mentioning specific cases of human rights violations, and passed a resolution, addressed to the Security Council, urging it to take "the necessary measures" to stop the systematic murder of Bosnian Muslims. Unfortunately, as in so many other occasions, it all ended with a simple declaration of good intentions. Although the war of ethnic cleansing continued unabated, at least the world came to know the names of Gorazde, Srebrenica, Zepa and Sarajevo, as sites of monstrous crimes against humanity.

Two weeks after this conference, I met in New York with minister Silajdzic. He told me that what he had experienced in Vienna reminded him of the intervention by Emperor Haile Selassie at the Society of Nations in June 1936, after Benito Mussolini's army had invaded Ethiopia and deposed him from his throne. The emperor had traveled to Geneva to denounce that aggression and to warn the world about the risks of an unimpeded expansion of fascism. Back at home, I searched my library for Haile Selassie's speech in Geneva.

"The Ethiopian government – he then said – never expected other governments to spill the blood of their soldiers to defend Ethiopia. Our warriors only asked for the means to defend ourselves. So, I now ask the big powers, who continuously promise security to all the nations of the world, what are you going to do to confront and stop the extermination of a people who are the victim of such barbarous attacks?"

Many years later, in October 1963, Selassie would once again address the international community, now from the podium of the UN General Assembly, to recall how "Twenty-seven years ago, I addressed the Society of Nations to ask for international help to defend ourselves against the fascist aggression. My warnings about what was at stake were ignored. History would very soon show the consequences of not having heeded my warnings in 1936".

The similarities between the cases of Ethiopia and Bosnia were huge. On the one hand, the overwhelming superiority of the aggressors' army. On the other, the refusal by the international community to assist the victim of the aggression denying it the resources and means to defend itself. In Ethiopia, the Italian aggressors employed asphyxiating gases and chemical products to poison the farmland. In Bosnia, the "savage means," as Selassie had called them, were ethnic cleansing, torture, rape, and concentration camps. History repeated itself with the same cruelty and the same indifference on the part of the international community. In 1936 it was Mussolini, now Milosevic, Karadzic and Mladic. The international community's passivity was the same, then and now. It was as if for the great powers moral issues were irrelevant since they did not pose a threat to international security and stability. For the same reasons, the international community did not understand then nor now the enormous cost that allowing the forced disintegration of one of its legitimate members would entail. I simply could not understand why the five Permanent Members of the Council, who had that privilege precisely because they were the victors of the Second World War, had learnt nothing from their past mistakes and continued to refuse to see the reality of what was happening in Bosnia.

The United States Supports the Non-Aligned

Towards the end of the month of June, the Non-Aligned Caucus held several meetings with the US delegation, whose positions were becoming closer to ours as time went by. So much so, that we agreed to explore the feasibility of preparing jointly a draft resolution to lift the arms embargo on Bosnia, the only way to level battle conditions between Serbian and Bosnian troops. Naturally, we were very much aware that providing weapons to the Bosnians would have consequences, as General John Shalikashvili, NATO Supreme Commander, acknowledged in a hearing before the US Congress. In his opinion, lifting the arms embargo would make the conflict more "egalitarian" but would also increase the level of violence. He believed that better options could be found but did not specify which. In reality, the general's views were similar to those of the French and British, and we knew the Pentagon was not in favor of lifting the arms embargo nor inclined to the use of force against Serbian military installations in Bosnia. Clinton shielded himself with these ambiguities and on May 21 declared "I will not send troops to a shooting gallery."

The Clinton Administration was divided over what to do about the situation in Bosnia. Declassified official documents indicate that, for example, between March and June, Ambassador Albright's positions were very different from those of the State and Defense Departments, as well as the White House:

"Although it is true that at the beginning we shared the European position, our current interest (Summer of 1993), is to definitively solve the problem, which is becoming much more serious for the interests of the United States. The failure of our European allies to solve the Bosnian crisis has revealed the inadequacies of their policy and produced a serious erosion of the trust of many nations in institutions as important as NATO and the UN. Our continued reticence to lead a collective effort to avoid the Bosnia crisis turning into a major conflict in Europe, has put at risk our global leadership, and shows that our failure to assist the Bosnian Muslims is blowing apart our relationship with moderate Muslim sectors and governments. We must place Bosnia within a larger political context and reexamine our inclination to leave the solution of the problem in European hands. Today, faced by what is happening in Srebrenica, Gorazde and Zepa, neither the Bosnian side nor international public opinion will understand and accept that we keep our distances from the Bosnian imbroglio. We must, therefore, take the initiative and draw up our own diplomatic and military plans to, at a minimum, try to reach a lasting peace in the region, and facilitate that the Bosnian government takes up its own defense. This will only be possible if we propitiate lifting the arms embargo and give its government the necessary political and material support."

In this way, as the only option to prevent the dissolution of Bosnia as a nation and the extermination of its Muslim population, Ambassador Albright argued in favor of replacing the peace plans sponsored by Europe with an American one. Unfortunately, her government did not share her views nor was it guided by them in the Security Council.

In the context of our increasingly shared views with Albright, the Non-Aligned decided to present a draft resolution authorizing the lifting of the arms embargo to Bosnia. Needless to say, our draft caused tensions among the fifteen members and was the cause of debates that brought to light the divisions within the Council. In spite of the strong confrontations, the pressures, and the efforts by Russia, France and the United Kingdom to prevent our initiative from reaching the Council floor for a vote, our draft was included in the agenda for Tuesday, June 29.

Some days before, we had met with the ambassadors of the Arab regional group, and with international and American media correspondents posted to the UN. We were confident that making public our initiative would have an important impact. An so it was. Not since the days of the Gulf War had the great hall of the Security Council registered such affluence. As soon as Spain's Ambassador Juan Antonio Yáñez-Barnuevo, President of the Council for the month, opened the session, he read the agenda for the day, which included the draft resolution presented by the representatives of Cape Verde, Djibouti, Morocco, Pakistan, Venezuela, and to the surprise of many, the United States, who had finally come on board with us. He then announced that the delegations of Afghanistan, Algeria, the Comoros, Egypt, Estonia, Latvia, Malaysia, Syria, Senegal, and Turkey had joined as co-sponsors. Twenty-three delegations had asked to take part in the debate.

As we had requested, the president gave the floor to introduce the draft resolution to Ambassador José Luis Jesus, of Cape Verde, who stated that "The lack of political will on the part of those that have the power and the means and bear special responsibility to carry out and ensure the implementation of the decisions of this Council, is a cause of major concern". It was the message we wanted to convey to public opinion. If the Security Council did not find it appropriate to defend the Muslim civilian population of Bosnia, it should at least allow its government to have access to the necessary means so they could exercise their right to defend themselves. "It has been said – he added – that the lifting of the arms embargo in favor of Bosnia is a policy of despair. But what kind of other measures are there to defend the lives of the civilian population...," murdered by the thousands in cold blood for over a year by the Serbian aggressors. He went on to say the Council was left with only two options. Either to let the Muslim people continue to die and disappear as a community, or to allow them to exercise their basic and inherent right to defend themselves. He concluded inviting the Council to approve the draft resolution, which, in the circumstances, was "the only realistic measure."

Then the Ambassador of Bosnia and Herzegovina, Muhamed Sacirbey, took the floor. In a defiant tone he addressed the ambassador of France stating that his arguments could have been used to deny the French people their right to liberate themselves from the Nazi occupation and the Vichy government. To the British ambassador, he asked whether in 1939 the only option left to the United Kingdom to survive as a nation was to capitulate to Hitler, as so many advised Winston Churchill to do. Ambassador Marker of Pakistan, when his turn arrived, said: "What happens in Bosnia will significantly influence the entire course of international relations. The Security Council's lack of decisiveness to respond effectively to the Serbian atrocities has emboldened the aggressor, which has continued to conduct its criminal campaign against the Bosnian people with impunity. Accepting the so-called reality created by the Serbian aggressor, will further incense the Muslims of the world, who have witnessed the systematic murder of their Bosnian brothers and sisters. The Muslim community will not let those crimes against humanity go unpunished. If aggression is allowed to stand in Bosnia, the forces of extremism will be strengthened." He added that "Pakistan and other Islamic countries will not accept the virtual extermination of a Muslim people in the heart of a continent that prides itself on its commitment to human rights, nor will it accept, after eighteen months of a most brutal and inhuman campaign against a defenseless people, a so-called new reality based on the acquisition of territory through the use of force and the practice of ethnic cleansing". To conclude, he accused those opposing the resolution of complicity with what in the eyes of the world was a genocide.

The tone of Marker's intervention plunged the great hall of the Council into deep silence, which only kept growing as other statements continued to reveal the prevailing indignation. Abu Odeh, Ambassador of Jordan, for example, speaking on behalf of the Group of Arab States, condemned the double standard prevailing in the Council when dealing with issues involving Muslim peoples. "We do not understand when it is said that lifting Bosnia and Herzegovina's arms embargo would only increase the violence and the number of victims, while at the same time accepting the killing of Bosnian Muslims. What kind of logic is that? The more powerful and influential members of the Council have seen fit to deal with the tragedy in Bosnia ignoring completely their ethical, moral and legal responsibilities. They hide behind grandiose slogans about laying the foundations of a world in which security and freedom may prevail but exclude Muslims from such a desirable reality."

As was to be expected, Dragomir Djokic, Ambassador of Serbia to the UN, opposed lifting the arms embargo on Bosnia, endorsing the European argument that it would result in the escalation of what his country called a civil war, and accused the sponsors of the resolution of denying Bosnia the option of a political solution to the conflict. David Hannay took the floor after him, and on behalf of the United Kingdom, repeated the reasoning endorsed by his European allies on the arms embargo, calling our proposal to have it lifted a desperate decision, which would not help the people of Bosnia but, on the contrary, intensify hostilities, thereby forcing withdrawal of UNPROFOR from Bosnia and a stop to the delivery of humanitarian assistance. "We hope this proposal will not pass and we regret the issue of the arms embargo should divide the Council." Then came the Ambassador of France, Jean-Bernard Mérimée, who reiterated, "in the name of peace", that the first consequence of lifting the arms embargo would be "the interruption of the negotiations under way in Geneva", with the mediation of Owen and Stoltenberg on behalf of Europe and the Secretary General of the United Nations, the withdrawal of UNPROFOR from the region and consequently the end of international humanitarian assistance to the civilian population of Bosnia.

The Ambassador of Spain took the floor to add his voice to the European perspective and to indicate his country would abstain in the vote. "We are convinced that anguish, frustration, even despair, should not make us adopt decisions that could have even worse and more damaging consequences for the Bosnians. We trust that reason will prevail and that the parties will agree on a negotiated solution to the conflict."

Ambassador Madeleine Albright, in reference to the Non-Aligned draft that it now co-sponsored, stated: "The United States, in voting "yes" on this draft resolution, reaffirms its belief that the Republic of Bosnia and Herzegovina has the right to defend itself. This is not a perfect solution, but the arms embargo mandated by the Council has had an unintended yet devastating effect in favor of the aggressor. We do not believe this organ should deny the Bosnian government the wherewithal to defend itself in face of the brutal aggression conducted by the Bosnian Serbs and their backers in Belgrade. We therefore regret that the Council was unable to adopt the resolution under consideration".

The Council Disregards Its Duties

My turn came five hours after the session had started. Over and over again, those who were against our draft resolution repeated the same arguments. Listening to their interventions gave me the opportunity to summarize and respond to their objections. I argued that the Council was not a debating society dedicated to philosophical speculation over theoretical scenarios, but an executive body the main duty of which under the Charter was to guarantee international peace and security. And that was, to the letter, what the Non-Aligned Caucus in the Council was trying to do, now with the support of the United States, by our proposal to lift the arms embargo, and thereby facilitate an effective and stable cease fire, first step towards a solution to the situation in Bosnia. I pointed out that the fifteen members of the Security Council, in voting in favor or against a proposal that would have a bearing on solving the crisis, faced that afternoon a responsibility of historical dimensions.

"I hope – I emphasized – that most of you will be up to the challenge and vote in favor of our draft resolution. We cannot imagine the world's most important political body failing to fulfill its duty for much longer. In the final analysis, what's at play with your vote are the lives of thousands of innocent civilians. Our proposal seeks to end the eighteen-months long war in Bosnia. I intend, therefore, to refute the arguments of those who oppose to militarily intervene in the conflict while at the same time refuse to allow the Bosnian government its legitimate right to self-defense against the illegal Serbian aggression."

Addressing those who sought to justify their opposition to lifting the arms embargo on the basis of avoiding further violence, I stated: "Is it not true that the passivity shown by the international community in relation to Bosnia has already caused more than two-hundred thousand civilian casualties? Is it not true that the policy of not stopping the Serbian aggression has brought about the forced displacement of more than two million people? The rape of twenty-thousand women? Or that the International Court of Justice and the World Congress on Human Rights have stated that Bosnia is the victim of abhorrent crimes against humanity, including genocide? Lifting the arms embargo will not increase violence. To the contrary. Up to now, the arms embargo has granted the Serbian aggressors a protective umbrella, one we have given them by depriving of defense the potential victims of the ethnic cleansing war conducted with total impunity by Serbia in Bosnia."

I recalled how, from the very beginning, from the first peace plan proposed by Carrington and Cutileiro, we had placed our trust in a negotiated solution to the conflict, and how it had only served to abandon the fate of Bosnia and of its martyred population into the hands of Slobodan Milosevic, Franjo Tudjman, Radovan Karadzic and Mate Boban.

"It is unacceptable – I argued – to consider the crisis in Bosnia as a civil war. The majority of the Bosnian population has been the victim of a foreign aggression. Even less can we accept the idea that what hinders a friendly resolution to the conflict is President Izetbegovic's obstinacy, when in practice he has been marginalized during the negotiations. It is the Serbs who have opposed the Vance-Owen Peace Plan, promoted by the UN and the European Community, and accepted by Bosnia's legitimate government. It is the Serbs who oppose the plan we bring today to the consideration of the Council as a legitimate proposal, not a desperate one, to release the Bosnian people from the unbearable weight of an arms embargo that condemns them to annihilation."

It was amazing to realize that such an undeniable reality did not move the international community's conscience. While in New York we were debating the arms embargo on Bosnia, in the Palais des Nations in Geneva, Owen and Stoltenberg were trying to have the occupation by force of arms of two-thirds of Bosnia legitimized, no matter the devastating political and humanitarian consequences. That very same day, June 29, Owen declared: "We have to stop this nonsense by President Izetbegovic, who refuses to take part in the negotiations. We'll have to address him as the President of the Muslim Party of Bosnia, which is how Karadzic and Boban call him."

Owen's rude statement, placing Izetbegovic at the same level as the unpresentable leaders of the Bosnian Serbs, the very same who were responsible for the massacre of the civilian population of his country, was a perfect illustration of the way in which Belgrade, the UN Secretariat, and the European members of the Council, were trying to force the approval of the false peace agreement they were promoting in Geneva. The plan amounted to having Bosnia stripped of all its rights as an independent, sovereign, republic. It seemed as if Owen and Stoltenberg were bent on re-living in Europe an old, failed, colonial policy.

To the argument that lifting the arms embargo would seriously jeopardize the delivery of humanitarian assistance to areas where the conflict was raging, I answered that it would be so only if the continued violation by Serb and Croat aggressors of the safety of those areas was not seriously confronted. It was to ensure the safe delivery of humanitarian assistance that the safe areas had been established, and it was regrettable to see them used by the international community as an excuse to avoid facing the true problem, which was its unwillingness to take the necessary political decisions. Food and medicines were not the answer to a political problem and would not solve the crisis. Clearly, safe areas – that were not safe – and humanitarian assistance – that was not allowed to reach the civilian population – were the schemes to which the Security Council resorted to create the illusion of an international community committed to the task of facing and solving the crisis.

The Safe Areas Deception

It was apparent that the safe areas were a fraud that placed the Security Council at risk of losing whatever credibility it still had. From the time of our visit to the Srebrenica safe area, at the end of April, we had denounced that the besieging Serbian forces had left the city without running water, gas, electricity, and even medical assistance. Epidemics were consuming thousands of its citizens, trapped between their cruel Serbian jailers and our inability to protect them. The same was happening in Gorazde, Tuzla, Bihac, Zepa, and even Sarajevo, all of them declared safe areas by the Security Council. All because the international community had refrained from adopting the measures needed to neutralize the voracity for land displayed by the Milosevic government. On this issue, I thought it would be appropriate to recall that the Council of Europe, meeting in Copenhagen a week before, under the chairmanship of Jacques Delors, had agreed that its members "Would not agree to any territorial partition imposed by the Serbs and the Croats on the Bosnians, and that any agreement must be based on the Vance-Owen Plan, particularly in relation to the independence, sovereignty and territorial integrity of Bosnia".

The resolution adopted by the Council of Europe allowed me to highlight the contradictions within European governments over Bosnia. Felipe González, for example, shared our position, as his statement in Copenhagen made clear. "If the international community is unable to solve the Bosnian crisis with the means at its disposal, while at the same time rejecting the option of an international intervention to solve it, we have to recognize Bosnia's legitimate right to self-defense." However, a few days after this statement, Ambassador Yáñez-Barnuevo, Spain's representative to the Council, was ready to vote against our proposal. The same happened with Francois Mitterrand, President of France. Mitterrand believed the Council and the UN Secretariat's passivity were the reason Serbia allowed itself to ignore the safe areas' status. In Copenhagen, Mitterrand declared that "If we were talking about the security of our countries, it would take us less than a couple of hours, not weeks, to take a decision. For whatever reason it might be, we are not, however, ensuring the safety of the Bosnian civilian population, even in the areas we have designated as safe areas. How then are we going to explain to the Bosnian government and to the Muslim Bosnian population that neither are we going to allow them to defend themselves from their aggressors?" Yet, the French representative in the Council, Ambassador Mérimée, was equally ready to vote our proposal down, labeling it a measure prompted by despair.

Helmut Köhl, the German Chancellor, also addressed the issue of Bosnia at the Council of Europe and stated that: "The international community cannot allow itself to turn its back on the Muslim population of Bosnia. To lift the arms embargo is a necessity and a moral duty." The Former British Prime Minister, Margaret Thatcher, took the same position. She considered it was "Intolerable to prevent people from defending themselves, unless one is willing to defend them oneself."

Before concluding, I reiterated that our proposal was, first and foremost, a declaration of principles, both ethical and political, and that we were therefore confident the Security Council would vote it favorably. That a UN Member State's defense of its rights would not enlist the approval of a majority of the members of the Council was inconceivable to us. "Not to rush to the defense of an independent nation such as Bosnia and Herzegovina, a victim of ethnic cleansing, and to do everything possible to obstruct its self-defense, carries ethical and political responsibilities of an extraordinary significance. Those who today deny that republic its right to defend itself will be, in the eyes of the world, in those of their own nations, and even in their conscience, burdened by an extraordinary and momentous debt."

I then overheard the British Deputy Permanent Representative, Ambassador Thomas Legh Richardson, telling a colleague in his delegation "It is unfair to criticize Lord Owen when he is not present to defend himself."

Neither was I in Geneva to tell him in person.

Twenty-Seven Ambassadors Condemn the P5

Never before had there been, nor would there be in the future, a more heavily attended session of the Council. Nor did I recall having witnessed such an intense debate. In favor or against, every intervention was passionate, no matter how different the positions about the situation in Bosnia were. From that day on, none of the members of the Security Council could plead ignorance of the scale of the crimes against humanity underway in Bosnia. As I waited for the vote to begin, I recalled the monstrosities I had witnessed in Srebrenica, Ahmici, Mostar, and Sarajevo, and wondered how some Permanent Members of the Council could argue that lifting the arms embargo on Bosnia was a measure of despair, when, in reality, it was our last opportunity to avoid its annihilation as a sovereign and independent nation.

I knew our position was the correct answer to the Serbian aggressors, both from a moral and a humanitarian standpoint. Even though there were no Venezuelan soldiers deployed in Bosnia, the British ambassador had no right to ask, "Why don't Venezuelan soldiers march from Caracas to Bosnia to stop the massacre?" as if it was not incumbent upon the Permanent Members to discharge their responsibilities under the UN Charter. To witness how more than half of the Council members did not care for the fate of a defenseless people, was a sad and terrible realization.

Yáñez-Barnuevo's call for a vote "on the draft resolution contained in document S/25997", brought me back from my musings. He then read out the results of the vote. In favor, six: Cape Verde, Djibouti, Morocco, Pakistan, United States, and Venezuela. Against: None. Abstentions, nine: Brazil, China, France, Hungary, Japan, New Zealand, Russian Federation, Spain, and United Kingdom.

Our proposal had been defeated. The session ended not long after, a few minutes before 9 pm, six hours after it had begun. The leaders and the people of Bosnia must have understood that with this decision they were abandoned to their fate by the international community. I felt truly desolate. I left the Council Hall overwhelmed by a feeling of embarrassment. The European powers had defeated us, certainly, but I was not willing to surrender. So, next day, in my capacity as coordinator of the Non-Aligned members of the Council, I convened a meeting to assess where we stood and consider our next steps. Even if we had not been successful this time, I knew not everything was lost.

We also had other issues on our agenda which concerned the Non-Aligned and which we could no longer postpone. The first was the extremely serious situation in Somalia where twenty-four Pakistani peacekeepers had been murdered by General Farrah Aidid's men. Aidid was one of the war lords disputing control of the country since 1991. The other was the situation in Haiti, where the Americans, with the Council's green light - the same Council that had denied Bosnia any assistance against the Serbian aggression - were planning to directly intervene to restore democracy and reinstate Jean-Bernard Aristide to the presidency, from which he had been deposed by force of arms by some colonels.

We met at the embassy of Pakistan on the afternoon of the following day. Previously, I held individual meetings with the ambassadors of Bosnia, Croatia, Jordan, Germany and Turkey, as well as with the Latin American and Caribbean Group, GRULAC, to brief them on our position in relation to the situations in Haiti and Somalia, but above all, on the situation in Bosnia after our proposal to lift the arms embargo had been defeated. I was concerned with the impact this might have on our group's mood. Ambassador Olhaye, who was the Dean of the Diplomatic Corps accredited to the UN, soon relieved my anguish. He opened the meeting expressing his satisfaction with all we had been able to accomplish in just three days.

"When have you seen – he asked – a public session of the Council in which twenty-seven ambassadors intervene, and all criticize, censure, and even condemn four out of the five Permanent Members? Never. It is a credit to our group, particularly so because the British ambassador had to admit that the Council is absolutely divided about what is truly happening in Bosnia." The Ambassador of Morocco added that "It was also worthy to note that the United States had co-sponsored our initiative, something without precedent." In this context, I expressed the view that, unfortunately, the United States had not exerted its influence to bring on board the three votes we lacked to have the resolution approved. Ambassador Marker intervened to bring to our attention that all the media had strongly criticized the lack of support to our draft by members of the Council, and the maneuverings by some Permanent Members and the Secretariat in support of the Serbian goals, thereby showing that our position on Bosnia and on its population's human rights, was gaining widespread support.

We knew the obstacles we faced when we proposed to lift the arms embargo on Bosnia. We could also imagine that, should our initiative fail, many Muslim nations would start helping their Bosnian brethren with weapons, even with combatants, and that Muslim radical groups would become active in the Balkans, which is to say, in Europe. Such a potential risk had to be contained, as the British Secretary of Defense, Malcolm Rifkind, indicated clearly when, in a statement to the press, he advanced the view, similar to that held by UN high officials and the Serbian commanders in Bosnia, that the conflict was in its final stages thanks to the Serbian occupation of most of Bosnia, and that it would be counterproductive to lift the arms embargo, since it would only serve to prompt the Bosnians

"To try to unnecessarily prolong the war in the hope of recovering some of the lost territory". It was a difficult position to understand and Vice President Ganic, once more, had to denounce "The international community's lack of concern for the genocide and other crimes against humanity committed on his country's Muslim community."

In the course of the meeting, we also touched upon the issue of the International Tribunal for the Former Yugoslavia, formally in place since May, but neglected by the Secretary General, so much so that the Tribunal still did not have a budget nor a roster of candidates. The first Prosecutor was to be the South African Supreme Court Judge Richard Goldstone, but he would not be available to take his position until August of the following year. Neither was Boutros-Ghali in a hurry to name the first High Commissioner for Human Rights, a lack of interest which was strongly criticized by many of the NGO's that took part in the Vienna Conference.

The Security Council went on to approve a series of resolutions on the obstacles faced by the delivery of humanitarian assistance to cities such as Mostar and Sarajevo, appealing to all the parties to cooperate with the mediators, Owen and Stoltenberg, so as to conclude "in the shortest possible delay, freely and by mutual agreement, a just and comprehensive political arrangement", exactly as France and the UK had insisted on during the informal consultations on our draft resolution. And with that they pretended to justify their opposition to President Izetbegovic's and the Non-Aligned position, based on the belief that it was simply impossible to reach a negotiated solution to the crisis in Bosnia as long as General Mladic's troops occupied and devastated two thirds of the country.

Bosnia Stands Alone

The pace and ferocity of the war picked up towards the end of June, just as Russia, the UK and France successfully sabotaged our efforts to have the Council lift the arms embargo on Bosnia. The war had been on-going for a year-and-a-half and continued to claim the attention of the international community. But now, in disregard of the ceasefire agreement with Bosnia, it was additionally fueled by the Bosnian Croat pretension to occupy Mostar, located in Central Bosnia, in order to make it the capital of an eventual Croat republic in Bosnia they called Herzeg-Bosnia.

The overall situation was rapidly deteriorating. The Bosnian Ambassador to the UN, Mohamed Sacirbey, denounced the upsurge of the Serbian offensive on all fronts, the brutal attacks on Mostar, and in the area of Mount Igman, close to Sarajevo. After consultations led by Ambassador David Hannay of the UK, then President of the Council, a Presidential Statement was issued on July 22 strongly condemning this escalade and designating Sarajevo as a Safe Area.

A Cornered Nation

The Presidential Statement demanded the Serbian aggressors to immediately halt their assault on the Bosnian capital and to withdraw to a safe distance, from where they could not endanger the safety of the city's civilian population. Both Serb and Croat forces were ordered to lift all obstacles to the delivery of humanitarian assistance and to the provision of public services to the besieged Bosnian towns. Finally, it also included two requests made by the Non-Aligned Caucus.

First, in evident reference to a possible use of force, to keep all options open, without any exception, to deter an aggression on the sovereignty of Bosnia and the safety of its civilian population. Second, to request the parties to meet in Geneva with the mediators, Owen and Stoltenberg, until a "Durable and equitable agreement is reached, based on the sovereignty, territorial integrity and political independence of the Republic of Bosnia and Herzegovina, as well as on the inadmissibility of ethnic cleansing and acquisition of territory by force of arms."

The Non-Aligned were obviously aware that a peace plan based on those terms, which guaranteed Bosnia the sovereign rights they refused, would be unacceptable for Tudjman and Milosevic. But such terms had to be upheld even if we understood Izetbegovic was not in a position to negotiate on an equal footing with Tudjman and Milosevic. Even though the July 22 Presidential Statement's terms were not enforceable, it sent a strong message around which the international community could rally. President Izetbegovic immediately announced that, in compliance with the Council's call, he would travel to Geneva on the next day. However, on that very morning, a barrage of heavy Serbian artillery fire on Sarajevo forced him to cancel his trip.

The Serbian shelling of Sarajevo was obviously intended as a reply to the Security Council's July 22 Presidential Statement. The bombing continued unabated until, on July 30, a mortar grenade seriously wounded Irma Hadzimuratovic, a five-year-old girl, and killed others, including her mother. Kosevo Hospital, the most important hospital in Sarajevo, was overcrowded and lacked the equipment and medicines to care for the extremely serious wounds Irma had suffered in her head, column, and abdomen. From its London headquarters, the BBC launched an intensive information campaign on the case. The British Prime Minister, John Major, found it impossible not to intervene, and sent an RAF Hercules plane to bring the little girl to a British hospital.

The Serbian artillery continued to pound Bosnia all throughout the week, causing a considerable number of fatal casualties on a daily basis, including children, and hundreds of wounded. Notwithstanding this, the British policy remained not to evacuate the wounded, even if they required specialized medical attention. In this context, Irma's evacuation came to be seen as just a showcase. ACNUR's spokesperson, Sylvana Foa, referring to Irma's case asked whether evacuation was just for wounded children, "Particularly if they are under six years of age, blonde, and blue-eyed," demanded that Sarajevo not be taken as a "supermarket" for photogenic refugees, and requested clarifications on the British evacuation policy. Dr. Patrick Peillod, Head of the UN Evacuations Committee, went as far as to declare that the UK government had until then treated the Bosnian children as if they were animals in a zoo, and that Irma's evacuation was simply part of a "public relations agenda." In an encounter with the international press, the Director of Kosevo Hospital, Faruk Kulenovic, declared that he found truly shameful that "Cats and dogs in the UK have more rights and receive better medical attention than the inhabitants of Sarajevo." To understand all this rage, one must remember that since the beginning of the conflict Serbian artillery and sharpshooters had been responsible for more than two-thousand deaths and more than fifty-four thousand wounded only in Sarajevo.

The Owen and Stoltenberg Peace Plan

While the war followed its bloody path, Owen and Stoltenberg went ahead in their strategy to secure a peace plan that would be palatable to Milosevic, Tudjman, Karadzic, and Boban. Izetbegovic steadfastly refused to sign any agreement that contemplated the partition of his country and now demanded a formal recognition of Bosnia's sovereignty before taking part in the Geneva summit. He knew well that, with the mediators' complicity, what Serbs and Croats really wanted was to make him agree to a transformation of Bosnia into a federal state, made up of three mini-states, each one based on its ethnic identity. Izetbegovic knew that would be the first step towards reducing Bosnia into a non-entity.

By way of Ambassador Sacirbey, we knew there were doubts within the Bosnian government about what to do. But also that leaders such as Vice President Ejup Ganic were adamantly opposed to allowing the diplomatic negotiations to delete Bosnia from the map of Europe. The risk of an internal crisis within the Bosnian Muslim leadership was viewed with concern within the Non-Aligned Caucus. Indeed, a very worried Sacirbey confided to me that President Izetbegovic, with whom he was permanently in contact, was seriously considering travelling to Geneva, although he insisted that he would only take part in the negotiations "To find a formula that would effectively end the conflict but without allowing for a political or territorial partition, since that would be akin to a collective suicide". That was how President Izetbegovic understood any peace plan had to be, if it was to be clearly "fair and just", while for the mediators, the UN Secretariat, and the Permanent Members of the Council, peace, at whatever price, was the absolute priority, even if it meant legitimizing the territorial conquests made by Serbs and Croats by force of arms and ethnic cleansing. If this approach were to be approved by the Geneva mini-Summit, the Bosnian Muslims would be left with only two terrible and unacceptable options: either the division of the republic along an ethnic lines or the continuation of the war under increasingly disadvantageous military conditions.

Foul winds were blowing over the Palais des Nations. The negotiations in Geneva simply did not offer any good options. Bosnia could choose to continue a war it could not win, or it could give in to the pressure and impatience of the big powers, keen to end the Bosnian crisis at whatever price. In the midst of all this turbulence, President Izetbegovic was informed that the United States was ready to support the Owen-Stoltenberg plan, even though it implied changing its prior staunch opposition to the apartheid model for Bosnia. Since the United States was Bosnia's only ally among the Council's Permanent Members, it was a development that forced President Izetbegovic to reconsider his nonattendance to the Geneva meeting.

Confusion reigned until Washington informed the Bosnian government that, no matter the results of the Geneva negotiations, it could rely on the economic and financial support needed to overcome the calamitous destruction brought on by the war. This, and the fact that all the Permanent Members of the Security Council were now behind the Owen-Stoltenberg plan, convinced President Izetbegovic of the need to travel to Geneva, which he finally did on July 26. The situation left Izetbegovic cornered, unable to either accept or reject the plan as a whole, while giving its mentors – the Tudjman, Milosevic, Karadzic, Boban quartet, with the blessing of Owen and Stoltenberg – an unfair upper hand.

Indeed, though the plan was in reality a false solution to the Bosnian issues, in the midst of such distressing circumstances it allowed its sponsors to try to push forward their advantage, as shown by their aggressive statements during those days. Radovan Karadzic, for example, declared that "If the Muslims reject the proposal, they risk losing everything, even the little territory they still control. If they do not sign, the Croats and us will carve up Bosnia for ourselves." Owen endorsed this menace by claiming that it was the Bosnian government's fault if this was the last opportunity the Bosnian Muslims had to be part of the new Bosnia, and warned that "If this agreement does not come through in the next few days, the offer of a negotiated division among the three parties will no longer be on the table, and the future of Bosnia will rest in the hands of the commander of the Serbian nationalist forces in Bosnia, General Ratko Mladic."

In the eyes of all these characters, the Bosnian Muslims had to accept all the Serbian and Croatian demands or resign themselves to be exterminated by the "Butcher of the Balkans," as Mladic was known. It all amounted to an ignominious intimidation of the Izetbegovic government, now put seriously at risk by a plan tailor-made for Serbia and Croatia. To add insult to injury, there was just a week to reach a final decision. Izetbegovic was aware that he was politically and militarily isolated and believed that the Serbs were taking part in peace negotiations only as a front, as they had always done. While the summit was taking place they were preparing for and threatening to launch a final offensive on Bosnia, with the military and political support of Croatia.

The Geneva Summit Fiasco

When we met in his office in Zagreb on April 27, President Franjo Tudjman told the members of the Security Council Mission to the Balkans that an alliance between Serbs and Croats against the government and the Muslim population of Bosnia would never happen. The Bosnian Croat leader Mate Boban in Split said the same. The fact was his irregular troops, with the total support of the Tudjman government, had just began one of the most vicious operations of the whole war on the Western flank of Bosnia and Herzegovina, close to its borders with Croatia. It would displace more than thirty thousand Muslims and their homes would be given to Croat refugees. Their Muslim inhabitants had to abandon them and go "to Turkey or any other Arab country." Hermann Tertsch, a Spanish journalist, described with a grisly phrase the results of this ethnic cleansing, "Everybody is now a Catholic, everybody is a Croat, and everybody is a dutiful follower of President Tudjman." On a subject as vile as ethnic cleansing, Croats and Bosnian Croats had quickly learnt their lesson.

As the plan advanced to erase from the map of Europe an independent but defenseless nation, and in view of such flagrant violations of every ethical and political principles, I could not fail to ask myself exactly what role the mediators Owen and Stoltenberg were playing in all this. To end the war as soon as possible by a negotiated agreement was obviously their mandate, but should it be done at any price? As mediators, were they acting as honest brokers when they cornered President Izetbegovic to have him accept what they called "the only realistic solution" to the conflict? Was this plan not, in reality, a death sentence on Bosnia and on the Bosnian Muslim population? To my mind, the worse was that Owen and Stoltenberg were not even acting independently.

They were doing the bidding of the main members of the Security Council, of the European Community, and of the UN Secretary General.

It all amounted, in fact, to a true international conspiracy with the purpose of covering up the annexation of Bosnian territory by neighboring countries, while placing Sarajevo under UN administration, and Mostar, chosen to be the capital of a future Croat Bosnian republic, under that of the European Community. When these aspects of the Geneva peace plan became public, an editorial in the Bosnian daily *Oslobodenje* (Liberation in English), signed by its director, Kemal Kurspahic, denounced that the peace negotiations in Geneva were in reality a way to force the Bosnian Muslims into accepting ethnic cleansing as a basis for a settlement in exchange for avoiding accusations as enemies of peace. "It would be a tragedy to divide Bosnia as is proposed in Geneva. Terror and violence – he added - will spread all over the country and it would amount to having endorsed Radovan Karadzic's brutal extermination policy". Unfortunately, events during the following two years proved him right.

In Geneva, the negotiations pushed the Bosnia and Herzegovina government against the wall, but their implications for the Western governments were no less serious. They now had to decide whether they were ready to accept the acquisition of territory by use of force and to be complicit to the extermination policies practiced on the Bosnian Muslims for ethnic and religious reasons or approve an international militarily intervention to solve the crisis.

As usual, the Non-Aligned members of the Council were denied appropriate information on what was truly taking place in Bosnia. Only thanks to my personal relationship with Ambassador Sacirbey were we brought up to speed daily on the conflict, and became aware that Haris Silajdzic, Minister of Foreign Affairs of Bosnia, who was in Geneva with President Izetbegovic, had just denounced that the international community was presenting Bosnia with an ultimatum, not with a peace plan. It was more a rendition than a peace agreement, like the Treaty of Versailles of 1919 had been. Beyond the obvious differences between both situations, there could be no doubt that the Geneva peace agreement proposal amounted to the rendition of Bosnia and Herzegovina to the stronger and more violent party.

During our almost daily conversations, Sacirbey confided that his president was "a wise man, although too old", who was in the habit of letting anyone approach him and hearing what they had to say, which placed him in a position to be manipulated. Sacirbey had a quite different education and background to that of the leaders of the Former Yugoslavia. He told me, in strict confidence, that before Bosnia decided on whether to accept or reject a plan based on the partition of the country into three ethnic regions, his government's lawyers had requested the International Court of Justice to declare invalid the Geneva proposal.

On My Way to Zagreb to Meet Franjo Tudjman

The scarce information available on the diplomatic and military developments in Bosnia and in Geneva kept the Non-Aligned members of the Council permanently worried and fearful regarding the situation in which the "Muslim side" might find itself in. In an urgent meeting convened by Ambassador Ahmed Snoussi of Morocco, it was decided that, in view of a coming trip to Europe to give a presentation at the Vienna Peace Academy, I should travel to Zagreb to meet President Tudjman and ascertain his position on the evolving realities in Bosnia, and then to Sarajevo, to exchange views with the president of Bosnia on our possible next steps as a group.

I decided to personally inform Kofi Annan, Under Secretary General for Peacekeeping Operations, and Boutros-Ghali, UN Secretary General, about the mandate I had been entrusted with and the reasons behind it. I formally requested that UNPROFOR be given charge of my transport and security needs in Croatia and Bosnia, in particular during my stay in

Sarajevo, a city still under attack by Serbian artillery. I also met with the Ambassadors of Croatia and Bosnia, Mario Nobilo and Muhamed Sacirbey, so they could inform their governments about my imminent trip, which I would be making with Víctor Manzanares, First Secretary at the Venezuelan delegation to the United Nations.

It was not my first time in Vienna´s International Institute for Peace. The subject of my presentation was the war and armed conflicts in the Former Yugoslavia, and I was able to verify that my perspective on those terrible situations, and in particular my criticism of the role played by UNPROFOR in Bosnia, was shared by growing segments of the European military establishment. We all agreed that it was absurd to reduce UNPROFOR´s mandate to the support of UN humanitarian activities, and to not allow it to play a role in the promotion of a stable ceasefire and the safety of the civilian population.

We then travelled to Zagreb by train. We arrived around seven pm, after a six-hours journey. Two UNPROFOR officers met us and took us to the hotel to drop our bags and then continue on to the Government Palace. Ambassador Nobilo had informed that President Tudjman and members of his Cabinet would receive me at eight pm at the same place where we had met the previous April. As on that occasion, we were greeted and sat at the same majestic table placed at the center of a hall with views on the beautiful gardens surrounding the palace. A smiling and cordial Tudjman addressed me:

— Mr. Ambassador – have you tried the tie adorned with the Croatian crest that I gave you and your colleagues as a present? Please remember that in Croatian, the word for tie is the same as for Croatia.

I wasn´t expecting to be greeted with a question like that, so I barely managed to reply that I would use it to celebrate when the war ended. We both smiled, knowing full well there would be truly little to celebrate, with or without a tie. It´s very obvious – I said – that we are still a long way from peace. I explained that my mission to Zagreb on behalf of my Non-Aligned colleagues was to follow up on the issues we had discussed during my previous visit two months ago, such as the need to bring to justice those responsible for the Ahmici massacre, a crime he promised would be investigated and punished, and the more recent assault by Mate Boban's troops on Mostar and on villages in the area of Medjugorje, twenty kilometers from the border with Croatia.

Mention of these issues made Tudjman fall into a deep silence. For a man like him, a Head of Government, and would be Father of the Croatian Homeland, it could not have been easy to be confronted with these truths, more so after I told him they harmed Croatia's international image and risked placing him at the same level as Milosevic and Karadzic, well-known promoters of the abominable ethnic cleansing policy in Bosnia. I told him that in the opinion of the Non-Aligned Caucus, he was not like Milosevic or Karadzic. His political standing, his academic credentials, and his military service record as a high-ranking Army officer, placed him at a quite different level. However, since in April we had agreed to speak frankly, I told him that should these serious crimes not stop immediately, "the Karadjordjevo agreement, which you deny, between yourself and Milosevic to carve up Bosnia would very much start to have a ring of truth to it."

Franjo Tudjman's friendly, and at the same time haughty smile disappeared. Both he and his Defense Minister, Gojko Susak, thought to be the main architect of the Croatian policy in Bosnia, and directly in charge of the support given to Boban's military forces, looked extremely annoyed. In their eyes, I was just a non-permanent member of the Security Council and represented a country that had no relevance in European politics. They of course could not forget that I spoke in the name of the six Non-Aligned members of the Council, and therefore for a large majority of the UN membership. Whatever the case, Susak was quick to reply that the Tudjman government had nothing to do with any of those situations, which they considered to be a responsibility of the Bosnian Muslim commanders in those areas. Ten days later, in a statement to the press, he would reiterate this version of events and insist that the Bosnians were harassing and attacking the

Bosnian Croats in Central Bosnia, declaring that "The Armed Forces of the Republic of Croatia were ready to protect the areas with a Croatian majority if the Muslims tried to carry out their threats of invasion."

Not too long after that statement, Boban would declare himself president of a non-existent Croat republic in Bosnia, named Herzeg-Bosnia, a development warmly welcomed by Tudjman, who would reiterate that his government "would help the Croats of Bosnia and Herzegovina to defend themselves from any Muslim aggression." I pointed out to Tudjman that any such military intervention in Bosnia by Croatia would bring about the adoption of the same economic and trade sanctions imposed by the Council on Serbia. I also reminded him that the recently established International Tribunal for the Former Yugoslavia was already conducting investigations on crimes against humanity committed in Bosnia by either civilian or military officials, no matter their nationality or their place in the chain of command. All to no avail. The President of Croatia, like his counterpart in Serbia, was absolutely convinced that the international community would not enforce any decision the Tribunal might adopt.

I was surprised to see that Tudjman's positions had become notoriously more radical since April. He referred to the Muslim Bosnian population with contempt, calling it simply "the Muslims." Twice, and with evident intent, I asked him to clarify if by that he meant the citizens of the Republic of Bosnia and Herzegovina, a member state of the United Nations, as independent as Croatia was, but he simply ignored the provocation. The only issue about which Tudjman expressed satisfaction was the one-year renewal of UNPROFOR's mandate in Croatia, omitting to mention its purpose was to deter further Serbian attacks on the historic city of Dubrovnik, as those that had taken place between October and December 1991.

Our meeting lasted two hours. As we said our goodbyes, I informed Tudjman I would now travel to Sarajevo to meet President Izetbegovic, with whom, I assured him, I would also be absolutely frank. Tudjman asked me to urge Izetbegovic to sign the plan Owen and Stoltenberg had presented in Geneva, as it was, in his opinion, the only way to bring the war to an end. I just replied that we understood extremely well Izetbegovic's refusal to do so, with Bosnia under siege and threatened to be erased from the community of independent nations. Tudjman pretended he did not hear my reply and, instead, asked me to meet with some dignitaries of the Croat Catholic Church. I told him I would do so with pleasure since I was - as he - a Catholic.

When I left the palace, I did so with the feeling I would leave Croatia without really knowing Tudjman's position on the conflict, and also that he must be the most amoral political leader I had ever met. Years later, Richard Goldstone, Chief Prosecutor of the ICTFY, would tell me that, in his opinion, only his death saved Tudjman from prosecution as a war criminal, at the very least for his responsibility in launching ¨Operation Thunderstorm¨, executed by the Croatian army in the Krajina region to regain enclaves occupied by Serbian Croat forces while under UN protection. Operation Thunderstorm represented the largest land battle in Europe since World War II and caused the forced displacement of about two hundred and fifty thousand Serbs, more than a thousand deaths, and the internment in concentration camps of thousands of Muslim Bosnian Croats. It was condemned as a "criminal action" by the International Criminal Tribunal for the Former Yugoslavia, which deemed it an operation conducted with the purpose of carrying out the ethnic cleansing of Serbs in Croatia. Tudjman's criminal actions almost equaled those ordered by Milosevic, but he hid his responsibilities with much more cunning and continued to be in power until his death six years later. By then, his prestige was absolutely tarnished and not a single foreign government was represented at his funeral.

Back in Sarajevo

The next morning, an UNPROFOR escort picked us up at the hotel and took us to the military section of Zagreb Airport. Two Catholic priests were waiting for us and identified themselves as representatives of the archbishop, who could not join us – they explained – because he was out of town and would not be back until the afternoon. I too regretted the situation, but since I had to take a plane to Sarajevo, I wasted no time and directly expressed my concern over the violence displayed by Mate Boban's troops, a concern I had brought to the attention of President Tudjman. "The Ahmici massacre was not just another episode of violence but one of the many war crimes committed during the Yugoslav wars. Crimes, by the way, that neither President Tudjman nor Mate Boban have even tried to investigate." To my surprise, both priests took exactly the same position as Tudjman and Susak, arguing that the media focused excessively on that event while silencing or barely mentioning the attacks by Muslims on the Bosnian Croat enclaves.

There was nothing further to talk about with the priests, so I took my leave and boarded the airplane. In an hour we were in Sarajevo and, once again, hurried along the sandbag-lined corridor towards the rundown terminal building. The same armed vehicles of the UN Blue Helmets took us to their Command's Headquarters, crossing a city even more in ruins than in April. It looked as if a devastating earthquake had hit it. Serbian artillery had destroyed all buildings, houses and schools. The city was desolate and not a single pedestrian was to be seen anywhere. Manzanares, sitting beside me, could not hide his astonishment. It was his first time in Bosnia, and he was not prepared for what he saw. It made an impression on him. A few days ago, as I was writing these lines, I called him to ask how he had felt on his first visit to Sarajevo, and he confided it had been something unforgettable since he had never seen the horrors of war up and close. "It was the most important experience in my life," he answered.

I was expecting to be greeted at the door of UNPROFOR Headquarters by Vere Hayes, the British general who had left me with such unpleasant memories, but instead it was the Belgian Francis Briquemont who met us. Just a few days before, he had replaced General Philippe Morillon as commander of the Force. The UN Secretariat must have tried to avoid new confrontations between us, so Hayes was nowhere to be seen during my visit. I felt very much at ease with Briquemont, and we had a pleasant meeting in his office. Sergio Vieira de Mello, a veteran Brazilian UN official, at the time Director for Civilian and Political Affairs of UN Forces in Bosnia, joined us shortly after and accompanied us during the day's activities.

Briquemont's personality was in stark contrast to that of his predecessors, Generals Morillon and Wahlgren. He was calm and always smiling. He started the conversation by expressing the wish that our meeting would be less uncomfortable than the previous ones, and I of course graciously returned his smile. I had been told that when Briquemont arrived in Sarajevo, a journalist had asked him if he came as a diplomat or as a general and he had replied that it depended on the time of day. He was very self-assured and did not mince his words. During our hour-long meeting, his opinions clearly reflected that he always acted as a general, no matter the time of day. Even if, as he said, he had not been in post for long, he had no qualms about sharing with me his opinions. "My experience as an officer in NATO tells me the UN is not structured to meet the challenges posed by the conflicts in the Former Yugoslavia." He was very critical of the press, which he found to be extremely aggressive, in particular American media such as CNN, and had decided to no longer hold press conferences, as Morillon and Wahlgren used to do. Even though I considered that to be truly a mistake, I preferred not to argue about it with him. I could imagine, however, that the Permanent Members of the Security Council and the UN Secretariat would be happy to have it that way.

I was also surprised to notice how not one of the other officers present in the conversation took part in it. Not even when Briquemont repeated the widespread opinion that the "Muslim combatants" were responsible for most of the ceasefire violations in the safe areas. In his published memoires, Owen holds that the international media and some NGO's lied, making false denunciations that distorted reality. Also, that the UN Forces had never displayed an anti-Muslim policy but rather had tried to bring some order into the chaos resulting from the war. In Owen's mind, it was the Bosnian Muslims who, by their actions, hindered the negotiations the most. As mediator in the negotiations, Owen's opinions should have been objective and independent, but the truth is that they were always at the service of the European powers, the United Kingdom in particular, a country that bears much responsibility for the inefficient and erratic management of the conflict in Bosnia.

We had been told exactly the same by General Wahlgren when we met in April, also in that office. Even though the UN deployed to the theatre of war highly competent civilian officials like Vieira De Mello, the Blue Helmet military commanders' perception of the conflict was the only one it was willing to consider, as if the United Nations were a military institution. For example, the first UNPROFOR commander, General Satish Nambiar, of India, went as far as to declare that the UN Forces had never acted in error and that, if something had to be changed, it was "the political will of the members of the Security Council." Although it was diplomatically inappropriate to say so, to a certain degree he probably had a point.

To prove it, a day before, while I was still in Zagreb, Ambassador Madeleine Albright, who chaired the Council during that month, strongly criticized a statement by General Briquemont on President Clinton's initiative to lift the arms embargo on Bosnia and conduct a multinational military action. Unfortunately, I only came to hear about it after my return to New York.

My New Meeting with President Izetbegovic

Before I travelled to Sarajevo, I asked UNPROFOR's officials for an update on the situation in Srebrenica. Their reports, however, were far from informative. They could just indicate that things had not changed much since my recent visit to that sieged Muslim enclave and had no precise information on the electricity and running water situations.

In view of this, I asked General Briquemont to include in my itinerary the Kosevo Hospital, and the editorial office of the Oslobodenje daily, in addition to my scheduled visit to President Izetbegovic and other members of his Cabinet. Little could I imagine at the time that four months later Briquemont would resign, profoundly disappointed with UNPROFOR's performance in Bosnia. In its January 22, 1994, edition, *The Washington Post* published an interview with Briquemont by its correspondent in Sarajevo, John Pomfret, in which the general strongly criticized the role played by the United Nations in Bosnia, calling it "Unfortunate and ill prepared, and probably prejudicial to future missions with similar mandates". He added that he discharged his duties in Bosnia in a state of permanent discomfort, knowing it was all simply an experiment by the UN, one "That had caused the useless death of dozens of his soldiers", and he harshly criticized the Security Council for limiting its participation to the enactment of countless resolutions "that read very well but do not go beyond that."

Briquemont's comments went very much in the same direction as my reiterated observations on the situation, with the exception of his praise for the Serbian military, whom he considered to have "Respected their engagements with UNPROFOR." However, he did not reiterate what he had confided to me in his office, that had United Nations truly wanted to bring the war in Bosnia to an end, it should have deployed a much stronger force and given it a much more precise mandate, in particular, once the General Assembly had admitted Bosnia and Herzegovina as an independent nation in

May 1992. The interview ended with Briquemont recalling that while in Bosnia he received instructions from his superiors "To do this and that, but they never provided the necessary manpower and equipment." He was replaced by the British General Michael Rose, who upon arrival declared exactly the opposite, stressing that he had all that was needed to fully discharge his mandate. It was the beginning of a tour of duty that fell under strong criticism by the Bosnian government, which Rose accused of pretending to have the Blue Helmets fight its wars. In time, Rose would be accused of being far too lenient towards General Mladic, whom he did not even consider to be a war criminal. Referring to Rose, Haris Siladjzic, at the time Prime Minister of Bosnia, said that "The United Nations, instead of taking action to ensure Bosnia stopped being a defenseless victim of Serbian and Croatian aggression, considered the war and the ethnic cleansing merely as a humanitarian catastrophe."

This background and the accelerated deterioration of the military situation gave my second meeting with President Izetbegovic in his office in Sarajevo a completely different tone to the one in April. The lack of political will by the Permanent Members of the Council to foster a just and equitable peace in Bosnia was now beyond any doubt. They limited their initiatives to the largely unsuccessful delivery of humanitarian assistance to the civilian population. In an attempt to overcome this situation, Joe Biden, at the time Chairman of the US Senate Foreign Relations Committee, proposed to establish a demilitarized zone around the besieged Bosnian capital, with a strong contingent of UN peacekeepers deployed as a buffer between Serb and Bosnian troops, but President Clinton did not support his initiative.

Truly discouraged, as I approached the Government Palace I felt like someone on his way to offering his condolences to a good friend. Indeed, I was not in a position to give President Izetbegovic the slightest hope about the future of his country. At the same time, I had to be very careful not to convey to my Bosnian counterparts any pessimism. So, I put on my best face while my good friend Vice President Ejup Ganic accompanied me to the meeting room where President Izetbegovic, a few ministers and General Rasim Delic, Chief of Staff of the Bosnian Army, awaited my arrival.

President Izetbegovic received me with his usual cordiality and thanked me for the role Venezuela had been playing within the Security Council. My notes about that meeting record I was left under the impression their welcome was a combination of hope and fear: fear about the ongoing situation and hope for the initiatives that, against all odds, I might be able to take once back in New York. Maybe that was the reason he received me with a smile, or maybe it was because he immediately announced "a very frugal lunch" would be served. It was a "War Menu," which, as the typewritten card announced, also included a "war soup," to be followed by vegetables instead of the traditional lamb of Muslim meals.

In the background, during this "State Luncheon", we could hear the blast of Serbian shells and heavy machine guns, but General Delic told us they were coming from other parts of town. President Izetbegovic seemed to have aged considerably. He was much thinner, and his face showed the burden he carried. And with reason. The so-called peace plan under discussion in Geneva was clearly a farce that did not even address the systematic eviction of the Muslim population from areas in which it was a majority. It evidenced how little there was to be expected from the Owen-Stoltenberg mediation. Both mediators were clearly exhausted after almost two years of useless peace plans. That was the reason why, President Izetbegovic told me, he had decided to travel to Washington in the coming days. After all, he said, the Clinton Administration represented the only powerful government that could offer some hope for the Bosnian cause, much more so now that the Republicans, by way of Senator Bob Dole, a presidential precandidate, had informed him that they too would support the Clinton-Gore Administration's position on lifting the arms embargo.

Ambassador Sacirbey and the Bosnian Prime Minister had informed on the efforts being done to secure this endorsement. And now Izetbegovic assured me his intention was to take advantage of this bipartisan support to request a meeting with the Security Council. I immediately told him that it was an excellent idea and that he could rely on the support of the members of the Non-Aligned Caucus in the Council: Venezuela, Pakistan, Morocco, Cape Verde and Djibouti.

I then shared a couple of observations. First, that I had the impression, following my meeting in the morning with General Briquemont, that the UNPROFOR commander did not entirely disagree with the Council's policy of limiting the possible use of force to the delivery of humanitarian assistance to the Bosnian civilian population. Second, that my meeting with President Tudjman the night before had left me with a very disappointing impression. President Izetbegovic was not surprised by Tudjman's attitude. "I know him far too well - he said – as well as his sidekick, Mate Boban. Even so, I believe it will be more productive to negotiate with the Croats than with the Serbians." This disconcerted me somewhat since precisely in those days, Central Bosnia was under heavy attack by Bosnian Croat forces.

General Delic then intervened to say he had information that the United States and NATO were considering the option of conducting attacks on the Serbian heavy weapons emplacements in Bosnia, and that if this came to pass, it would have a decisive impact on the war. In his opinion, we should prepare for an escalation of hostilities, since only a long-drawn-out war would allow the recapture of Serbian occupied territory, something that now seemed out of reach by only diplomatic means.

It was not up to me to say so, but I totally agreed with General Delic and Vice President Ejup Ganic's support of that position. President Izetbegovic evidently enjoyed the strong support of his collaborators, which made me take the opportunity to reiterate that I was there on behalf of the Non-Aligned Caucus and, at the same time, to request to be kept informed of his position in the Geneva talks in order to avoid any contradiction between his position and ours.

In short, Izetbegovic believed that to sign a peace plan basically designed by Milosevic and Tudjman, and endorsed by Owen and Stoltenberg, would be the equivalent of signing the rendition of Bosnia, and that his government, no matter the heavy losses incurred, both human and territorial, would not under any circumstances approve such a misguided plan. That was why, he insisted, it was of the utmost importance to enlist the support of the United States, even if, he feared, it might not be enough given the importance Clinton gave to his British and French allies′ position.

— I truly doubt that the United States would act unilaterally, he conceded.

Vice President Ganic intervened to say that given the way at least four out of five Permanent Members of the Council conducted the Geneva talks, they would end up rewarding Serbia′s ethnic cleansing policy. It was not by chance, he added, that while we were there, Stoltenberg was on his way to New York to enlist the Council's endorsement of what by then he and Owen called "the Geneva package."

Speaking on this thorny issue, I told them that both mediators were concerned about a possible Non-Aligned Caucus initiative to significantly modify the "package." I then shared with them that early in the morning I had spoken with Venezuela's Deputy Permanent Representative, Ambassador Carlos Bivero, who had confirmed that the P5 had agreed to support Stoltenberg's request and that the Non-Aligned would reject it if the plan included the recognition of Serbian sovereignty over territories occupied by use of force and by ethnic cleansing, adding that, unfortunately, we were still in a minority position within the Council.

President Izetbegovic then added that that was the reason why he had included in the agenda of his planned visit to the United States meetings with important members of Congress, where the Bosnian cause was followed with empathy, and that he would try to build a bipartisan agreement, which by itself would not be enough to change the Council's position, but would at least disclose to international public opinion the

Permanent Members′ passivity, and in some cases, complicity with Serbia. As our meeting ended, President Izetbegovic confirmed his intention to travel to Geneva and cautioned that before deciding on whether to sign "the package," he would present it to the consideration of the Bosnian parliament.

To close, Ejup Ganic stated: "It they want to liquidate us as a sovereign, independent nation, and the world goes with it, then so be it. But do not ask us to leave to future generations the legacy of us agreeing."

As we left the Government palace, one of President Izetbegovic's collaborators approached me and said: "You might remember that when you came at the end of April you were welcomed by a group of children, applauding you and the Blue Helmets. Now, the same children throw rocks at the Blue Helmets, whom they no longer consider the protectors of the city or its people."

The Horrors we Witnessed at Kosevo Hospital

I left the Presidential Palace more convinced than ever that the meetings in Geneva would not bring an end to the war in Bosnia. There was an increasingly notorious chasm between the reality of the situation in Bosnia and the international community's perception of it. As I was heading towards Kosevo Hospital, the buildings in ruins, some still smoldering, and the hauntingly solitary streets confirmed this. It was impossible not to be overwhelmed by feelings of impotence and frustration. Sergio Vieira De Mello had been by my side since my arrival at UNPROFOR headquarters. Ten years later, as UN High Commissioner for Human Rights and widely considered as a future UN Secretary General, he would die in Iraq, the victim of a terrorist attack by Abu Musab al-Zarqawi on UN offices in Bagdad. That day, as the UN armored vehicles arrived at the main gate of the hospital – a ten-floor building, with shattered windows and walls pierced by shells – he would comment, full of bitterness, that the Serbian aggressors would stop at nothing and attacked even civilian targets, like that hospital, to which they had also cut running water and electricity.

Months before, in October 1992, *The New York Times* had published an article signed by John Burns, titled "A Sarajevo Hospital Works in Horror Beyond Anything". It was this articled that had prompted me to visit Kosevo Hospital. Burns had interviewed one of the doctors who told him how, the previous winter, without electricity, he "Had slept in a freezing cold, woke up with cold, and even surgical operations had to be done in conditions of several degrees below zero temperatures." The hospital was located on one of the city's more exposed mountain flanks and for months on end its patients and medical personnel lived with the threat to be killed or wounded by Serbian artillery fire.

The Director took us through the hospital, and we saw how seriously injured patients received care while on stretchers or sleeping pads placed even on the corridors' floors. I had never witnessed so much pain and desolation in a single place. Only the memory of the charred remains of Muslim families murdered by Mate Boban's Bosnian Croat troops at Ahmici came close to what I witnessed at Kosevo Hospital. In all of its ten floors the same terrible scenes of suffering and sacrifice were repeated. When we arrived at the rooftop, the Director showed us a nearby football field and told us it had been converted into an improvised war cemetery.

It seemed to me simply unimaginable that the Security Council could remain, by its own will, uninformed and indifferent to situations such as that of this hospital, located at the center of a theater of war. We had never been informed of situations such as that. Even less conceivable was that UNPROFOR should stand aloof and do nothing to put a stop to all the Serbian barbarities. I was ashamed beyond limits by so much indifference and cruelty, and for being a part of the world's leading political body. I did not know how to say goodbye to the hospital's director, although my face said it all. There was no need for words.

At the Oslobodenje Daily´s Newsroom

We left the hospital and headed straight to the newspaper's headquarters through the city center, leaving behind the bridge where archduke Francis Ferdinand of Austria was murdered. The *Oslobodenje* was Bosnia´s most important newspaper. It had been founded in 1943 as an expression of the country´s anti-Nazi sentiment, and had never missed an edition, not even during the grim times the city was living in. To me, it embodied an unshakeable commitment to freedom and a daily reaffirmation of a will to fight to preserve it. In my previous visit to Sarajevo in April, I had been interviewed by one of its heroic journalists who wanted to know my thoughts on the war, and also because he knew that years before, in Venezuela, I had founded and directed *El Diario de Caracas.*

For security reasons, we held our meeting in an area of the building the least exposed to risk of attacks. Just as it had been the case at the hospital, the meeting was held by candle lights. About my exchanges with the paper´s editors I particularly remember their criticism of the UN and its Protection Forces' unexplainable conduct. Two months later, the newspaper would be distinguished with the Sajarov Prize and New York´s World Press Review would honor its directors, Kemal Kurspahic and Gordana Knezevic, naming them International Directors for 1993, in recognition of their "courage, tenacity, and commitment to the principles of journalism". During the three years of the war against the Serbian aggressors, five members of the newspapers´ team had been murdered and twenty-five had been wounded. To have met them, even as bullets rained, was an incredibly special and unforgettable experience.

We left the building under the protection and close surveillance of our Blue Helmets escort, who led us all the way to the plane that would take us to Zagreb. The day after, I flew to Paris, still under the strong impression my visit to a devastated Sarajevo had caused me. I was the guest of the writer Bernard Henri-Levy, with whom I had struck a good friendship the year before thanks to our shared commitment to the cause of freedom. We had met at the premiere of his film *The Death of Sarajevo,* invited by my best French friend Jean-Luc Lagardère, one of the most prominent businessmen of his country. At his request, a digital copy of the film was to make its way to the White House thanks to Madeleine Albright, to whom I sent a small note asking her to have it delivered to President Clinton, if necessary, "through a crack in a window of the White House." To my surprise, a few days after I received a note by President Clinton in which he said that Bernard Henri-Levy's film had made it to his hands, not through a crack in a window, but through the front door of the White House, and that he "had to admit that watching it had caused him a strong impression."

In Paris, on the same day of my arrival, I was interviewed by Henri-Levy. We talked about another film he was then making, to be named *"Bosna!"* which he hoped would become a *"Cri du Coeur"* about the massacre of Sarajevo's civilian population since the beginning of the war in April. The film recounts in real time the genocide suffered by the Bosnians, as well as the West's indifference and, most importantly, the Bosnian determination not to surrender.

My interview for the film focused on my experience as coordinator of the Security Council mission to Bosnia. The film would also include interviews with General Philippe Morillon and the director of the Sarajevo morgue.

By day's end, I joined a rally in support of Bosnia, organized by Henri-Levy in front of the Quai d'Orsay, the French Ministry of Foreign Affairs, to protest Europe's passivity over that conflict and, forgetting my high diplomatic status, I even gave a short speech in support of the denunciation. From there the rally moved to the French National Assembly to convey the same message. To have taken part in these events on the eve of my return to New York made me enormously proud.

The Reckoning

When I returned to New York on August 21, I was met with an official note signed by General Fernando Ochoa Antich, Minister of Foreign Affairs of Venezuela, notifying me I had been relieved of my post as Ambassador of Venezuela to the United Nations, effective on the 30 of that same month of August.

The news did not surprise me. We had drifted apart since June 4, when the Council passed Resolution 836 on the Safe Areas. The minister had repeatedly called me while the session was on, and I had chosen not to take his calls. I had been informed, a few minutes before, that Ochoa was in a meeting with the ambassadors to Venezuela of the United Kingdom and France, and I feared they were there to put pressure on the minister to change our vote on the issue. The minister had sent word, in no uncertain terms, that Venezuela should vote in favor of the Resolution, never mind it made a mockery of the conditions a safe area should meet in accordance with the guidelines defined by the UN Secretariat and the UN High Commissioner for Refugees.

By refusing to take the minister's calls, I was able to abstain in the vote and not incur in open "insubordination." In this way I spared Venezuela the shame of giving its vote in favor of a resolution that, to this day, is considered to be the most irresponsible ever adopted by the Security Council. Given the minister's professional background, I knew I would be relieved from my post sooner than later. I could not imagine, however, that this would come to pass just a few days before I was to become once more president of the Council.

With time I have come to understand that my call back home was prompted, not so much by a general's annoyance with an ambassador, but rather by the need to ensure that I did not continue to defend, in the name of Venezuela, the right of the Bosnian people and government to their self-defense. My minister-general had no qualms about separating me from my position in order to satisfy the interests of the French and

British, which I had strongly confronted in the Security Council. My views had been fully shared by President Carlos Andrés Pérez, who had a clear understanding of the values of democracy and of his international responsibilities as head of a UN member state. Once President Pérez was no longer in power, I lost that critical support. From then on, Venezuela's positions would be aligned with the national interests of the Permanent Members of the Council. In *Quiet Diplomacy*, his memoirs as a lifelong Pakistani diplomat, Jamsheed Marker notes how after my replacement Venezuela ceased to play a similarly active role within the Non-Aligned Caucus in the Security Council. All the above also explains why I was the only ambassador Ochoa Antich replaced during the seven-months long transition presided over by Ramón J. Velásquez.

My Assignment at the United Nations Ends

In just a few days, I would leave the United Nations. I would, however, always remain committed to the causes I had supported and had been fully engaged with in the General Assembly and in the Security Council. Among these, the sequels of the First Gulf War, the peace process in El Salvador, the sanctions on Libya for its role in sponsoring international terrorism, the Security Council Summit of Heads of State and Government, nuclear disarmament, the fight against drug trafficking, decolonization and the Malvinas and Puerto Rico cases, peace in Cambodia, sanctions on Iraq, the situation in Palestine, the international intervention in Somalia, the debate on the Permanent Members of the Council's veto right, the International Court of Justice, the cases of crimes against humanity committed in Bosnia and Herzegovina, the reinstatement of democracy in Haiti, the conflicts between Azerbaijan - Armenia - Nagorno-Karabakh, UNICEF, North Korea's denunciation of the Non Proliferation of Nuclear Weapons, the peace processes in Angola and Mozambique, the growing challenges in the fields of economic development, international cooperation, and technology, the situation of human rights in Cuba and in Iran, the Earth Summit in Rio de

Janeiro, the establishment of the International Criminal Tribunal for the Former Yugoslavia, the end of apartheid in South Africa, the development and consolidation of what came to be known as the Arria Formula and, of course, the exceptional experience of presiding over the Security Council.

They had been two years of an exceptionally intense activity and I must acknowledge my satisfaction at having had the opportunity to take part in the intricate doings of international affairs. My time in the United Nations had allowed me to accumulate a wealth of extraordinary experiences. And so, notwithstanding the impact my cessation had on me, on that same afternoon I attended the informal Council session where Thorwald Stoltenberg was scheduled to present what everybody now called "the Geneva Package", a plan both he and Owen proposed and drafted to satisfy the Croatian and Serbian governments' requirements, with the complicit indifference of the so-called P5.

In that "informal" meeting, Stoltenberg reiterated the arguments both mediators had been using throughout the last few months. Assured of the support of a large part of the international community, they continued to present their peace plan as "the only possible option to end the war in Bosnia." At the Non-Aligned Caucus we had decided not to confront Stoltenberg and to support whatever position the Bosnian government presided by Izetbegovic, the true victim of the conflict, decided to take. Next day, the Council would pass a new resolution knowing full well that it would not help to bring the negotiations in Geneva to a happy conclusion nor end the war.

The Security Council Stays Complicit

Ever since January 3, 1992, when I first ventured into the Security Council hall, I was acutely aware that decisions by the Council had an impact on issues of capital importance for international peace and security. That made me highly sensitive to the weight carried by everything one said and by how one voted, since one represented one's own country. Never in the course of those two very intense years did I stop feeling a profound commitment and emotion in the discharge of my duties as ambassador of Venezuela to the United Nations.

I keep a very special and fresh recollection of the June 4, 1993, session of the Council, when I took the floor to announce that Venezuela would abstain on Resolution 836, since its purpose was to leave aside the international community's obligation to protect both the territorial integrity and human rights in any of its member states, an obligation that had led to the designation as safe areas of those areas where the civilian population lived under highly dangerous conditions. That session sealed my fate as Permanent Representative of Venezuela to the United Nations. But I felt pleased to have done what needed to be done, as the tragic events in Srebrenica proved two years later, in 1995, when Bosnian Serb troops, under General Mladic's command, murdered in cold blood more than eight thousand men and children for the sole reason of being Muslim. It was a genocide that found its origins in the Security Council's continued refusal to act in accordance with Chapter VII of the UN Charter and adopt coercive measures, including military action, to keep or restore peace. It had done so when it authorized a multinational military force to confront Saddam Hussein's troops in occupied Kuwait. Yet, that was precisely what the Council refused to do in any of the long string of resolutions it adopted on the situation in Bosnia, even while it recognized and demanded, over and over again, respect for the territorial integrity and political independence of the Republic of Bosnia and Herzegovina.

True enough, Resolution 859, of August 24, 1993, approved after my return from Sarajevo, represented an unmitigated condemnation of the war crimes and violations of international humanitarian law committed in Bosnia, and reiterated "The profound concern of the Council in face of the deteriorating humanitarian situation in that republic, especially as a consequence of the siege that Sarajevo, Mostar and other cities are under". It also declared that the annexation of territory by force of arms and the conduct of the abhorrent policy of ethnic cleansing were unacceptable, and that all those involved in war crimes would be held personally responsible and placed on trial at the newly established tribunal for Yugoslavia in The Hague. The resolution even stated that any change to the name or to the way the Republic of Bosnia and Herzegovina was organized, that might affect its UN Member State condition, would not be accepted. Sarajevo was recognized as its legitimate capital and its multicultural, multiethnic, and multi-confessional character could not be altered in any way by anyone. However, the resolution went no further than exhorting the parties in conflict to cooperate with the Owen-Stoltenberg duo, endorsed as mediators in the negotiations taking place in Geneva, in order to "Conclude as soon as possible with the adoption of a politically just and fair agreement."

Whoever takes time to read the full text of the resolution will be surprised by the ability of its drafters to hide the profound discrepancies between the goals the Council purported to pursue and the proven lack of will on the part of its more powerful members to do what had to be done to ensure all commitments to the values and principles of the Charter and international justice were honored. For them, the priority was to sign a peace agreement without delay, and to preclude the option of an international military intervention, even if it was fully justified in order to guarantee the territorial integrity of Bosnia and its sovereignty.

By now it was obvious that both the Security Council and the UN Secretariat managed the crisis in Bosnia without much regard to the Organization's fundamental political and ethical values. In the real world, to divide a sovereign nation into pieces and give the larger part of its territory to its aggressors almost as a reward may also qualify as a crime against humanity. Even more so if condemnations are followed by inaction. For Bosnia, it was as if the organization simply did the contrary to what it said. The purpose of the arms embargo was, from the very beginning, to make sure Bosnia did not have the means to defend itself from foreign invasions. As a result of such a contradiction, the many resolutions passed by the Council had only served to prolong the conflict until the stage was set for Resolution 859, centered on making the Bosnian government accept a peace plan based on its enemies' demands. This was so much so that in one of its most offensive sections, the resolution states that the agreement's purpose was to find "a just and equitable solution," which it does not define, thereby taking for granted, by its very ambiguity, the annexation of Bosnian territory by force and the ethnic cleansing practiced.

Cynicism and Impudence

Before opening the final round of interventions on the resolution, Ambassador Albright announced that the Permanent Representative of Bosnia and Herzegovina, Ambassador Muhamed Sacirbey, had requested to take part in the debate, and that she would give him the floor without the right to take part in the vote. At the center of the Council's attention, my good friend Sacirbey started by thanking Venezuela and, in particular, myself, for our efforts to bring justice and peace to Bosnia. He used the same terms he had used in the letter he had sent that morning to President Ramón J. Velásquez, "Venezuela has become the international conscience's voice on the crisis in the Former Yugoslavia, and Diego Arria, its Ambassador to the United Nations, has strengthened its leadership in the promotion of the rights of the Republic of Bosnia and Herzegovina, and in the reestablishment of a state of law and justice". He then added, "Without Venezuela's leadership in the Security Council, Bosnia would be in a very worse situation. Ambassador Arria's leadership in the case of Bosnia has made it possible for many countries, from East, West, North and South, Muslim and Christian, to come together, leaving aside all considerations of a political nature, and adopt a common position in the defense of international justice and human rights. As Bosnians, we are saddened and, frankly speaking, concerned, by his replacement in the Security Council, and by such replacement taking place in a most critical moment for my country's destiny. All Bosnians would feel much more at ease to see Ambassador Arria once more as president of the Security Council."

He then broached the issue at hand. "The draft resolution to be shortly put to a vote has a special importance for us because it underlines the need to restart in Geneva the talks that may allow us to reach in a peaceful manner a stable and just peace. For this to be so, the Council must make sure that Owen and Stoltenberg include that condition in the agenda of the negotiations. I say so because the first objective of the agreement must be the cessation of the crimes committed by the Serbian aggressors in the name of a supposed ethnic purity in the occupied Bosnian territories, among others, the rape of more than twenty thousand Bosnian Muslim and Croat women, practiced as a policy, to fertilize them and, as the perpetrators proclaim, produce Serbian children. To make sure this practice was even more humiliating, they told their victims that they would remain kidnapped until their pregnancy was sufficiently advanced, and they could no longer have an abortion without risking their lives." Sacirbey insisted that these and other similar crimes against humanity would continue to be committed in Bosnia until it was insured the negotiations would bring a just and equitable solution to the crisis.

The Ambassador of Djibouti, Roble Olhaye, then took the floor. "Once again, the world is witness to another attempt to make the unfortunate Republic of Bosnia and Herzegovina accept what in reality is simply an ultimatum disguised as a peace plan. It comes adorned with a map of scattered bits and pieces, in what amounts to a grievous acknowledgment that violence and aggression pay well. The most grotesque part of this peace proposal is its almost inexistent reference to the many lofty ideals and values reiterated in every resolution on Bosnia passed by this Council. We have tolerated every kind of atrocity, including ethnic cleansing. The international community's indifference leads us to believe that what is wanted is that Bosnia cease to exist as an independent and sovereign nation. The negotiations in Geneva simply mask that objective and condemn the Muslim population to death or exile. And while we discuss what fate awaits them, Sarajevo, Mostar, Zepa, Srebrenica and other towns and villages die. It is a tragedy that puts Izetbegovic under the obligation to negotiate what might be the closing chapter in one of the worse hoaxes of our time."

We all remained under the shock produced by these words. Then Ambassador Marker, of Pakistan, added: "The Non-Aligned members of the Council insist on the urgent need to acknowledge this state of affairs, because during the past eighteen months Bosnia, notwithstanding it is a United Nations member state, has been and continues to be savagely attacked and mutilated, as the world had not seen since the end of the Second World War."

It fell on the ambassadors of the United Kingdom and France, Richardson and Jean-Bernard Mérimée, to respond to these three strong interventions. The French ambassador argued: "We are on the eve of a crowning moment in this history. Either reason prevails and the Geneva agreement makes true the wish for peace, or the irresponsible extremism of the few prevails." Mérimée, no doubt to avoid responding to those serious accusations, preferred to shift the blame onto the Non-Aligned, accusing us of obstructionism and of an "irresponsible extremism" by not endorsing the Owen-Stoltenberg proposals. Richardson, on his turn, referred to Stoltenberg's presentation during the informal consultations held the day before and repeated the argument that "if any of the parties rejects the map included in the package, it would only be fostering the continuation of the war, since the proposal was the only alternative to war." He then added that his government would "only accept an agreement that is freely approved by all the parties," an obviously cynical statement since to argue that there was no alternative to the Owen-Stoltenberg proposal meant that the so-called peace plan was nothing more than a maneuver to try to make the Serbian and Croat strategy prevail. Indeed, Richardson went on to say: "Owen and Stoltenberg have made every possible effort in their struggle for peace in Bosnia. They are the ones dealing with the parties on a daily basis, trying to have them reach an agreement. For that simple reason, they deserve our recognition and respect."

The idea that a rejection of the proposal ment choosing war was how France and the United Kingdom chose to put pressure on the Bosnian government. It was their tortuous way of conveying to the Serbian and Croat aggressors the notion that the best way to avoid a possible international intervention in the conflict was to keep alive the Geneva negotiations. All the considerations, exhortations and demands included in Resolution 859 were in reality nothing more than embellishments to sweeten the decision to put the legitimate Bosnian government against the wall. Either it signed the agreement as it stood, or Bosnia would be annihilated by its enemies. That was the twisted way in which the Council had come to understand its "primordial duty" under the Charter to preserve peace and international security. Plain cynicism and effrontery.

My Last Intervention in the Security Council

I took the floor before the debate closed. It was my last intervention in the Security Council, and I started by denouncing the fact that the Non-Permanent Members of the Council had had absolutely no contact with Stoltenberg until we met him the previous afternoon in the informal consultations, one of the ways the P5 used to keep the process under their control. It was also for that reason that Boutros-Ghali had kept us on the outskirts of the negotiations for as long as possible. Therefore, I felt that the Council needed to be reminded that ever since the Carrington-Cutileiro negotiations started, Bosnia's tragedy had served as the steppingstone for Serbia towards its dream of a Greater Serbia. I added that Owen and Stoltenberg, instead of discharging their responsibilities as mediators, had taken upon themselves to foster the implementation of a plan of racial and religious domination conceived by Milosevic, Tudjman, Karadzic, and Boban, the quartet of aggressors. I concluded that the resolution to be put to a vote would not help at all to reach a "just and equitable" agreement between the parties, but rather exactly the opposite. What it did pursue was to ensure the Council´s endorsement of the life-or-death ultimatum the Serb and Croat aggressors were giving to their Bosnian victims.

— If we give our support to the Owen-Stoltenberg plan, Bosnia will most certainly pay the very steep price of losing its independence by choosing not to die trying to defend its legitimate right to be a sovereign nation. However, the international community will pay a much dearer price in political and ethical terms, even if such things do not seem to be of concern to those in a position to do justice by a defenseless member of the United Nations.

"How is it possible, I asked, that the Council chooses to entrench itself behind a wall of indifference and not acknowledge the upsurge in violence by Serbs and Croats? How can it accept to offer Bosnia's legitimate authorities a proposal based on the brutish policy of ethnic cleansing? Is that the reason Owen had tried to save his plan with the argument that, even if it might suffer from a few legal deficiencies, its goal is to end a seventeen-months long bloody war? Can this Council take decisions outside the realm of the law and not abide by the principles of the Charter? I do not believe that to be the case, and I will always continue to do so."

I made a pause before going ahead with my remarks. "I wish to make it clear that my delegation is under no doubt that allowing the aggressors to get away with it in Bosnia will degrade us all as members of the Security Council, but particularly its Permanent Members. We have tried to highlight the wrongs about to be righted by the Geneva agreements, but everything points in the direction that it might already be too late to avoid it. I must however insist that the Council cannot admit the use of force as a source of law. If we do, then the members of this body will be in part guilty of the consequences this unforgivable mistake will have."

The fact that neither the Owen-Stoltenberg "package" nor the draft resolution about to be approved made any reference to the International Tribunal for the Former Yugoslavia, established, precisely, to deal with the serious and notorious human rights violations that were taking place in the Balkans, was foremost in my mind. That was why, before concluding, I stressed: "If we wish to bring peace to Bosnia, and make it lasting, we must first of all acknowledge what gives the Tribunal its reason to be and its importance. The credibility of the Council rests on the Tribunal beginning to operate immediately to discharge its responsibilities."

I expressly brought up the ITFY because it was by then quite evident that neither the UN Secretary General, nor the Council, wanted such a critical legal institution to begin operating before the Geneva negotiations had concluded. I was convinced the Tribunal's exclusion from the Geneva talks was to insure that "not a single Serbian be extradited to be judged by that tribunal" as Radovan Karadzic asserted in a private talk with Owen held on November of that year. As future events would prove, the aggressors underestimated the Tribunal's determination to fulfill its mandate, while overestimating their own impunity in committing war crimes.

As I begun to draw my remarks to a close, I purposely made mine the accusation voiced in those days by George Zarycky, Executive Director of Freedom House, who had said: "Bosnia is a horrible lesson. Moral evasions, when they eclipse our ability to see and respond to evil, will undermine our values and our fundamental beliefs at a time when the world is shrinking and so many are looking to the West for leadership." As it was my last intervention in the Council as ambassador of Venezuela, I took the opportunity to say my farewells, and to put on record that: "I have discharged my duties under circumstances that, I believe, have been extremely difficult and compromising. I have endeavored to be of service to the international community and uphold my responsibilities as a member of the Council. To be Venezuela's Representative to the Security Council has been my greatest pride as a public figure. I am immensely grateful to President Carlos Andrés Pérez for giving me this privileged opportunity, and wish to tell you, distinguished colleagues and friends, that I cannot leave without sharing with you what I believe to be the implications of our decisions, and emphasize that my hope is that tomorrow, when contemplating the devastation and remains of what used to be the peaceful nation of Bosnia and Herzegovina, we will not be obliged to recall Shakespeare's lamentation in Henry V when after the battle of Agincourt he said: "Shame and eternal shame, nothing but shame."

The Tragedy's Thankless End Approaches

The day after this session of the Council, a meeting of the Non-Aligned Caucus was convened by Ahmed Snoussi, Ambassador of Morocco, to agree on our next steps. We did not want the false impression to prevail that the resolution had been adopted by unanimity without objections on our part. During the debate, the Permanent Members had abused the argument that the war and the extermination of the Bosnian Muslim population would continue unheeded if the Izetbegovic government did not sign on to the agreement. It was their way to corner President Izetbegovic and those who supported him, and to accuse us as enemies of peace and promoters of division within the Council.

Not long ago, I revisited David Owen's memoirs, published in 1995, and I still fail to understand why, after the initial efforts he made, joined first by Cyrus Vance and afterwards by Thorwald Stoltenberg, he surrendered to pressure and left the final stages of the negotiations in the hands of Milosevic and Tudjman. It is also noteworthy that Owen, in the many references he makes to the reports he systematically sent to the European Union and to many Heads of State and Government, could not hide the fact that France and the United Kingdom led the negotiations, and did so guided by their national interests. The Security Council was in fact just a fig leaf on that reality and on the complicity of the Secretary General and the P5. This jealously manipulated strategy required that the Non-Aligned members of the Council be kept far from the orchestra playing the tunes, in a party that had to last as long as needed. Even if this reality had become painfully evident since the very first debates on the safe areas and on economic sanctions, it would be from April 1993 onwards that it became of critical relevance during the Council's informal consultations. Even from the outside, the game of shadows played by the Council became obvious, forcing the Dutch Hans van den Broek, European Commissioner for Foreign Affairs, to accuse Owen and Stoltenberg of fostering an unacceptable policy of appeasement and non-resistance towards the Serbian and Croat aggression.

Five days later, on August 29, the Bosnian parliament, with a Muslim majority, finally voted to reject the "Geneva package". The vote was 75 to 0, and it thereby gave implicit approval to the continuation of the war for as long as it took. The Bosnian Serb leader, Radovan Karadzic, had already threatened of new attacks inside Bosnia unless the parliament approved the Owen-Stoltenberg plan. President Izetbegovic had warned parliament that Bosnia should not expect any saving intervention by the United States. "The United States is with us – he said – but will not send a single soldier to defend us. We should not forget that the Serb military has deployed a thousand tanks in Bosnia, and that if we fail to quickly find a political solution to the conflict, Bosnia will be destroyed." That even under such a terrible admonition, all the seventy-five members of parliament would oppose the signing of the Geneva Agreement, was unmistakable evidence of the will of Bosnia and Herzegovina to fight to the death for its sovereignty.

When news of the vote reached him, Franjo Tudjman, President of Croatia, declared that the war would continue without any respite. Owen, in turn, declared that even if the Geneva proposal did not satisfy every expectation, reality being what it was, it was the best option the Bosnian government and population had, adding that it would not be on the table for long. The alternative would be "The country's fragmentation, the rule of anarchy, the resurgence of chieftains, and overall chaos."

A week later, on November 7, President Izetbegovic met with President Clinton at the White House. He did so in the hope that the United States would lend Bosnia, whose cause had been buried in Geneva, support that went beyond rhetoric and, in particular, set a deadline for the Serbians to lift the asphyxiating siege of Sarajevo, already in its eighteenth month. Clinton´s answer was that there was nothing he could do without the support of the other four permanent members of the Council and suggested that Izetbegovic "Should return to the negotiating table in Geneva and try to reach the best possible agreement."

Izetbegovic did not make any statements after his meeting with Clinton. He did not expect to be so rebuffed. The following day, he received me in his room at the Roger Smith Hotel in Manhattan, where he had just arrived, in the company of Ejup Ganic, his Vice President, and his ambassador to the United Nations, all of them absolutely surprised by President Clinton´s turnaround. Ganic said it had felt like "a bucket of cold water", and that it was "a turnaround in US policy that leaves Bosnia on the other side of the street in relation to Clinton." Izetbegovic, on the other hand, felt that not everything was lost, and that the meetings he had held with Members of Congress allowed him to still hold on to some hope, a hope neither Ganic nor Ambassador Sacirbey shared. They did agree on the need to manage the situation with utmost care, and to try not to damage in any way whatsoever the future of relations with the United States. First of all, because good relations with the US would always be a dissuasive force for the Serbs and Croats and second, because they knew that if the siege of Sarajevo continued to worsen, they could only rely on the US for help.

A few hours later, invited by Jamsheed Marker, Ambassador of Pakistan, President Izetbegovic took part in an informal session of the Council convened under a modality I had first established in March 1992, that would come to be known from 1994 until today, as the "Arria Formula". It was the first time that a Head of State from a country at war came to the Council. He took advantage of it to warn its members about the consequences of the international community's passivity in the face of what was happening in Bosnia.

— I am under the impression – he said – that no one in this room is in a position to impose compliance with Security Council resolutions, and that neither is there any one to impede it. If the Council is not willing to enforce its own resolutions, it must then lift the arms embargo that so seriously hampers the exercise of our right to self-defense. In other words, either you defend us, or you allow us to defend ourselves, because you do not have the right to deprive us of both options at the same time. You have even less the right to force on us an unacceptable so-called peace plan, that in essence legitimizes genocide and promotes the ethnic partition of Bosnia, a disaster that will ignite blind violence and a ferocious desire for revenge. Any peace plan that does not address the causes of war will only allow, in the best of circumstances, for a temporary cessation of hostilities but not for a real solution to the conflict. This Council cannot continue to ignore that one of the parties, Bosnia, is the sole victim in this war of extermination.

Izetbegovic's words were met with silence, prompting Ambassador Albright, President of the Council, and visibly moved, to ask "Does anyone have anything to say?"

THE PRICE OF PEACE

On August 10,1995, two years after the frustrating Security Council meeting of June 4 and my untimely departure from the United Nations, as I left the Council on Foreign Relations in New York, where I was a *Diplomatic Fellow,* I watched a shocking report on CNN: Madeleine Albright, who was still the US Permanent Representative, had shown the Security Council, meeting in informal session, three aerial photographs taken by an American U2 aircraft of what looked like vast land movements at the outskirts of Srebrenica. According to Albright these were huge pits the Serbian military had used to bury the remains of more than eight thousand Bosnian Muslim men and teenagers, murdered in cold blood by orders of General Ratko Mladic.

The pictures, and Ambassador Albright's comments, made headlines all over the world, causing much impact on the public at large. I, on the other hand, was not surprised as already in 1993, I had publicly called attention to developments in Srebrenica. My reaction was therefore one of indignation, rage and sorrow. At the time, very few political or diplomatic leaders had paid any attention. Now they all feigned outrage while at the same time they tried to turn a crime against humanity into just a current incident. No matter how one may wish to look at it, the genocide perpetrated in Srebrenica was clearly foreseeable. Upon learning it had indeed happened, I could only think about its people. We had promised them protection in the name of the United Nations and now they lied buried in common graves.

The pictures would forever record the shocking reality of a genocide but, for me, they were even more scandalous from an ethical perspective. Particularly so because what happened was a direct consequence of the appeasement policy followed by the Permanent Members of the Security Council and the United Nations Secretariat. Such policy resulted in the abandonment of Srebrenica's fate and that of other Safe Areas in the eastern part of Bosnia into the hands of their Serbian aggressors. Many inconsequential Resolutions with no impact at all on the search for an end to the conflict and countless rhetorical statements to the press were employed to try to hide the responsibilities incurred.

The Serbian Invasion and Occupation of Srebrenica

The undeniable reality is that ever since the first peace plans were drafted, back in 1992, and up to the November 1995 Dayton Agreements, the core issue behind the political conflict, the hostilities and the negotiations was the ethnic partition of Bosnia-Herzegovina, and how to prevent its people, predominantly Muslim, from creating a Muslim State in the heart of Europe. Equally undeniable is the role played by the Non-Aligned Caucus in the Security Council, of which Venezuela was a member. Had we not tried to safeguard the young republic's sovereign rights and its people's human rights, in spite of the objections we faced from within the Security Council and the failings of the United Nations, Bosnia-Herzegovina would have probably ceased to exist as an independent nation and its people would have been totally bereft of protection.

The outrageous double standard followed by the Security Council and the European governments in dealing with the republics of the Former Yugoslavia made them accomplices to the sinister ethnic extermination policy practiced by the Serbs. Had the international community displayed a minimum of resolve, it could have stopped from the very beginning the brutal Serbian aggression from escalating to genocide, with Srebrenica as its final episode. Something could have been done to stop the concentration of troops and heavy weapons around Srebrenica before General Mladic ordered the takeover of the UNPROFOR observation post on the outskirts of Srebrenica on July 6, 1995. It was the UN forces' passive stance that conveyed to the Serbian aggressors the clear message that the Blue Helmets would not act, not even to protect their own.

The highest responsibility for what happened on that occasion falls on General Bernard Janvier, Commander General of UNPROFOR, who did not authorize the aerial attack on the Serbian heavy artillery and on the troops concentrating around Srebrenica, as had been already agreed by NATO. The concentration of troops and weapons was obviously in preparation for an assault on Srebrenica, which finally took place on July 9, without armed opposition of any kind. General Janvier cynically justified his decision by arguing that Thomas Karremans, Commander of the Dutch battalion deployed in Srebrenica and its surroundings, could repel any Serbian attack without aerial support, something he knew full well amounted to a suicide mission.

The French general's decision made it possible for General Mladic's battalions to enter triumphantly into Srebrenica, unobstructed by any kind of military resistance. During the following three days, Mladic, empowered as never before, took it upon himself to carry out Karadzic's July 1993 threat that rivers of blood would flow on the streets of Srebrenica should it ever fall into his possession. That was exactly what came to happen, as later excavations of burial pits revealed the dismembered remains of countless victims. The victims of that shameful massacre were the Muslims who had sought refuge and protection at the Blue Helmets' barracks at Potocari. They were kidnapped by the Serbian soldiers and then murdered in cold blood in an orgy of hate. It was a tragedy that could have been avoided had the international community acted in a timely manner. Srebrenica's premeditated rendition marked the beginning of the end for the war in Bosnia. It would become formal a few months later with the peace agreement signed in Dayton, but at the high price of allowing the Serbian and Croat aggressors to retain almost two thirds of Bosnia's territory.

The International Community's Complicity

One cannot fail to wonder why the United States waited until August 10, 1995, to reveal the magnitude of this crime against humanity, a massacre witnessed in real time by the CIA through satellites keeping watch over the war in Bosnia's most critically important areas. The images were never officially made public, but they were certainly leaked. They show civilian prisoners murdered by Mladic's troops and then thrown into huge, hastily dug common graves. Such deeds were confirmed in June 1995 by Jovica Stanisic, Head of Milosevic's Serbian Intelligence Service, also a CIA agent, later condemned to twelve years imprisonment, in his statements to the International Court at The Hague.

The date to leak the images and the news was not chosen at random. On the contrary, the American planners made it coincide with the visit to London by Anthony Lake, National Security Advisor in the Clinton Administration, charged with meeting the representatives of the British and French governments to give a final revision to the new, Washington-made, peace plan for Bosnia. The plan, although seriously flawed, would serve as the basis for the peace agreement signed later at the Wright-Patterson US Air Force Base, at the outskirts of Dayton, Ohio.

In the meantime, on July 11 of that year, Boutros-Ghali, displaying his astonishing indifference towards the situation in Bosnia, declared to the BBC: "(The Serbian occupation of the Srebrenica Safe Area) is a humiliation, but we'll just have to live with it", immediately adding, as if to lessen its importance, "In a few days it will all be in the past". Yasushi Akashi, who at the time was the Secretary General's Personal Representative in Bosnia, speaking two days later from Dubrovnik where he was on vacation during those dismal days, reacting to the persistent rumors about war crimes committed by Mladic's men in Srebrenica, told Kofi Annan on July 13 that "He was not aware that Srebrenica's civilian population was mistreated by General Mladic's men but rather - according to his information - that they had given sweets to the children and cigarettes to the adults". The truth, according to Akashi, was that the Serbs had evacuated thousands of civilian refugees up to then considered to be missing persons, and his conclusion was that the United Nations did not have to fear any international reproach since "UNPROFOR's vehicles had not been used" in that operation. Akashi came to acknowledge that there was cause for concern only some days later when, on July 19, he received a communication from Annan, worried about reports of atrocities committed by Serbian troops in occupied Srebrenica. Akashi admitted that at that time the estimated number of disappeared persons ranged "between four and eight thousand civilians."

Kofi Annan's increased worries were prompted by a July 17 report by Robert Block for the London newspaper *The Independent.* Block relayed information included in an audiovisual report on the atrocities aired by a Belgrade TV station "That made your blood freeze in your veins." Block told how the Serbian TV commentator pointed out that what at first sight appeared to be sacks, randomly piled up along a bullet-sprayed wall "Were bodies, not bundles." To begin to fathom the meaning of this atrocity, it is worth recalling the moving statement made by Mevludin Oric, one of the very few survivors of the massacre. He told the American investigators that were trying to reconstruct what had happened, that the Serbian soldiers "Had them stand in lines of about twenty to twenty-five individuals and, after executing them, dealt with the following line… When my turn came, I fell to the ground and hid among the bodies of the dead falling all around me. I lay there for the rest of the day and at nightfall I managed to slip away."

Kofi Annan's Report on the Srebrenica Genocide

Years after, Kofi Annan, by then the seventh UN Secretary General, presented to the General Assembly, at its request, a report on Srebrenica. In his report, titled *"The Fall of Srebrenica"*, dated November 15, 1999, Annan argues that "The main reason for the Secretariat's failure to act as decisively as the situation required was its miscomprehension of the Serbs' true war aims. Because of this, UNPROFOR was not able to perform its duties in defense of Srebrenica, a town whose Bosnian Muslim population was under threat of mass extermination." On the next day, *The Washington Post* observed that the Annan report – one hundred and fifty-five pages long, including classified UN documents and interviews with more than one hundred UN officials - showed that "The United Nations, by following a policy of appeasement had unwittingly contributed" to making the Srebrenica genocide possible. However, this appeasement was not, as Annan states, an unintentional mistake, since after a brutal four years Serbian aggression, it can hardly be argued that it was difficult to ascertain the true aim of the Serbian military.

Such arguments cannot justify the position adopted by the Security Council and they completely invalidate the Annan report, including the title it carries, since what really happened was not simply "the fall" of Srebrenica as a consequence of mistakes and misunderstandings, but the failure of the Security Council to discharge its institutional duties. The Council chose to deny the possibility of a Muslim republic, as was the wish of the majority of Bosnia's population and bowed instead to the interests of three of its permanent members, even though that implied the territorial division of that independent republic and, by implication, the green light to a perverse system of ethnic cleansing in the very heart of Europe.

A number of officials and personalities who, in one way or another, had had something to do with the situation in Bosnia, received an advanced copy of the report before it was made public. I naturally read it with utmost attention, particularly because it acknowledged the mistakes the Organization had made and even criticized its performance. It was an unprecedent initiative. Never before had a UN Secretary General publicly acknowledged faults and mistakes in managing a situation as complex and delicate as that was. However, it was also the least he could do to justify before the

General Assembly and international public opinion the inappropriate behavior by the Secretariat and the UN Security Council throughout the almost four years of the war, ending with the atrocious massacre of civilians in Srebrenica. It was undoubtedly important for the Secretary General to be accountable to the General Assembly, even if I doubted the objectivity of Kofi Annan's conclusions. Maybe it was too much to ask that those responsible for that nefarious policy of appeasement openly confess their misdeeds and to pass judgment, even if indirectly, on Boutros-Ghali, on Annan himself, and on the governments of the Permanent Members of the Security Council, mostly France and the United Kingdom. That was the reason all the grievous charges included in the report are of a general nature, and no individual responsibility is placed on any official or government. It was also the condition under which Annan accepted to draft a report of such an illuminating nature, as the American journalist and freelance writer James Traub reveals in his 2006 book *The Best Intentions: Kofi Annan*, on the power struggles inside the United Nations during his mandate as Secretary General.

The U.N. General Assembly Has its Say

A month later, on December 16, in keeping with this "diplomatic" understanding to avoid blaming anyone in particular for what happened in Bosnia, the UN General Assembly passed a resolution in which it welcomed the report "for its thoroughness and candor." The text of the resolution makes it plain that the Assembly did not debate on the report. Only ten out of ninety-three delegations took the floor, and none referred to those governments that could have done something to prevent the tragedy. Neither did any delegation point out that while the Dayton Agreements did indeed restore peace to the region, they did so at the expense of surrendering to Serbia and Croatia's inadmissible territorial demands, giving legitimacy to an undisguised apartheid regime in Bosnia. Three entities - Bosnian, Serbian and Croat -

now replaced the single independent, sovereign republic, recognized as such by the United Nations only five years before. The contradictions between the principles stated in every Security Council resolution and the Dayton Agreements simply indicate that the United Nations was not really committed to solving the issues at the heart of the crisis, and neither was the UN keen to assign responsibilities as to how the long-lasting conflict had been managed. The report's purpose was to turn the page on Bosnia and to start focusing attention elsewhere, for example, Kosovo, where Serbia had unleashed a new and very violent conflict, or Eastern Timor, where pro-independence sectors were facing strong opposition.

While on December 16, 1999, the General Assembly had reaffirmed the independence, sovereignty and territorial integrity of Bosnia and Herzegovina and the equality of its three constituent peoples, dwelling extensively on the Peace Agreement signed at Dayton and ratified in Paris on December 14, 1995, in the resolution it approved it mentions only in six lines the appalling magnitude of the human tragedy that occurred before and after "the fall of Srebrenica." This amounted to an exercise of collective complicity which did not go unnoticed. The Ambassador of Jordan to the UN, Prince Zeid Ra'ad Al Hussein, expressed his astonishment at the "candor" of a report that broke the silence that had prevailed throughout the many years the war had lasted, a silence that had the intention of erasing from the collective memory what had happened in Bosnia.

The EU representative considered the report to be honest and impartial, while the representative of Russia expressed his disagreement with how it assigned the greater share of responsibility to only one of the parties, the Serbians, and with how it highlighted the genocide in Srebrenica as it if were the only unfortunate episode in a war that saw many other atrocities. In the Russian representative's opinion, to open old wounds would only hinder the complex reconciliation process. In 2015, when the twentieth anniversary of the Dayton Accords was commemorated by the Security Council, the

Russian representative vetoed a statement to be issued by the Council because it reiterated that what happened in Srebrenica in July 1995 was a genocide.

In this tortuous way, an undeniable war crime was turned into a perfect crime thanks to the UN Secretariat's usual makeup skills. However, no matter how many times the Secretariat might have expressed its regrets, the cover up failed, and the Srebrenica tragedy will forever tarnish the United Nations' reputation.

David Harland and Ahmed Salman were two brilliant UN officials working on the "Annan Report", and in this context they sought my opinion. During our meeting they mentioned that after approval of Security Council Resolution 819 in April 1993, "Five of its members had the rare opportunity, to which there was no precedent, to ascertain on the ground the situation in Bosnia. They travelled as a delegation under the coordination of Diego Arria, Ambassador of Venezuela, and arrived in Srebrenica on April 25. At their return, they reported to the Council and gave a vision of the conflict quite different from the one prevailing within the Organization. On behalf of the Non-Aligned members of the Council, the Venezuelan ambassador took the opportunity to demand to know if the UN would or would not use force if the Serbs did not abide by the Council's mandates but did not receive a satisfactory answer. Arria was critical of the Council's position, indicating that it only had to "Take preventive measures, establish safe areas, conduct a rigorous border surveillance, strengthen the sanctions, establish a no-fly zone over Bosnia for military aircraft, and create an international criminal tribunal to sanction crimes against humanity committed during the war."

Harland and Salman also referred to my question as to whether the Permanent Members believed that with resolutions that did not go beyond rhetoric, they would be able to "convince the Serbian aggressors to graciously relinquish the territories they had conquered by force of arms." During my interview, I reiterated the proposals and denunciations on the situation in Bosnia I had made during my time in the Security Council, but they were not included in the report's conclusions, no doubt owing to their critical tone.

With the December 16, 1999, General Assembly resolution on the Situation in Bosnia and Herzegovina, the 193 members of the United Nations, without any explanation, agreed to ignore the relinquishing of Srebrenica and other safe areas to Serbian interests, and the dissolution of an independent, sovereign nation. According to Kofi Annan's report, what happened in Bosnia was not that the UN failed to discharge its most fundamental duties, but rather that it had suffered some kind of unintentional accident, and no one was to blame. In the end, in Dayton, the international community rewarded war criminals of the ilk of Milosevic, Karadzic and Mladic by granting them forty-nine percent of Bosnia's legitimate territory, as was their wish.

The Background to the Genocide Cover Up

The establishment of "safe areas" in Bosnia, to assist in immediately ending the systematic harassment and forced displacement of its civilian population, was proposed in August 1992 by Cornelio Sommaruga, at the time President of the International Committee of the Red Cross, during the London International Conference on the Former Yugoslavia. The Conference unanimously endorsed the proposal and included it in its final document. The members of the Non-Aligned Caucus in the Security Council took advantage of this circumstance to push for approval of the April 16, 1993, resolution that declared Srebrenica and surroundings a safe area. Unfortunately, this resolution would only serve to prove that the world powers had absolutely no intention to abide by their own mandates.

Indeed, that might have been just the reason they did not raise objections to our draft resolution. At the same time, however, the mediators on behalf of the UN and the EU, Cyrus Vance and David Owen, argued that the establishment of safe areas in Bosnia would only "promote an intensification of ethnic cleansing in those areas." The same observation, but from a military perspective, was made by the UNPROFOR High Command, which argued that the UN military forces deployed in Bosnia did not have the means to defend such "safe areas."

The Permanent Members' ambivalence regarding the safe areas issue became apparent on May 6, 1993, when the Council approved Resolution 824. Presented only a few days after our return from Belgrade, it "welcomed" our report, and in particular our recommendations concerning the treatment as safe areas of Sarajevo and the towns of Tuzla, Gorazde, Bihac, and Srebrenica. Years later I would learn that the UN Secretary General Boutros-Ghali, acting behind the back of the Council, instructed the Commander of UNPROFOR about the resolution's implementation, indicating that it did not "provide for the use of force to ensure its mandate is fulfilled." He did this notwithstanding the resolution was adopted under Chapter VII of the Charter, which provides for the use of force, and that it expressly required the adoption of "all measures necessary" to ensure its full implementation in relation to the security of those areas.

I have absolutely no doubt that Boutros-Ghali gave such instructions to the UN military commanders in Bosnia only after consulting the Permanent Representatives of the United Kingdom and France in the Council, since most of the UN troops deployed in Bosnia were British and French. On the other hand, everyone was aware that at the highest echelons of the Secretariat there was widespread opposition to the establishment of safe areas in Bosnia based on the belief that to do so would violate the Organization's neutrality, to my mind a very partial and immoral understanding of that concept.

As I write now about this sad business, I must quote Michael Dobbs, historian and journalist, Director of the Simon-Skjodt Center for the Prevention of Genocide. In his article for *Foreign Policy,* he states: "The Srebrenica genocide did not happen offhand, nor did it take anyone by surprise." In Dobbs view, the repeated violations of the most basic human rights in Bosnia by its Serbian aggressors since the conflict started should have alerted the international community, with ample time to take preventive action. Dobbs is adamant in pointing out that the Western governments chose not to take seriously the signs of what inevitably came to happen, and reminds us that Bill Clinton, in August 1992, while still a candidate to the presidency of his country, in reference to the crisis in Bosnia, held: "We cannot afford to ignore what seems to be the implementation of a policy of deliberate and systematic extermination of human beings based on their ethnic origins". And he additionally recalls that the first mention at the international level of what was happening in Srebrenica in April 1993 was made by "the international mission sent by the United Nations to Srebrenica, whose coordinator, Ambassador Diego Arria, of Venezuela, had denounced from Srebrenica that ′a slow-motion genocide′ was taking place over there." He concludes his considerations on the Security Council's unexplainable attitude by asking why nothing was done to prevent the tragedy given that as early as 1992 some credible observers had anticipated what came to happen in Srebrenica.

To this day, not one of the governments implicated in what I have called the UN's most gross cover-up, has offered a convincing reply to Dobbs' questions. To a considerable extent, this book responds to the need to clarify the reasons for such a disconcerting silence. Even though these events are now in the past, it is important to try to do so, if only to help ensure that similar crimes never take place again. Therefore, it is never too late, and particularly so given that those events happened under the watch of the United Nations. If the United Nations today is a much-diminished organization, it is so because the veto right enjoyed by the five Security Council Permanent Members prevents it from acting with independence when confronted with atrocities such as those committed in Bosnia.

That is why I found it relevant to examine what happened in Bosnia in detail, why it happened with absolute impunity, and to shed light on the network of sinister complicities woven in the Security Council that allowed the Secretariat and, to a greater extent, the governments of France and the United Kingdom with the cooperation of the United States and Russia, the power to decide the outcome of the crisis in Bosnia.

Regarding this conspiracy within the Security Council, one of the critical developments that needs clarification is why the UN Secretariat held back the very revealing exchange between Radovan Karadzic and Ratko Mladic, in which the latter received orders to "as soon as possible isolate the Bosnian enclaves of Srebrenica and Zepa and cut off their communications." The UN Secretariat equally silenced Karadzic's standing orders given on June 2, 1995, to "wipe out the Muslim defenders of Srebrenica and Zepa". That was exactly the criminal goal he had announced in Pale a year before in a speech to the Srpska parliament, when referring to the Bosnian Muslims, he vowed to "make all the Turks completely disappear." This exchange of mail and this speech prove beyond any doubt the real motivation behind the Serbian aggression on Bosnia and the Srebrenica genocide and make us wonder why Boutros-Ghali and the UN Secretariat's most senior officials, routinely chose to ignore the extreme, evil motivations of individuals such as Milosevic, Karadzic, and Mladic.

To roundup the overview of this perverse manipulation of the truth, it is useful to recall the May 24, 1995, correspondence that General Janvier sent to Boutros-Ghali, in which he informed him that UNPROFOR was not equipped nor had the manpower to defend the safe areas of Srebrenica, Zepa, and Gorazde. Why was it that neither the UN Secretary General, the United States, France, or the United Kingdom, did anything to try to remedy the situation in which the UN forces in Bosnia found themselves?

Maybe because once Bosnia had declared its independence it became more urgent to ensure the territorial fragmentation of the new Balkan republic than to enforce the Council's resolutions they themselves had approved. At least, that is what a recently declassified report by US intelligence agencies reveals. In a May 27, 1995, secret telephone call, the British

Prime Minister John Major, Presidents Bill Clinton and Jacques Chirac, agreed to immediately halt NATO air strikes against Serbian positions concentrated in the areas surrounding Srebrenica. Moreover, a "For Your Eyes Only" Memorandum addressed by Anthony Lake, US National Security Advisor, to President Clinton, recommends to keep the decision absolutely secret. "Privately, we may admit that we are temporarily halting Srebrenica's air defense, but we may not do so openly."

Alexander Vershbow, also a Clinton advisor, considered the military defense of Bosnia to be impossible, and therefore suggested reaching an agreement with Serbia by surrendering some small enclaves in Eastern Bosnia, such as Srebrenica, in exchange for allowing the Bosnian government to keep a significant part of its territory. These documents clearly point to an understanding among all three governments not to fight to save Srebrenica, and that what the UN and EU mediators, as well as the United States, really aimed at, was to reach a settlement where the Serbian and Croatian forceful occupation of two-thirds of Bosnia and Herzegovina would become legitimate, as would be the case in November, with the Peace Agreement signed at Dayton. The international community was indeed resolute to make peace, no matter at what price, to the detriment of an independent and sovereign republic.

Was the Srebrenica Genocide Impossible to Foresee?

To pretend that it was impossible to foresee what happened in Srebrenica in 1995 is absolutely unacceptable. By March 1993, Henri Jacolin, the French Ambassador to Bosnia, had fully briefed his government on the criminal methods used in Bosnia by General Mladic to wipe out the Muslim population. How is it possible that such a compromising report was not duly taken into consideration by the French military commanders active in the region? And how could Jean-Bernard Mérimée, former Representative of France to the Security Council in those turbulent days, state during the 2001 inquiry by the French National Assembly: "As a member of the

Security Council, I knew nothing about what happened in Srebrenica between July and August 1995"? It was such a surprising statement that the National Assembly was forced to conclude that "After hearing Ambassador Mérimée, we must ask ourselves if what happened was the consequence of incompetence by all the ambassadors to the Security Council, by Ambassador Mérimée, or of the pervasive apathy of the United Nations."

On July 9, in this murky environment of indifference, while the Serbian troops under General Mladic's command readied themselves to begin the massacre of thousands of defenseless civilians in Srebrenica, General Janvier held a meeting in the Croatian town of Split with the British General Rupert Smith, Commander of UNPROFOR in Sarajevo, and Yasushi Akashi, Personal Representative of the UN Secretary General in Bosnia. At the meeting he briefed them, as he already had Boutros-Ghali, on the advisability of "relinquishing the safe areas in Eastern Bosnia to the Serbian aggressors," based on the rather amazing reasoning that, for military professionals such as them "it was the best decision, even if he could also understand that the international community would not accept it."

Therefore, it was not by mere chance that a day after this meeting, the Indian Ambassador Chinmaya Gharekhan, the UN Secretary General's most trusted advisor in the Secretariat, "informed" the Council that "a group of Bosnian Muslims had attacked several UNPROFOR vehicles" in the streets of Srebrenica, something immediately denied by the Bosnian command. That day Gharekhan also went on to say that the Blue Helmets had the situation in Srebrenica "under control," even though by then it was common knowledge that General Mladic's troops were at the city gates and that there seemed to be no one willing to stop them. Where did Chinmaya Gharekhan get this information? Did he have his own sources, or did he act under instructions from Boutros-Ghali?

I knew Gharekhan well. We had been colleagues in the Security Council, and I am sure he did not act without consulting Boutros-Ghali or Kofi Annan. His intentional manipulation of the facts can indeed be presumed because as the Serbian battalions entered Srebrenica, General Janvier sent a note to General Mladic from his headquarters in Zagreb, expressing his concern about the security of his men, omitting any mention of the extremely serious situation of the so-called displaced, that is to say all the people of the enclave, later to be massacred. And why was it that out of the three days the massacre lasted, it was only on the second day that the Council came around to express its "profound concern" on the deteriorating situation and the hardships experienced by the civilian population? The statement issued by the Security Council underlined the need for the Serbian troops to "put a stop to the attack on Srebrenica and to withdraw from the enclave," although the Council knew perfectly well that both mandates were impossible to satisfy if they were not backed by a real and credible threat of the use of force.

On July 9, NATO fighters flew over Srebrenica at 6 am, ready to take out the Serbian positions in the outskirts of Srebrenica, but soon returned to their base in Aviano, Italy, when General Janvier denied authorization for the attack. Only when the Serbian occupation of the enclave had become evident, did Akashi inform that Janvier had finally approved the NATO airstrikes, and this only if Mladic's troops attacked UNPROFOR positions in Srebrenica and surroundings.

A Surrender in the Name of Peace

The undeniable truth is that thousands of Muslim adults and teenagers would have survived the genocide ordered by Mladic if Akashi and General Janvier had authorized the NATO airstrikes. They would have survived had the authorization been given on July 10 or even early on the following day, which was when Akashi informed Kofi Annan that he received a call from the German Minister of Foreign Affairs, Klaus Kinkel, informing him that the Dutch government demanded that all the military operations in Bosnia, conducted with their prior approval, now be immediately suspended.

On the night of July 12, after Srebrenica and its surrounding areas had been taken, Lieutenant Colonel Thom Karremans, Commander of the Dutch battalion entrusted with the defense of those enclaves, informed General Janvier and his Minister of Defense that he had met twice with General Mladic at the Fontana Hotel, at Bratunac, eleven kilometers from Potocari, and in both opportunities Mladic warned him that should NATO carry out airstrikes against his positions he would shell and obliterate the Dutch positions. Videos of the two encounters show closeups of Karremans' terror-stricken face as he hears Mladic's threat and of Mladic, later trying to calm him down, offering him a shot of *Rakia,* the Serbs' favorite liquor.

Karremans, in his report to Janvier and to his national authorities, justified his passivity and his fears with the well-worn argument that his battalion did not have the necessary means to defend the refugee civilians in Potocari, and expressed the opinion that the only way out of the situation was for the parties to engage in negotiations under UN mediation. He also called to their attention that two months earlier, on May 25, he had warned that the situation in that area had become so desperate that his mission no longer made sense as he was in no position to carry it out. The next day, July 13, having received no answer from his superiors, Karremans surrendered his battalion to General Mladic. The Serbian aggressors, in what amounted to a purposeful humiliation, stripped the Dutch soldiers of their uniforms, Blue Helmets and weapons. On August 15, 1995, the BBC aired a documentary based on a report published a week earlier by the London daily *The Observer,* accusing the United Nations of destroying a video showing Dutch soldiers and officers at their Potocari base while Serbian soldiers organized the forced evacuation of thousands of Muslim refugees. This deprived the International Tribunal for the Former Yugoslavia of evidence that would have allowed for the identification of many of those responsible, one way or another, for the genocide in Srebrenica. Not surprising, unfortunately. Ever since 1992, on to that fateful 1995, the Council had not been presented with a single video or photograph of the very many atrocities committed during the three years of the war in Bosnia.

The truth is that UNPROFOR's commanders in the region, General Janvier in Zagreb, and General Hervé Gobilliard, in Sarajevo, both French nationals, had not drawn up any plans for the contingency of a Serbian offensive against the safe areas, probably because it was simply not a priority for them. Add to that their unjustifiable surrender of authority, and the occupation without any opposition of Srebrenica and Potocari became possible. The immediate and criminal consequence was that Mladic's military units proceeded to separate the women from the men in the Potocari Muslim refugee population, and then forcefully took the latter to the nearby woods where they were executed.

Not long ago I watched the extraordinary film *Quo Vadis, Aïda?* by the Bosnian director Jamila Zbanic, Oscar finalist for 2021, which shows heartrending sequences, filmed in direct, of desperate mothers, their children brutally taken from their arms by Serbian soldiers. I have also watched videos showing Mladic soldiers forcing adult men and teenagers to kneel, their hands tied behind their backs, and then murdering them by shots from behind. Hundreds of pathologists and forensics have since been trying to find their remains, a task that has proved to be extremely difficult since the killers dismembered the bodies and dispersed them in common graves. To the day, specialists at the International Tribunal in The Hague have managed to identify almost eight thousand victims of that genocide. Information has also surfaced that almost twenty-thousand workers, hired by private companies, were employed to lorry the future victims and then to excavate with heavy machinery the pits for the common graves. Not one of those private sector companies, nor their employees, have been investigated nor taken to court as accomplices to the crime of genocide and concealment of genocide.

A year later, on July 6, 1996, Colonel Karremans participated as witness in the International Tribunal for the Former Yugoslavia's criminal proceedings against Radovan Karadzic and Ratko Mladic. A judge asked him whether, in his opinion, the United Nations and NATO did everything they could to save lives in the enclave, to which the Dutch officer replied: "No, they did not, even if they were constantly informed about the terrible reality on the ground." Another judge asked him to summarize the meetings he had held with Mladic between July 11 and 21, and he answered that the Bosnian Serb general had yelled at him saying that only the surrender of their weapons would save their lives, otherwise they would be killed. Another judge asked him if he had, at any of his meetings with Mladic, inquired about the Bosnian civilians taken away by his troops, to which Karremans replied he had not because he did not know then what had taken place. What he did ask Mladic was why he had requested a list of all the male Muslims refugees aged between sixteen and sixty, to which the general had cynically replied that it was to verify if there were any war criminals among them. Just to clarify, by the time Karremans held his last interview with Mladic, the massacre had been going on for nine days. He insisted, however, that he knew nothing about it and that therefore he was unable to report it to his superiors.

It is an open secret that neither the P5 nor their governments' intelligence agencies shared the detailed information they had about the Bosnian conflict, including developments in Srebrenica, with the Non-Permanent members of the Council. General Raymond Germanos, Chief of Cabinet of the French Minister of Defense, in reference to this situation, declared to the French National Assembly, that, indeed, "It had been criminal to censure information about the atrocities committed in Bosnia. If such facts had been known in time, measures could have been taken to save tens of thousands of lives. Evidently, the national interests of the Permanent Members weighed much heavier than the obligation to save lives and uphold human rights." Even if somewhat late, the truth about the Srebrenica genocide caused a strong public opinion reaction in the Netherlands and, years later, brought down the government, while its tribunals passed sentences that, even if not condemning anyone, at least granted compensation payments to hundreds of families that had lost a loved one in the massacre perpetrated during that somber month of July. However, no one, nor anything, has come to disturb the sleep of the governments of France and the United Kingdom, as if their generals, who were the highest UN military authorities in Bosnia, had never been in that country. Neither has the United States ever admitted any responsibility in what happened, even though its intelligence agencies kept the White House, the Pentagon and the State Department informed on all developments.

No matter the systematic cover up, many serious accusations have come to the fore in relation to the Srebrenica genocide. A case in point is the statement given on July 10, 1995, by Joris Voorhoeve, former Minister of Defense of The Netherlands, on the occasion of the twentieth anniversary of the Srebrenica massacre. He said: "A month before the genocide took place, the leaders of the Western Powers knew about the Serbian intention to invade in the coming weeks the safe areas of Srebrenica, Zepa, and Gorazde", and two of them – he added - the United States and the United Kingdom, for whatever reasons, chose not to share that information with the other members of the Security Council. David Harland, main author of the draft of the Annan report to the General Assembly, told me in confidence, and later declared as a witness for the prosecution in the ITFY, that "Thousands of the Bosnian Muslims murdered in Srebrenica would be alive today had it not been for the lack of courage of General Janvier and Yasushi Akashi."

The most relevant among these denunciations was made on October 24, 1995, by President Alija Izetbegovic, in his speech to the Special Session of the UN General Assembly to commemorate the Fiftieth Anniversary of the United Nations. In it he stated that "The UN has always been a source of hope" but warned that "It has also been a source of disappointment. If, indeed, it is the biggest and most lasting international alliance in history, it has also proven itself to be the most ineffective, and no one can deny that because of its hesitations and indecisions my country has paid an exceptionally high price, a circumstance that puts us under the obligation to call an aggressor, aggressor, and a genocide, a genocide. We cannot forget that since 1993, when the first pictures of the concentration camps set up by the Serbian aggressors in our territory were made public, the world reacted with indignation and surprise, but the UN, which knew full well the size of the brutal abuse inflicted on Bosnia's sovereignty and on the human rights of our citizens, kept silent, an increasingly guilty silence in the same measure the aggression became increasingly more brutal."

A few days ago, as I wrote these lines, I called my friend Ejup Ganic, who at the time was Vice President of Bosnia, to ask him why his government had taken so long to make this denunciation, and he replied that what was truly serious was not the timing but the fact that, "Knowing the imminence of that tragedy, no one had done anything to forestall it". His words point to the key issue of why the United Nations and the governments of Europe and the United States have never provided answers to the most important questions about the war in Bosnia. Those questions still lack appropriate answers. Access has been given only to some of the relevant information, through recently declassified documents by the United Kingdom, France, and above all, the United States. However, most of the potentially more revealing data has been censured. Maybe because, as cynically put by Yasushi Akashi, one of the important players in the Bosnian tragedy, to justify the unjustifiable performance of the international community, the United Nations' mission "is not to take people to heaven, but to save them from hell."

The Twentieth Anniversary of the Srebrenica Genocide

Precisely to fill this information void, to shed light on why the international community failed to prevent that tragedy, and to draw some conclusions that may serve to avoid its repetition, more than forty government officials, diplomats, and members of the Armed Forces who played a significant role in a war that led to the Srebrenica genocide gathered from June 29 to July 1, 2015, invited by the Simon-Skjodt Center for the Prevention of the Crime of Genocide, the US Holocaust Memorial Museum, and The Hague Institute for Global Justice. Among those present were Yasushi Akashi, former Special Representative of the UN Secretary General for Bosnia; Carl Bildt, former EU peace negotiator for Bosnia; Rupert Smith and Vere Hayes, former British Commanders of UNPROFOR; Muhamed Durakovic, survivor of the Srebrenica genocide; and three former members of the Security Council, active during those days, David Hannay, of the United Kingdom, André Erdos, of Hungary, and myself, from Venezuela. Hasan Muratovic, at the time minister in charge of relations with the international community, and Zlatko Lagumdzija, former Deputy Prime Minister and Minister of Foreign Affairs, represented the Bosnian government. Also present were Wim Kok, former Prime Minister of The Netherlands, Joris Voorhoeve, his Minister of Defense, and Colonel Thom Karremans. The UN Secretariat was represented by Shashi Tharoor, Kofi Annan's right hand during the war, and Zeid Al Hussein, UN High Commissioner for Human Rights, who was the UN's Advisor for Civilian Affairs in the region during the war in Bosnia.

For me, the occasion was truly a special one. It allowed me to come into the knowledge of documents that until then I did not know existed, and to have the opportunity to exchange views with former colleagues in the Security Council, such as Ambassadors Hannay and Erdos, and even with General Hayes, with whom I had serious disagreements when we met in Bosnia. Unfortunately, neither Kofi Annan, nor Boutros-Ghali, nor the French Generals Janvier and Bertrand de La Presle, took part in the meeting. I honestly did not miss them. For me, it was more than enough to listen to Muhamed Durakovic, the miraculous survivor of the Srebrenica genocide, whose testimony embodied the Bosnian people's condemnation of all those directly or indirectly responsible for a tragedy that could have been avoided.

Among the documents we had access to, two stand out. The first, from the archives of the ITFY, were extracts from the personal diary of Ratko Mladic. In these pages, the general notes the dialogue he had on May 15, 1995, with the UN's chief civilian affairs officer in Sarajevo, the Russian UN official Victor Andreyev, on the issue of a possible Western and UN intervention in the conflict. Andreyev, in a conversation that was both surprising and remarkable, tells Mladic: "What you should do is, first of all, to not obstruct humanitarian assistance. Then, everything will go your way." Andreyev, who had access to privileged and confidential UN information, goes on to give Mladic assurances that the possibilities of a US or NATO military intervention were minimal, because, on one hand, the United States and Europe disagree on the issue, and on the other, because Russia would not allow it. He adds: "Diego Arria has presidential ambitions in his country and for that reason he takes a highly defiant stand during our meetings. He has the support of the Non-Aligned members of the Council, who are the most radical and only want to intensify the war." Mladic also includes in his diary suggestions made to him by the Russian which led him to say in jest: "Victor, I should name you my advisor. I am no good at politics", to which Andreyev replied, "No, general, you are an excellent politician, you are great." I wasn't overly surprised by this scandalous relationship between the UN Political Advisor in Sarajevo and the "Butcher of the Balkans." Although it followed the usual pattern of Russian conduct within the Council, I never imagined this UN high official would dare reveal to Mladic, the military representative of one of the parties at war, confidential UN information. I am sure that, had it been among its powers to indict UN officials, the International Tribunal for the Former Yugoslavia, would have indicted Victor Andreyev on the charge of high treason.

The other document is the highly surprising confidential report sent by Urs Boegli, the International Committee of the Red Cross' Representative in Sarajevo, to his superiors in Geneva in April 1993, in which he states: "Ambassador Arria has been critical about the leadership and strategy of

UNPROFOR during the negotiations between the parties. He believes that the Force´s goal is to unilaterally disarm the Muslim military, a purpose he judges to be truly a disgrace." He goes on to say, not relying on any source other than his personal opinion: "We are conscious that, in doing so, Ambassador Arria is just trying to strengthen his position in favor of an international military intervention. He believes that our support of the decision to not allow international media representatives to enter Srebrenica is to inhibit reporting on what is truly taking place in that enclave." Finally, he accuses me of acting and making statements during our mission as if I were the only representative of the Security Council, without ever mentioning the other members of the delegation, "To eclipse them and monopolize everyone's attention." In Boegli's opinion, my conduct showed how far I was willing to go in pursuit of my alleged personal ambition to become president of Venezuela. It was on that basis, he goes on to say, that I declared that it was because of UNPROFOR's incompetence that Srebrenica had become "an open jail, a slow-motion genocide case, he accuses us of shedding crocodile tears for something that was only the sequel of a ´population outflow´."

Needless to say, this is an inadmissible value judgment by a high official of an international humanitarian organization that enjoys universal prestige. It is even more unacceptable that Boegli´s report was made available to the international conference´s organizers by General Hayes, Chief of UNPROFOR´s General Staff at the time Boegli sent his confidential report, once more revealing the complicities that made possible the cover up of war crimes. So much so, that the date of Boegli's vile report coincides with that of the note sent by Sadako Ogata, who in those days was ACNUR's Representative in Bosnia, to Boutros-Ghali, warning him about the imminence of a tragedy of great proportions in Srebrenica.

At the end of the three-day meeting, some journalists approached me to enquire about my opinion on the outcome reached by the important group of civilian and military officials that were somehow involved with the war in Bosnia and the Srebrenica genocide, its abominable consequence. Naturally, I carefully considered what my answer would be. When I did reply, I did so to acknowledge that after hearing and taking part in those sessions, what struck me the most was the generalized indifference the tragedy elicited, as if all the participants were agreed in keeping the atrocity and its significance at arm's length. A good example of this cold distance from reality was given by Shashi Tharoor, Kofi Annan's closest collaborator as UN Under Secretary General for Peacekeeping Operations at the time of the war, who appeared profoundly indifferent to what had happened. Some may argue that that is what "diplomacy" is about. Be it as it may, in a war such as that, in which ethnic cleansing and crimes against humanity were a critical part of the policy guiding one of the parties, it is unfortunate to ignore, under the guise of neutrality, the moral dimensions of the tragedy. When all is said and done, both documents help to prove that the Bosnian Muslims were up against not only Serbian and Croatian invaders, but also the UN's high military and diplomatic officials, and important international organizations such as the International Committee of the Red Cross.

The Srebrenica Mothers

In July 2005, I went back to Srebrenica to take part in the ceremony commemorating the genocide's first decade. I was invited by "The Mothers of Srebrenica," a group of mothers, wives and sisters of the victims, who since 1995 campaign to make sure that crime against humanity is not forgotten. I was moved by the gesture since only those few who had supported their cause from the very beginning received an invitation.

The main events took place in the buildings that had served as headquarters for the Canadian battalion deployed at Potocari. They have been preserved just as they stood when the massacre took place ten years before. I will never forget the pain I felt in addressing the wives, sisters and mothers of those men and youngsters assassinated in July 1995, many of them present when, two years before the events, I had given them guarantees on behalf of the Security Council that the United Nations would protect them. The promise was not kept. How could we have been so foolish? I can still hear the words of Prince Zeid Al Hussein, UN High Commissioner for Human Rights, speaking in the Security Council on occasion of the twentieth anniversary of the Srebrenica massacre - July 8, 2015: "We did not take corrective measures to avoid future repetitions of the Srebrenica genocide."

The UN is guilty of a conduct that included not allowing the circulation of videos and photos taken during the war in Bosnia, even going as far as destroying them. The same was done by the government of the United States, that only allowed three images taken by its U2 planes - or maybe by its satellites – to be divulged and did so after holding on to them for a month. The US government's policy of not showing the crimes committed in Bosnia went so far that in 2001 a Federal Appeals Court denied a judicial request by the organization Students Against Genocide and prohibited to divulge graphic materials documenting war crimes in Bosnia.

Towards Peace in Bosnia

On October 25, 1995, President Alija Izetbegovic, addressing the UN General Assembly, announced that "A few days ago, by initiative of the government of the United States, negotiations have begun to bring an end to the war in Bosnia - a war we did not start, a peace that my people very much need and wish for." The news made me realize that the images shown by Ambassador Albright to the Security Council and the NATO airstrikes against Serbian heavy weapons located around Sarajevo in immediate response to the ruthless mortar attack against that city´s Markala popular market, were part of the US plan to pressure President Milosevic into accepting to debate a true and lasting peace agreement in Bosnia. President Izetbegovic rejoiced because "The international community has finally started to do what it should have done a long, long time ago."

On that occasion, I had the opportunity to talk at length with President Izetbegovic. He assured me that only the peace plan put forth by the United States' government, after three years of war, could have a decisive impact on a process until that moment under the control of the United Kingdom and France. After taking this decision, President Clinton named Richard Holbrooke, a career diplomat, as head of his negotiating team, and General Wesley Clark, Head of Strategy of the US Joint Chiefs of Staff, as his chief advisor. He then went on to convene Presidents Slobodan Milosevic, Franjo Tudjman and Alija Izetbegovic for a meeting with Holbrooke and Clark on November 21, urging all not to leave the table until a peace agreement was signed. An so it was that on November 21, Milosevic, Tudjman and Izetbegovic signed the agreement later to be countersigned in a solemn protocolary act held in Paris, on December 14 of that same year.

The Dayton Agreements replaced the Republic of Bosnia and Herzegovina with a state made up of two independent entities, the Croat-Muslim Federation of Bosnia and Herzegovina, and the Serbian Bosnian Srpska Republic. This territorial division, imposed by fire and blood, bolstered the Serbian apartheid system and, instead of condemning the aggressors, rewarded them by giving legitimacy to the illegal Srpska. Adding insult to injury, the agreements included Srebrenica among the areas that ceased to be a part of Bosnia to become part of the Serb's now independent republic. In the new maps agreed upon by the three parties to the conflict, fifty-one percent of Bosnia's original territory was allotted to the new Bosnia and Herzegovina Federation, made up of Bosnian Muslims and Croats who had joined in alliance against Milosevic during the last months of the conflict. The other forty-nine percent was allotted to the now legitimate and sovereign Srpska Republic, governed by criminals such as Radovan Karadzic, its President, and Ratko Mladic, Commander of its Armed Forces, both currently serving life imprisonment sentences in the UK and in Holland for crimes against humanity in Bosnia.

In private conversations with former high officials of the Bosnian government, I came to know that in Dayton Slobodan Milosevic represented not only Serbia's interests but also Karadzic´s, and that on behalf of both of them he had threatened Richard Holbrooke, only days before the agreement was to be signed, to withdraw from the negotiations if the United States persisted in its refusal to create the Serbian Srpska republic. The extortion forced President Izetbegovic to give in to the Serbian demands. Dayton, and later on, Paris, gave Milosevic a setting and an opportunity to portray himself to the world as a promoter of peace in the Balkans. Four years later, his successful aggression in Bosnia would lead him to try to do the same in Kosovo. Only this time the international community finally put him in his place, helping to topple his government and putting him in jail and then on trial in The Hague for war crimes.

When we talked in October 1995 in New York, President Izetbegovic had confided that the peace negotiations were about to begin, this time in Dayton, and that there was some urgency to it, to forestall a Bosnian military triumph. Beginning in July, in reaction to the Srebrenica genocide, his government had started to receive weapons in sufficient quantity to decisively change the course of the war, and the Croats had promised their support to expel their Serb enemies from Bosnia. I did not want to argue, but I was sure a military triumph by the Bosnian Muslims would not be acceptable to the governments taking part in the peace negotiations. President Izetbegovic's optimism reminded me of General Rasim Delic, Commander of his army at the time of my visit to Sarajevo, who believed that only a long, drawn-out war would allow the legitimate Bosnian government to take back the territory seized by force by the Serbian invaders. That was the reason for the urgency with which Holbrooke, as mediator, wanted to reach any kind of agreement to bring the war to an end. In the end, for the United States as well, a fragmented Bosnia was preferable to a military triumph by Muslim Bosnia.

In retrospect, it could be said that the international community's irresponsible conduct throughout the almost four years of war led to what was finally agreed in Dayton. To a certain degree, the conflict was cruelly extended by countless and useless Security Council resolutions. Moreover, the universal scandal caused by the Srebrenica genocide, as well as the need to prevent further tragedies, forced the hurried compromise signed at Dayton Airbase.

When the twenty-one days Dayton confinement was about to end, a new obstacle came up that almost killed the agreement. Without any doubt, the terms demanded by the Serbs implied an extremely harsh sacrifice for the Muslim Bosnians, making President Izetbegovic call it "an unfair and bitter agreement." To this, Holbrooke replied: "It's a good agreement and you will not get a better deal." Warren Christopher, the US Secretary of State, in an attempt to settle the issue, and losing somewhat his renowned composure, raised his voice to put President Izetbegovic into a bind: "You have one hour to decide. Either you sign or we have reached the end of this process." He then stood up and left the room. The next day President Izetbegovic signed the agreement.

The Bosnian Drama's Denouement

The main beneficiary of the Dayton Peace Agreements were the people of Bosnia. The terms of the agreements and the final text were drafted by US State Department officials. The American historian Derek Chollet, in his book *The Road to the Dayton Accords*, available since 2003 on social media and based on a large number of recently declassified documents, argues that Dayton came about as a consequence of radical changes in American policy and of challenges to its NATO leadership's credibility. "During the three and some years that the war in Bosnia lasted, the United States' position was to not get involved in the efforts made to solve the conflict, and it justified its passivity with the confidence the budging alliance with its European partners provided to solve the problem on their own. However, the way Europe had till then taken on the

Bosnia challenge was marked by serious irresponsibility. Washington was no less responsible until the Clinton Administration, in search of a quick foreign policy success, suddenly made peace in Bosnia its top priority, a goal it finally reached in Dayton."

Chollet's research represents the most comprehensive study on the Clinton Administration's management of its peace plan for Bosnia up until its final stage in Dayton, even though the plan implied significant costs for the international community. Chollet abstains from any criticism of the multiple irregularities in the process, such as the transfer of a sizable part of Bosnian territory to Serbia and Croatia, or the occupation of more than half of Bosnia by military and paramilitary Serbian and Croatian troops that led to the frightful policy of "ethnic cleansing", the most appalling example of which was the mass murder of more than eight thousand Bosnian citizens.

Representatives of France, the United Kingdom, Germany and Russia were present during the Dayton meetings held in November. Their presence was, however, mostly of a purely testimonial nature since the Americans managed all the negotiations. This upset the British Representative, Pauline Neville-Jones, who complained that the negotiators never consulted with them even while informing on a daily basis about the advances made in the course of the negotiations. So much the better, in my opinion. We must remember that what was agreed in Dayton had an impact on the lives of almost three and a half million Muslim Bosnians, and that they still live in one of the most fragile states in the world, under great economic difficulties and a political stalemate. The Dayton Agreements provide a complex and ineffective constitutional arrangement for the current Bosnian Federation, with a rotating presidency of Serbs, Croats, and Bosniacs, with ethnic quotas in all public institutions, and different doors in schools for each different ethnic group of students. This fragility is compounded by the constant pressure brought to bear on it by the Srpska Republic in its unrelenting push for the annexation of the other half of the Bosnian territory and the creation of a

Greater Serbia. How ironic it would be if the Dayton Agreements turned out to be the way to make this Milosevic-Karadzic fantasy come true. At the end, with these agreements, they came out as winners. Beyond all the shortcomings of the agreements, the international community can rest satisfied for having helped to bring the war to an end, even if peace was reached at the cost of perfecting an apartheid regime in the very heart of Europe.

THE BEGINNING OF THE END FOR MILOSEVIC

Just as the Srebrenica genocide brought about the Dayton Agreements and the end of the war in Bosnia, the upsurge of aggressions against the small province of Kosovo by Slobodan Milosevic's government in 1999, brought about its downfall. Milosevic was detained and, on June 29, 2001, transferred to the Scheveningen maximum security jail, at the outskirts of The Hague, awaiting trial by the International Tribunal for the Former Yugoslavia.

Since 1991, I had closely followed Milosevic's wanton obsession to establish a Greater Serbia at the expense of other Balkan republics, taking advantage of the international community's shortcomings and complicities. When in April 2003 I was surprised by Prosecutor Carla Del Ponte's telephone call inviting me to become involved in the trial against Milosevic, I realized that the opportunity to fulfil the commitment I made to the Bosnian people, was finally available.

My First Trip to The Hague

The day after my first telephone conversation with Del Ponte, I received a call from two of the Prosecutor's Office main officials, Prosecutor Geoffrey Nice, in charge of Milosevic's case, and Inspector Bretton Randall, the Tribunal's Head of Investigations. They briefed me about what the prosecution expected from my participation and told me that during the period prior to the trial, they would assist me in preparing the written deposition that, in keeping with the Tribunal's rules, I would need to submit to the judges, the prosecution and the defense, before my appearance in court. In the case at hand, the Prosecutor's Office was particularly interested in my recollection of the many instances in which the horrible massacre of thousands of unarmed civilians in Srebrenica could have been avoided had the international community taken timely action to prevent it.

With the assistance of Randall, an experienced professional, I devoted the following months to the complex task of recovering, from my files and my recollections, the information needed to rise to the immense legal and moral challenge I faced, which was to provide evidence that proved Milosevic's responsibility in unleashing a war of ethnic extermination in Bosnia.

With Randall's counsel and support by my former colleagues in the Security Council, Ambassadors Jamsheed Marker of Pakistan and Roble Olhaye, of Djibouti, I was able, a few weeks later, to complete the task of attesting to the international conspiracy to deprive a nation of its territorial integrity and place its citizens under a brutal regime of racial discrimination.

On Friday, September 19, 2003, I finally travelled to The Hague. After my arrival, I could not resist the temptation to immediately take a look at the Tribunal's headquarters, formerly those of an important Dutch insurance company, located in an unremarkable building at about one kilometer from my hotel. The setting was certainly not that of the magnificent palace where the International Court of Justice resides, but the tribunal's appeal was not based on its appearance but on the kind of justice dispensed within its walls. For the first time since the Nuremberg and Tokyo trials, the world would be able to witness legal proceedings against the main culprits of ordering crimes against humanity.

The building was not well lit and discreetly protected by just a few guards. I circled it several times and ended sitting in a bench in front of its main entrance. I felt hugely proud of having been one of the more active sponsors of the creation of this tribunal. Suddenly, I could not help exclaiming aloud: "My God! I cannot believe I am here!" Within three days, Slobodan Milosevic would be transferred from Scheveningen prison, and I would have the opportunity to help dispense justice for the hundreds of thousands of innocent victims of his arrogant racial supremacy policies. I don't believe I had ever experienced such a strong emotion and once back in my hotel wrote the following letter to my three daughters: Karina, Camila, and Manuela.

"I want to share with you the profound satisfaction I felt today at the knowledge that very soon, in a jail located close to where I am, the former Head of State of the Former Yugoslavia, will be placed on trial. He is the same individual who for years on end has scoffed at an international community that today places him on trial as a criminal and an agent of genocide. That is, without any doubt, the fate awaiting all such monsters. The world has become too small for them to make fun of their victims indefinitely. When my country and the circumstances of life placed me in the Security Council, I fully accepted the responsibility of standing up for humanity's core principles. I would not have had it otherwise. I would never forgive myself if someday any of you came to think that I was not up to the trust placed on me by my country and by the world. I believe that to never have made concessions in the discharge of my responsibilities as a member of the United Nations Security Council, the world's foremost political body, is an important part of what I may leave behind for you."

The morning after, I met Prosecutor Geoffrey Nice and Inspector Bretton Randall, to polish the final draft of my written testimony, and then, two days afterwards, early in the morning, with Prosecutor Del Ponte. Her first words after welcoming me to her office and thanking me for accepting to be part of her team, were to tell me she had bad news for me:

— When Mr. Milosevic heard that you had arrived at The Hague and would be a witness for the prosecution, his blood pressure went up so much that we were forced to postpone the process. Since we do not know when we will be able to resume, I am afraid you will have to return to New York until then. I am deeply sorry.

To compensate for the unwelcome news, Del Ponte proposed that I meet with all the Tribunal's staff and informally share with them my experience during those years of war in Bosnia. On the afternoon, I met with almost two-hundred officials. I told them how embarrassing it had been for me to be a part of an international community that, in the case of Bosnia, had acted with a deplorable combination of indifference, racial prejudice and guilt, making it possible to inflict on an independent and sovereign nation such as Bosnia, a discrimination system akin to apartheid. I also told them that in April 1993, I had met at the Srebrenica municipality with a large delegation of its townsfolks, to which, in good faith and in the name of the Security Council, I announced that they were under UN protection.

I must admit that we did not keep the promise. That is why I accepted to become a witness of charge against Slobodan Milosevic. Not to make amends, because the harm done has no repair, but at the very least to give my personal cooperation to the effort to make those guilty of such crimes accountable and help insure they never take place again.

Next day, awaiting Milosevic's recovery, I flew back to New York.

Summoned to the Milosevic Trial Once More

I would be back in the Netherlands four months later, once again called to appear in court as a witness for the prosecution in the trial against the former Serbian ruler. My court appearance was scheduled for the afternoon of Friday, February 10, 2004. On Tuesday 6, I was greeted at the Amsterdam airport by a security officer assigned by the tribunal to take me to my destination. A sense of deep emotion overwhelmed me during the short trip. I was the only witness to have been a member of the Security Council at the time of the Serbian aggression in Bosnia, and to have proactively contributed, ten years earlier, to the tribunal's creation. Milosevic was finally on trial.

It was a turning point of historical significance in the field of international penal law. For the first time, those guilty of crimes against humanity would answer, not to their victors in war, as was the case after the Second World War in Nuremberg and Tokyo, but to their victims. Nothing would allow them to escape justice: not their former high positions, not any political interests. It was, truly, an exceptional opportunity.

Since the beginning of Milosevic's trial, which started on February 12, 2002, I had followed its development as if it were a TV series, and I had seen how he had unfortunately turned it into a show in which he played the leading role. The judges, the prosecution, the witnesses, and the media representatives, all played the roles of supporting actors charged with highlighting his lead. Milosevic's body language and his unending interventions had the sole purpose of belittling judges, prosecutors, and witnesses, and of showing his unbounded ego. I arrived at The Hague determined not to play that kind of secondary role.

Milosevic had great political talents, and he used them, among others, to indefinitely delay the trial's development, and consequently, his public appearances. He did so appealing to two legal sophistries. One, to continuously deny the tribunal any legitimacy on the basis that the charges, in particular those relating to crimes against humanity committed in Kosovo, were solely of a political nature, and had the sole purpose of destroying his image and his legacy. "An ocean of lies made up by the West", he would say every so often; a West that had forced him to put up "A heroic defense to confront a political and military aggression by NATO." His purpose was to turn the trial into a debate of a more or less rhetorical nature, in part literary, in part philosophical, addressed to his followers in Serbia, who closely followed it on TV. Second, to take advantage of his hypertensive condition to slow the proceedings, as was the case months before when the trial's postponement for alleged medical reasons had forced me to travel back to New York. His legal ruses were so grotesque that the Tribunal president, Judge Patrick Robinson, of Jamaica, more than once had to chide Milosevic for his conduct, calling it "petulant and childish."

Chief Prosecutor Del Ponte was of the same opinion. In her book *La Caccia,* she recalls how for their first encounter she had ordered Milosevic be taken to an empty room and how "His arrogance was always that of a Mafia *capo di capi.*" While he was no longer the arrogant and self-sufficient ruler who, for years, had fooled diplomats and politicians from all over the world, she recalls that he still displayed an arrogance that now served the sole purpose of making continued protestations and complaints, like a brat. So unsufferable was his behavior that only a few minutes after joining him, Del Ponte ordered him to be taken away and left. As she has stated, never, then or in future occasions, did she shake hands with him.

The Serbian Excesses in Kosovo

On the morning of the 10 th of February, Bretton Randall came to pick me up at my hotel. It was early but he wanted us to have time for breakfast with Prosecutor Nice. At the entrance to the Tribunal's seat, he led me directly to the checkpoint. After verification of my credentials as United Nations Assistant Secretary General, at a second checkpoint some fifty meters down the corridor I was issued my credentials as a witness and was instructed to wear it at all times inside the building. When we arrived at the cafeteria, Nice was already waiting for us. At nine o'clock, he guided me to a small and not very well lit waiting room.

I had to get used to the idea that soon I would be face to face with Milosevic, indicted for dozens of crimes. In the Security Council I had tirelessly denounced his criminal behavior during the two years I had been Venezuela's Permanent Representative to the United Nations. Milosevic was at the end of his murky political life. It had begun to unravel on March 24, 1999, almost four years after the Dayton Agreements. On that day, free of the political and diplomatic contamination that had skewed its decisions, NATO launched Operation Allied Force, an air raid on Serbian military objectives located around Belgrade. It was labeled a humanitarian relief operation, launched to protect the people of Kosovo, a small province of the Former Yugoslavia whose inhabitants, mostly Albanians and Muslims, were the object of continued abuse by Milosevic's Serbian military.

The conflict's origin could be traced to 1989, when Milosevic cancelled the autonomy Kosovo had enjoyed within Serbia, granted after the Second World War by Marshall Tito. The situation in Kosovo had deteriorated continuously since then, and by 1999 it had already caused more than fourteen thousand deaths and eight hundred thousand refugees, most of them in Albania and Macedonia, fleeing from the same ethnic and religious cleansing that Milosevic had successfully applied with impunity in Bosnia and Herzegovina.

A few days before, the United States, the United Kingdom, France, Germany and Russia had made a final effort to find a political solution to an increasingly explosive situation and to avoid taking military action. At their invitation, the parties met at Rambouillet, France, for a meeting that lasted two weeks. The Yugoslav Federation was represented by Milan Milutinovic, President of Serbia, and not by Slobodan Milosevic, President of the Federal Republic of Yugoslavia, who stayed in Belgrade. The delegation of the Kosovo separatists was headed by Hasim Thaci, a former member of the Kosovo Liberation Army, now Prime Minister of the Kosovo Interim Government. The British and French Foreign Ministers, Robin Cook and Hubert Védrine, chaired the Conference, occasionally joined by the US Secretary of State, Madeleine Albright, and by Joshka Fischer, Germany's Foreign Affairs Minister.

The draft agreement that provided for the reinstatement of Kosovo's autonomy, although with some limitations, was rejected by Belgrade since Milosevic considered it would give ground for another independent republic within the Yugoslav Federation. Also included in the proposed agreement was the Serbian military and police withdrawal from Kosovo, to be replaced by a NATO stabilization force to guarantee the peace. As was to be expected, the Rambouillet proposal was accepted by the Kosovar delegation but absolutely rejected by Milosevic´s representatives.

Maybe his previous experience in Bosnia made Milosevic think that the only consequence of his refusal to sign would be a string of rhetorical threats by the international community and nothing more. A serious error! It was senseless to believe that NATO, under the decisive influence of the United States, would act the same way as the UN Security Council. The NATO air raid proved that Milosevic had made a fatal and irreversible miscalculation. NATO´s decisions simply did not have to satisfy the usual diplomatic compromises that were customary within the UN. President Boris Yeltsin joined in and gave Russia's unqualified support to Operation Allied Force over Serbia.

NATO Puts an End to Serbian Impunity

From March 24, when Operation Allied Force started, to its end on June 11, almost a thousand aircrafts, belonging to ten NATO members, conducted thirty-eight thousand combat missions against Serbian military targets. Just as President Clinton had sternly warned when the operation was launched: "If President Milosevic is not willing to make peace, then we will limit his capacity to make war." On the 9 th of June 1999, seventy-eight days after, Milosevic was forced to surrender and sign the Kumanovo Treaty, which provided for the withdrawal from Kosovo of Serbian troops while forty-five thousand NATO troops went in to guarantee the province´s stability and the consolidation of the new state. This was all possible thanks to the United States doing what it had not done in Bosnia and Herzegovina.

In an interview published by London's *The Daily Telegraph* on June 28, 1999, former Secretary of State Henry Kissinger admitted that the draft agreement discussed in Rambouillet, by asking Serbia to accept the presence of NATO troops in its territory "Was a provocation and an excuse to begin the air raids on Serbia since it was obvious that was unacceptable for any Serbian".

Ten years after, thinking about her performance as Chief Prosecutor of the Tribunal for the Former Yugoslavia, Carla Del Ponte admitted that at the beginning she, as others, had questioned the legality of the NATO attacks, but Milosevic's quick surrender in Kosovo had proved the failure of the diplomatic approach in Bosnia when dealing with situations that, in the final analysis, can only be solved with determination and air power. Exactly the same consideration is made by the historian John Keegan when he writes that Kosovo marked a turning point in the history of the great international crisis that came to an end on February 17, 2008. On that day, one hundred and ten countries, out of the one hundred and ninety-two members of the United Nations, recognized the independence of this former Yugoslav province, and turned it into the seventh Balkan republic, at a par with Serbia, Slovenia, Croatia, Macedonia, Montenegro, and Bosnia and Herzegovina. Few days later, Vojislav Kostunica, former President of Serbia, in a speech given in Belgrade to an inflamed crowd, asked: "What is Kosovo? Does anyone know where it is and to whom it belongs? Is there anyone among us who thinks Kosovo is not ours? Kosovo belongs to the Serbian people from time immemorial, and so it will be forever."

Milosevic is Overthrown and Held in Custody

The International Tribunal reacted quickly to the Serbian aggression against Kosovo. So much so that on May 27, 1999, while NATO was fully engaged in Serbia, it charged Milosevic with war crimes and crimes against humanity. These would be the first charges it would bring against Milosevic based of the decisions he made since May 1989, acting first as Head of State of the Republic of Serbia and then, from 1997 to September 24, 2000, as President of the Yugoslav Federation. In the 2000 elections Milosevic was amply defeated by Vojislav Kostunica but refused to acknowledge his defeat and continued to do so even after October 5, when a massive popular, nonviolent, civil disobedience movement deposed him.

Five months later, on March 31, 2001, the Tribunal sent a request to the new Serbian government demanding the handover of Milosevic. He locked himself up in his Belgrade house, paradoxically named Villa Pacific, and warned that if the police tried to arrest him, he would kill his wife and daughter and then himself. The new Serbian government was aware of Milosevic's tragic family history: his father, mother and uncle had committed suicide. Fearing Milosevic would deliver on his ultimatum, it proposed that he give himself up under the guarantee that he would be judged in Belgrade. For the next two months, Milosevic remained in the custody of the new Serbian government, which was divided on the issue of extradition. While the Prime Minister, Zoran Djindjic, was in favor of his handover, President Kostunica, a professor of Constitutional Law at Belgrade University, believed that his extradition would be illegal since the handover would be to a United Nations organization and not to another country. The debate on the issue within the Serbian government went on until the United States gave it notice that the financial sanctions imposed on Serbia in 1992 would not be lifted if Milosevic was not handed over within the next two months. On June 26, Prime Minister Djindjic ordered his transfer to The Hague under a cloak of secrecy, so much so that even President Kostunica heard about it on the radio. The date chosen by Djindjic was not random; it was the feast of Saint Vito, the most important in the Serbian liturgical calendar. He probably wanted to have more than one motive for celebration.

Milosevic is Put in Jail

Milosevic's trial begun eight months after his arrival at The Hague, airlifted under NATO custody. It was not an easy task. Many, like Ambassador Holbrooke, considered Milosevic a national leader with whom the United States would always be able to reason and negotiate. This gave Milosevic reason to believe he could shirk answering for the many charges filed against him by Prosecutor Del Ponte. In her book *Confrontations with Humanity's Worst Criminals and the Culture of Impunity,* originally published under the title *La Caccia* by *Feltrinelli Editore,* Del Ponte comments how others, like Hubert Védrine, Minister of Foreign Affairs of France, insisted to the very end that Milosevic should be judged in Belgrade in order to avoid an insurrection. On the other hand, personalities like General Colin Powell, at the time US Secretary of State, and the Serbian Prime Minister Djindjic, did not fall under Milosevic's spell and made his transfer possible.

As I waited to be guided into the courtroom, I was filled with jubilation. No matter how you might want to look at it, this was a man who barely ten years before, on June 28, 1989, had led a million followers in support of his claim to suppress Kosovo's autonomic status, at the Gazimestan monument in Kosovo the largest political rally ever in the Balkans since the liberation in 1945. Now, defeated in a democratic election by his own countrymen, he was answering to international justice. This was something out of the ordinary. Milosevic was the first head of state and government to be imprisoned without any special treatment and the first to be tried by an international criminal court. He was a prisoner like all the others, identified by a number, number 39.

For four months I waited in New York for a new court summons. Meanwhile, in The Hague, Milosevic argued repeatedly that he was a victim, a nationalist hero who American imperialism sought to humiliate. Fortunately for him, unlike the Nuremberg and Tokyo trials, the Hague tribunal could not deliver a death penalty. Milosevic's show in

The Hague probably had some bearing on the High Criminal Court of Iraq when, three years later, in November 2006, it sentenced Hussein to death.

Prosecutor Carla Del Ponte Indicts Milosevic

On February 12, 2002, the first day of the Milosevic trial, Chief Prosecutor Del Ponte opened arguments by stating: "The law is not an abstract concept. It is a live instrument charged with the protection of our values and the regulation of order in a civilized society. As Chief Prosecutor, I give this tribunal the accused, Slobodan Milosevic, indicted by the international community. The trial that begins today will serve to conjure the terrible fate suffered by millions of Croats, Bosnians, and Albanians, victims of Milosevic. This tribunal will write only one chapter of this tragedy, maybe the most heartrending, but it will also serve to give notice to other possible candidates to fall into the temptation to commit violations to international humanitarian law."

Milosevic took the floor for the first time two days later, on February 14, and did so to deny the legitimacy of the Tribunal, arguing it had no legal standing to judge him since it had been established by a Security Council decision and not by law.

Milosevic was a lawyer by training though he never practiced law and based on this the Tribunal allowed him to represent himself. However, back in Belgrade he had a legal team of his absolute trust. It became evident that the defense had decided not to answer directly to any of the charges and, instead, take advantage of the fact that the trial was televised in Serbia to send his political messages, accuse his detractors of distorting reality, and promote his image as the great pacifier of the Balkans who had been betrayed by his former allies in the international community. Every time he appeared in court, Milosevic, then aged sixty-two and suffering from "dangerously high blood pressure," feigned he was in danger of suffering a stroke at any moment and, on this pretext, frequently cancelled his court appearances. When he did appear, he gave unending speeches, mostly of a political nature, addressed to his followers in Serbia. Milosevic knew perfectly well that from a legal standpoint he could not successfully argue against the Prosecution, and thus appealed to his ample political experience to manipulate the trial's development in the Serbian press. Of this I was fully aware as I travelled to The Hague.

At Last, I Confront Milosevic

It was Tuesday, February 10, 2004. At nine a.m. sharp, an usher and two security agents came to pick me up at the small room where I had been placed in isolation half an hour before and took me along a narrow corridor to a staircase that led to the courtroom. As I entered the courtroom through a lateral doorway reserved for witnesses, I paused a few seconds to take in the view. To my left was a thick armored glass "wall," behind which sat about a hundred journalists and general public. To my right, in the foreground, was the table reserved for the prosecutors and their assistants. Facing the glass wall was the witness stand and, in a slightly higher position, a dozen meters away, the judges' bench. To my left, in the dock, was Milosevic, under the custody of two UN agents, dressed in a blue suit and sporting a red tie, the customary outfit of the Serbian political echelon. He looked at me straight in the eyes, raising his prominent chin in ostensible imitation of the defiant way Mussolini used to challenge the world. It was a ridiculous gesture. Milosevic must have practiced it in the mirror a thousand times. In the end, what mattered most to him at such a crucial moment of his life was how he would be portrayed in photographs and TV cameras.

For a few seconds, we looked at each other carefully. I had been, to my satisfaction, one of his more severe critics but now, ten years later, I saw him differently. Milosevic looked at me with a glint of satisfaction. I wondered if this was his way of expressing his intimate conviction that the international community would not go as far as to convict him, nor would it lay down a decisive precedent to help prevent a future repetition of similar atrocities. At any rate, during those initial moments Milosevic showed a cold indifference and seemed to be far removed from the reality of the trial.

His attitude made it difficult for me to try to correctly understand his mood. I had been warned by diplomat friends that had dealt with him, but I had the feeling that what lay behind his cool attitude had to do with indifference and even contempt for others. As the hours and minutes passed, I begun to feel that the lion was not as fierce as it pretended to be. After a long and successful political career in his country and warm relations with the international community, he probably had reasons to believe he was, even now, above the fray. He certainly gave me the impression that I was not one to merit his attention. In truth, it was as if no one did. Whatever I or anyone else might reply to his statements made no difference. The only thing that apparently mattered to him was to endlessly repeat his arguments, which amounted to political slogans turned into value judgments. It was the same posture I had seen him adopt on many occasions on television. As his own defendant, he initiated the "dialogues" he kept with the witnesses, the judges and the prosecutors. By his defiant attitude he managed to also convey to his people in Serbia that, notwithstanding the circumstances, he was still the invincible leader he had always been. Sometimes, however, as I looked sideways at him while speaking, I had the impression he was trying hard to concentrate and understand what I was telling him.

With time, no matter how he wished to portray himself, I came to see him as he really was: a man loaded with sorrows, who was a shadow of his former self. Through his mask of false superiority, I saw the horrors I had witnessed in Sarajevo, Ahmici, and Srebrenica. I could only regret that other evil criminals, such as Karadzic or Mladic, were not in the dock with their master. I also regretted that some important representatives of the international community were not also there with him, given their complicity with and indifference to those abominable crimes.

Sir Geoffrey Nice, the prosecutor to whom I turned later on to help me better understand the trial and Milosevic's behavior, believed that the Serbian leader's detachment and apparent indifference had to do with not wanting to be seen by his countrymen as a fallen idol, humiliated by his enemies and condemned to end his days in a Dutch prison cell.

I wanted Milosevic to know that I would do everything in my power to help make justice for the hundreds of thousands of victims of his raving obsession with an imperialist and ultranationalist "Greater Serbia." I wanted him to know that for me it was worth it to be there, to have travelled to The Hague, therefore, before taking my place, I glanced at him and nodded.

As I took my place facing the judges and with the public at my back, I felt accomplished and satisfied with the knowledge that the international community could now rely on an independent International Tribunal to establish the personal responsibilities of those who, abusing their power and in all impunity, had committed crimes against unarmed civilians. As had been the case for Bosnia, such impunity had been fostered by the automatic complicity of the international negotiators, more interested in reaching an agreement between the parties than on securing justice for the victims. In a distortion of ethical values that made possible the Nazi horrors all over again, Milosevic's civilian and military personnel were able to commit crimes against humanity in Croatia, Bosnia and Kosovo.

The unadorned setting of the courtroom, devoid of decorations, almost monastic, granted it majesty, as befitted the importance of the proceedings. As the Croat writer Slavenka Drakulic would comment after sitting in several sessions of the trial, its setting gave gravitas to the proceedings. Indeed, it helped the international community rise to the challenge of doing justice for all those whose only crime had been to be different.

My thoughts were suddenly cut short by an officer of the court who handed me a simultaneous interpretation kit in order to follow the proceedings in the three Court-approved languages: Serbian, Croat and Bosnian. As his self-appointed defense lawyer, Milosevic would interrogate me in Serbian, while the judges′ working language would be English. The most absolute silence filled the courtroom. The same usher that had showed me in, reappeared from a lateral door and requested all, in French and in English, to stand as the judges, Patrick Robinson, of Jamaica, and O-Gon Kwon, of South Korea, dressed in their black robes with red shoulder stripes and white collars, entered the courtroom and took their seats. Judge Robinson then gave the floor to Geoffrey Nice, Chief Prosecutor in the case.

Prosecutor Nice Takes the Floor

In his initial remarks to the court, Nice introduced me as his witness for the day′s proceedings:

— "His name is Diego Enrique Arria Salicetti, a Venezuelan national, who was his country′s Ambassador and Permanent Representative to the United Nations during 1991, 1992 and 1993. He is a former Governor of Caracas and is currently Assistant Secretary General and Special Advisor to the Secretary General of the United Nations, Mr. Kofi Annan.

The judge then asked the usual question: "Do you solemnly swear to tell the truth, all the truth and nothing but the truth?"

— I swear, I answered.

Nice proceeded to inform that the judges and the defense had been given copies of my sixty-four pages long written deposition, a summary of what would now be my statement to the court and, turning slowly towards me, asked whether I confirmed all the accusations included in the document.

— "Of course I do!", I firmly stated, while he went on to remind me that in my testimony I stated that the international community's more important countries had withheld highly important information about developments as despicable as the Srebrenica genocide, and that I accused them of not taking timely action to stop the ethnic cleansing carried out by Bosnian Serb civilian and military authorities with support from Belgrade, in order to facilitate the illegal appropriation of a greater part of the territory of the independent republic of Bosnia. He also reminded me that in my written deposition I highlighted how the Security Council and the UN Secretariat fostered the climate of impunity that made possible the slow-motion genocide that took place in Srebrenica and surrounding areas where thousands of Bosnian Muslim men and male teenagers were massacred.

I cut short the Prosecutor and stated that I wished to confirm everything he had already summarized as well as each and every part of my deposition, no exceptions made: "All these denunciations are based on my statements to the Security Council more than ten years ago. I also wish to clarify that when in my testimony I refer to the existence of a vile culture of impunity, I stress that it was the result of decisions by the UN Secretariat and powerful members of the Security Council, who made it official UN policy. The absolutely unjustifiable coverup of Hakija Turajlic's murder on January 8, 1993, by Serbian soldiers while under the protection of French Blue Helmets, proves the point".

When his turn arrived to take the floor as his own defense lawyer, Milosevic did not waist time in formalities, and went on to reiterate his thesis about the origin of the Bosnian conflict:

— As you know, this unfortunate war was the consequence of the premature fragmentation of the Yugoslav Socialist Federation and the establishment of a number of small independent republics. Do you agree?

— I do, I replied, knowing that his questions would from then on require only a yes or a no for an answer, a litigator's tactic to avoid giving a witness room to expand on his testimony. That was the reason I then turned around and spoke directly to the judges: "As I state in my deposition, my country was always in favor of preserving the territorial integrity of Yugoslavia. We did so until the day Belgrade put an end to its policies in favor of the federation, as had been the case under Josep Broz Tito. The war in Bosnia started, as it had done before in Slovenia and in Croatia, by decision of the accused, a man who by initiating the Yugoslav wars in 1991 proved not to be worthy of any comparison to Marshall Tito. Let us recall that those wars included the long and brutal shelling of Dubrovnik, a Croatian town declared by UNESCO a World Heritage Site. Let me also clarify that I do not consider the Yugoslav people as a whole to be collectively guilty of the criminal practices fostered by the government presided over by the accused."

Ever since the very beginning of the trial, Milosevic insisted on characterizing the conflicts in the Former Yugoslavia as a civil war, resulting from the fragmentation of the old Federation. It was an argument I absolutely rejected. If that had been the reason, Serbia would never have been sanctioned by the Security Council, nor made the object of more than fifty resolutions by that UN organ. "The Yugoslav wars, Your Honors – I insisted – were not the result of domestic conflicts, but of an aggression initiated by the accused in order to annex to Serbia large parts of the other now independent republics of the Former Yugoslavia, preceded by their ethnic cleansing. It is because he unleashed all those wars, with all their terrible consequences, that the accused is here on trial."

Once again, Milosevic appealed to his worn-out interpretation of events, but Judge Robinson interrupted him:

— "Enough, Mr. Milosevic! – I have urged you several times not to insist on that point. It is not up to us, nor up to you, to define the true nature of those wars."

I could not let the opportunity pass. I argued that Milosevic employed a double thronged strategy. On the one hand, he went into unending perorations about issues that had little to do with the facts he was accused of, while on the other hand, he tried to put the proceedings in an exclusively political context. His strategy had succeeded in pushing back for years an international involvement in the crisis in Kosovo. It was only as a result of his troops' excesses that the United States and Europe's patience ran out. Only, in this case they did not appeal to the United Nations in search of an appropriate response but acted within the framework of NATO.

— Thanks to this fortunate decision – I added - today we have Mr. Milosevic with us. He was rejected by his own people, who put him in jail and sent him to The Hague to be judged by an international tribunal. To my relief, I must admit. As many others, filled with anxiety and a sense of urgency, I waited for the day when this would happen. I was greatly relieved when the Serbian people finally toppled him, tired of his abuses. Now I can rest at ease in the knowledge that, as it has happened with the accused, other war criminals still at-large will soon be here too.

Immediately, Milosevic replied that the Bosnian authorities had hired American public relations consultants to distort reality and that my participation in the trial was a part of that scheme.

I cut him short.

— "I am here, Your Honors – and I again turned my back on him and addressed the judges - to assist the Prosecution and with the sole purpose of making sure the crimes and atrocities committed under the orders or with the support of the accused do not go unpunished. That is the only reason I accepted to take part in this trial as a witness for the prosecution.

Then Prosecutor Nice intervened and asked me, for the benefit of all present, to clarify what impact had the many Security Council resolutions on Milosevic's and Serbian responsibilities in the start and conduct of the war in Bosnia had. To which I replied that almost none.

— "All those resolutions very clearly signaled that although the United Nations condemned the Serbian aggression on Bosnia, it would never take military action to stop it. It was the reason Belgrade just continued its attacks on an independent and sovereign nation, by then recognized as such by the international community."

However, nothing could make Milosevic deviate from his ultranationalist and heroic version of events, and he took every opportunity to repeat it over and over again. Only when I compared him to Marshall Tito very unfavorably did he appear to lose his composure, but very quickly recovered it. He always addressed himself to me with an air of superiority and indifference, and not once during the six hours that my deposition as a witness lasted, did he address me violently. He behaved as a psychopath absolutely convinced of his innocence would and also, as someone who knew it was not worth the while to challenge specific accusations because it was impossible to counter "the international conspiracy" against him. All his interventions focused on trying to discredit my testimony and to make me lose my patience. He asked me questions that were not such, but rather, pompous political statements that I naturally ignored. So much so that I asked the judges to tell Milosevic "To ask the witness questions and not political statements to which he, as such, has nothing to say." A call he did not heed. All along, he continued to try to enter into a political debate with me in the interest of conveying his political message to his devoted sympathizers in Serbia, who closely followed the trial on TV.

Since those six hours of questions and answers would make an exceedingly long and very boring book, I have tried to summarize and reorder our interventions as found in the trial's official records.

A Summary of my Confrontation with Milosevic

To avoid falling into Milosevic's strategy, I decided to give the judges a summary of the manipulations used to turn all the initiatives taken by the Security Council on the situation in Bosnia into a continued denial of facts, even if we all knew what was taking place on the ground, particularly since the return of our inspection mission to the theatre of war and our detailed report to the Council. It was, I insisted, a false contradiction. Ever since the conflict started, some members of the Council, notably France and the United Kingdom, feared the establishment in the center of Europe of a state with a Muslim majority, a prospect they felt endangered the region's political interests. They even chose to forget that Sarajevo had been the most multicultural capital in Europe and decided to blame for the conflict a false and supposedly ancient confrontation between Christians and Muslims.

The Non-Aligned members had watched with alarm how the Council's policy on Bosnia differed completely from that followed long before in the case of Iraq's invasion of Kuwait. In my remarks, I stressed that, beyond the political and human differences between both situations, Bosnia was just as much a victim of military aggression as Kuwait had been. The only difference was that Bosnia was not an oil producing country, and consequently its war had never been a priority for the international community. Therefore, the Bosnian government had to appeal to the International Court of Justice (ICJ) to ensure the Serbian state was indicted for its involvement in the genocide.

I then brought to the attention of the tribunal that on April 8, 1993, following Bosnia and Herzegovina's request for the adoption of Provisional Measures, the ICJ ordered the Federal Republic of Yugoslavia to take all measures within its power to prevent the crime of genocide, and to immediately desist from all acts of genocide, including, but not limited to: murder, summary executions, torture, rape, ethnic-cleansing, the bombing of civilian population centers, and the detention of civilians in concentration camps.

Milosevic´s reaction was defiant.

— "Mr. Arria. Is it not true that you are quoting only in part the International Court of Justice's decision? Do you deny that what you are quoting is the fabricated version of the conflict publicized by the Bosnian government with the biased intention of hurting Serbia´s position?

Addressing myself once again to the judges, I underlined that for the first time in its history the highest tribunal of the United Nations had taken a decision in a case of what I had termed slow-motion genocide, and that it had done so based on the overwhelming evidence placed at its disposal. I then added that I had indeed quoted the ICJ's decision only partially, "But, if Your Honors so wish, we could take time to read the Court's decision in its entirety."

Judge Robinson intervened to ask Milosevic whether he was referring to the possible similarity between paragraph one hundred and seventy-nine of my deposition and the text of the request for Provisional Measures made by the Bosnian government's legal counsel to the ICJ, a text that "In your view, cannot be attributed to the ICJ during this trial."

Milosevic immediately replied.

— Mr. Robinson, as you very well know and, given his diplomatic experience, I hope Mr. Arria equally does, when the International Court of Justice issues Provisional Measures, it does so only because it is under the obligation to abide by the mandates of the 1948 Convention for the Prevention and Punishment of the Crime of Genocide.

After allowing a long exposé by the accused on the issue, Judge Robinson finally interrupted and urged him to continue to other matters, reminding him that the judges were fully aware of the decision made by the ICJ, and that they "had already taken a decision about its relevance."

Milosevic changed his line of defense and now argued that he had never been informed of the atrocities his accusers said were committed in Bosnia. In response, I brought to the attention of the judges that in my deposition I recalled how the Ambassador of the Serbian government in Caracas had complained to the Minister of Foreign Affairs and President Carlos Andrés Pérez about my denouncing of those policies in both the Security Council's closed and open sessions. Therefore, the accused was made privy of the scope of those discussions and was "always well informed about the situation in Bosnia."

He now attacked me directly, arguing that my criticism of Boutros-Ghali for not fully sharing with all the members of the Security Council the information he was privy to, sent by high civilian and military UN sources deployed in Bosnia, "Was just another unfounded allegation by Mr. Arria." I had to remind the judges that even though the Security Council had named Srebrenica a safe area and placed it under the protection of UN Blue Helmets, during the inspection mission sent by the Council to the region in April 1993, we were unpleasantly surprised to find that the UNPROFOR military did not have the situation under control.

— "It was the Serbian military and the Bosnian Serb paramilitary who were in control of the situation in Srebrenica and in other parts of the Bosnia-Herzegovina border areas, a situation about which the UN Secretariat had not informed us at all. Neither had General Vere Hayes, Chief of Staff to General Morillon, who had accompanied us in Bosnia, whose true mandate, under instructions by the UN Secretariat or from his London superiors, was to hide information and to not allow us to truly ascertain what was taking place in those areas. It was then, Your Honors, that I came to understand why the UN had never before sent missions to a theatre of war. To gauge the scope of this situation it might be enough to recall that UNPROFOR, before entering Srebrenica, requisitioned all the photographic equipment the members of the delegation had with them. Only I disregarded the instruction and was thus able to take many photographs that I later gave to the Reuters' correspondent, who was part of our delegation, to be published later by international media. It was for the same reasons that the international press correspondents were not allowed to travel with us to Srebrenica, thus preventing them from witnessing how the city had become a huge concentration camp, in which the Blue Helmets, in practical terms, played a role similar to that of the *kapos* in Nazi concentration camps. These were all clear warning symptoms. It was very clearly possible to anticipate the genocide that would shock the world two years later. So much so that I could denounce it there and then as an ongoing process. Our mission report gave a detailed account of what we found, and it was presented to the Council on April 30, 1993. Today, I may add that the report was simply not debated or analyzed within the Council, a clear indication that the UN Secretariat and the Permanent Members chose to ignore reality to avoid being under the obligation to act in defense of the Bosnian Muslim population. No one can plead ignorance because the only crime that was not committed, as Bertrand Russell once said, was "The crime of silence."

Milosevic then asked me if my oral deposition was made to fit the interests of the prosecution and even loudly wondered if that was the role I had been given. His inability to respond to my accusations was such that I chose to simply ignore his insulting remarks. Addressing the judges, I once more reiterated that as a witness for the prosecution my testimony exclusively reflected the positions I had firmly held ten years before as a member of the Council.

— Your Honors – Neither in my written testimony nor today in my oral depositions have I added anything to what at the time I had denounced in the Council meetings. That is the reason why the accused, instead of giving straight answers to my denunciations, limits his replies to the allegation that my accusations regarding the UN Secretariat and the Permanent Members obey interests that don't have the truth as their goal, and that I maliciously blame Boutros-Ghali and his closest collaborators for hiding from the public most of the relevant information about Bosnia. Allow me then to take this occasion to reiterate that that was indeed the case: most of the information available to the UN Secretariat and to the Permanent Members of the Security Council about the situation in Bosnia was kept from us and from the public. That was why I had denounced it as the greatest cover-up in the history of the United Nations. So much so, that it is only today, here in The Hague, that I became aware that on March 18, 1993, Sadako Ogata, UN High Commissioner for Refugees, alerted the UN Secretary General Boutros-Ghali of an imminent humanitarian catastrophe in Srebrenica and urged him to report the situation to the leaders of the international community. Although obviously incredibly important, the situation was not reported to the Council by Boutros-Ghali, as he was dutybound to do. He certainly did not inform the Non-Permanent members. However, I am sure, You Honors, in light of what happened in Srebrenica, that even if Boutros-

Ghali had shared that information, nothing would have been done because the decision not to take any measure had already been taken by the main powers, as the Secretary General must have known.

Many might wonder why was it that Milosevic continuously defended Boutros-Ghali from my accusations about concealing relevant information on war crimes and human rights violations in Bosnia. His strategy was to portray me as an opponent of official UN policy and therefore as an unreliable witness for the Prosecution. Milosevic knew his line of defense would not impress the judges but, as I have already said, his interventions had little to do with the judicial proceedings against him and more with his country's public opinion.

He forgot that when on May 23, 1993, the Security Council approved the establishment of the International Tribunal, I had given my vote in favor, and had done so with the clear intention that all those indicted for serious crimes, as was now the case, be brought to trial. And anyway, it was not Boutros-Ghali nor any other leader within the international community who was on trial, but Slobodan Milosevic.

— Your Honors – The accused, whom I have for years denounced, is the only person indicted in this trial. To my knowledge, neither Boutros-Ghali nor other members of the international community are on the dock, although they certainly have much explaining to do for their irresponsible appeasement policy and their lack of actions regarding the enormous tragedy lived by the Bosnian civilian population. It was, if I may add, Mr. Milosevic who provided his Serbian Bosnian associates with the tanks, munitions, weapons and uniforms that proved to be so critical for carrying out the atrocities.

Milosevic interrupted.

— That is completely absurd, Mr. Arria. But let's continue.

And so, I continued.

— Allow me to add, Your Honors, that from the very first days of the conflict and of the plans to divide Bosnia into ethnic-based areas, the Serbians, with the support of the UN and EU-named mediators, had placed Srebrenica in the area Belgrade claimed as Serbian. That was the reason for the harassment of Srebrenica's civilian population, Muslim in its majority, and later on for the 1995 genocide. Ever since the Dayton negotiators agreed that the Srpska Republic would include Srebrenica, as was reflected in the maps of the future Bosnia-Herzegovina drawn up in Belgrade, the fate was sealed for the thousands of Bosnian Muslims in the town and in its surrounding areas. They had to be wiped out to avoid reactions against the illegal appropriation of those territories, an appropriation legitimized by the agreements. Only if this condition were satisfied would the Serbs agree to sign the Dayton agreements. It was non-negotiable, and thus President Izetbegovic was forced to sign. As he had warned, that was the price of peace in Bosnia.

Milosevic then asked me: - Do you mean to say, Mr. Arria, that the Dayton peace agreement was a bad agreement?

— I do not know how the accused feels about it, but I am certainly very satisfied to know that the death toll has ended. However, for the Republic of Bosnia-Herzegovina the Dayton Agreements could not have been worse. But we are not here to pass judgment on the international community, a pending task for a future better-informed public opinion. We are here to consider the crimes committed in Bosnia by its Serbian aggressors and, more particularly, the Srebrenica genocide.

An Ally of the Accused

After a brief recess, Milosevic referred to a report by Boutros-Ghali, unknown to all except himself, exonerating his government of responsibility for the dispatch of Serbian weaponry and military personnel to Bosnia. This allowed me to bring up and extensively quote Kofi Annan's November 1999 report to the UN General Assembly. In it, Boutros-Ghali's successor as UN Secretary General, states that the greater part of the Bosnian Serb army of the Srpska Republic was in its majority made up of officers and troops from the regular Serbian army, and that its artillery, tanks, airplanes and other military equipment, had been transferred by the accused to that false republic. Once more, Milosevic appealed to the Boutros-Ghali report, saying that Ambassador Peter Hohenfellner, who had been Permanent Representative of Austria to the UN and at the time President of the Security Council, had ordered the report not to be circulated among its members in order to ensure its exculpatory contents did not hinder the approval of the sanctions against Serbia.

The judges decided to put an end to the confrontation between myself and Milosevic since it did not provide any new input to the proceedings and called the British lawyer Steven Kay to the witness stand. Kay had been named by the tribunal as one of the three ***Amicus Curiae***, available to the accused to ensure his access to expert and impartial legal advice. These experts were allowed to perform a very wide set of tasks, including that of interrogating the witnesses. Taking advantage of this, Kay soon displayed a substantially different conduct, more akin to that of a defense lawyer than that of an expert counsel. His real colors showed as soon as he made his opening statement, a particularly dangerous one.

— Did you know – he asked – that President Izetbegovic, in early 1993, had prohibited the population of Srebrenica to leave since the number of refugees entering town had substantially swollen?

I replied that I did not have that information, although I had to admit I would not be surprised if the president took such a decision since most of the inhabitants of Srebrenica must have wished to leave a place where they suffered so much. Kay, however, using the same tactic as Milosevic, insisted over and over again on the same issue with the clear intention to make the judges doubt.

— Kay went on - I do not know how many inhabitants Srebrenica had at the time nor the number of refugees that it received within a short period of time. Maybe you can correct me, but I have been told that Srebrenica had a population of around ten thousand and that the sudden refugee influx was of more than forty thousand. Are these numbers correct?

— I cannot dispel your doubts – I answered – What I can tell you is that the population of Srebrenica before the war was between fifteen and twenty thousand inhabitants, and that when I visited in April 1993 its living conditions were not apt for even five hundred. Before it became an infernal war scenario, Srebrenica was a pleasant town for both its inhabitants and for visitors.

— But I understand – Kay insisted – that Srebrenica and its surroundings were designated as safe areas precisely because the number of refugees it sheltered went quickly over the town´s capacity.

— This is the first time I hear such an absurdity – I replied – Srebrenica swelled with refugees, but they were not there to visit. They were fleeing from the pitiless ethnic cleansing practiced by the Serbians wherever they went. And, for the record, Mr. Kay, I cannot understand why you refer to them as if they were just "imported goods," when in reality they were human victims forced to flee from Serbian harassment.

— Be as it may – Kay once more argued – was it not the horrible conditions relative to water supply, food and medicines and the lack of housing to manage this sudden and excessive population growth the cause of all that would later happen in Srebrenica?

— Of course not – I countered – It was the other way around. There was scarce housing because the continued pounding by Serbian heavy artillery deployed around Srebrenica had destroyed much of it. And there was no water supply, no medicines and no electricity, because the Serbian military authorities had cut the supply of all public utilities to the city. You cannot hide the truth with twisted arguments, nor by calling the victims "imported." The Serbian aggressors were the only ones responsible for the Srebrenica tragedy.

It was very unpleasant to have to confront Kay's cynicism. However, I could not ignore the perversity of his questions. Even less when he went as far as to lie to the court by arguing that the Bosnian Serbs defended the city from the daily attacks the Bosnian Muslims had been launching against it for years. It was the classic manipulation practiced by totalitarian regimes whereby the victim is accused of the very crimes it suffers. Kay's gross lies forced me to remind the court that during my visit to Srebrenica in April 1993, its defenders were armed only with light weapons, and at that, evidently old ones, as UNPROFOR had the opportunity to verify when it proceeded to unilaterally disarm the Srebrenica's Bosnian defenders. I reminded the Court how both José María Mendiluce, ACNUR's Representative in Bosnia, and Sadako Ogata, his superior ranking official, had informed us that in addition to the continued Serbian bombardment, it was the siege the town was under that had turned Srebrenica into a gathering place for the victims of the war of ethnic cleansing practiced locally by its Serbian aggressors.

— That was the cause, Your Honors, not the consequence. Based on that the Security Council passed the resolution declaring Srebrenica and then other neighboring towns and even Sarajevo, Bosnia's capital, as safe areas.

Kay finally changed the subject and went on to ask me why, after visiting Sarajevo, we went to Belgrade and met with Radovan Karadzic but not with Milosevic, the head of the Serbian government. I answered that we had chosen not to interfere with the negotiations that were underway at the time between Milosevic and the mediators, Owen and Vance. "We believed, as I still do today, that Milosevic's blind ultranationalist fanaticism was responsible for the crimes committed in Bosnia and in other republics of the Former Yugoslavia."

— Kay returned to the issue of Srebrenica and pointed out that Karadzic had offered to turn on the water supply and to give safe passage to humanitarian convoys and that "Doctor Karadzic's argument that in April 1993, given the obvious superiority of his forces and of the means at his disposal, he could have taken Srebrenica without much trouble", seemed convincing.

— Karadzic was not lying - I replied – We said so in our Mission to Bosnia report. However, it is also true that his forces were slowly but surely strangling the city, decimating its inhabitants. As I stated not long ago, a few days before storming the city, his forces already had total control over the enclave. When General Mladic finally entered the city at the head of his battalions, what he found was in reality an open jail. So much so that when I visited in April 1993, I had to do so in an armored UNPROFOR vehicle. Following us in another was General Hayes, in friendly conversation with Colonel Rodic, the Serbian military commander of the area. I was extremely embarrassed by the possibility that people might think that the Security Council ambassadors were friends and allies of their executioners. If that does not show the degree of Serbian rule and control of the city, I fail to see how else it could be explained.

Kay jumped from his seat.

— It is not the same thing to monitor the city streets as to control them, control its government, its infrastructure! – he said.

— Which streets is Mr. Kay talking about? – I asked the judges – In Srebrenica there were no practicable streets left, nor any infrastructure available. There were only people desperate because of the lack of housing, water, medical attention, food, and medicines, all of them defenseless victims of epidemics, of artillery shelling, easy prey for those taking the enclave by assault with absolute impunity. If Mr. Kay had been with us, he would not have said what he just said. By the way, the Russian ambassador to the Council, who was a member of the mission, notwithstanding his known alignment with Serbian interests, signed without any reservations the report in which we denounced the tragedy Srebrenica was living.

Judge Robinson, as might be expected since he had never heard Kay's interpretation of the living conditions and overpopulation in Srebrenica, asked me whether the unlivable conditions in the city obeyed to these or to other causes.

— Your Honors, Mr. Kay has offered quite a different vision of what was taking place in Srebrenica to what the reality was. Just to illustrate the point, allow me to inform you that five days before our arrival in Srebrenica, the same officer in command of the Serbian contingents that kept the city under siege, ordered a heavy mortar battery to shell a school. When we visited it, we saw in horror the remains of children, dismembered by the shells that hit the schoolyard. It was a horrific sight, and we would not have seen it had it not been for Mr. Mendiluce's, ACNUR's representative in the mission, private suggestion to demand General Hayes take us to that dismal scenario. To put it plainly: Srebrenica and its inhabitants were at the mercy of an army of assassins who believed, as Karadzic had publicly declared, that they had the city's Muslim inhabitants "trapped as rats." Your Honors, by April 1993, the inhabitants of Srebrenica hardly survived in the streets and had no hope at all of salvation.

Maybe to end the turn of the supposedly impartial Friend of the Court, Judge Robinson then gave the floor to Prosecutor Nice. He asked me how I could prove that the vision the accused and his defense team had given the court was absolutely contrary to reality, and that the alternative vision that I and other witnesses gave of the conflict in Bosnia was not part of a public relations campaign by the Bosnian government to have Mr. Milosevic indicted and condemned for crimes he had not committed.

— Your Honors, my vision of the conflict in Bosnia has nothing to do with a sinister propaganda campaign to cover up what truly happened. Since I became a member of the Security Council, I acted with the clear understanding that I represented my country in the eyes of the international community. I took it upon myself not to be a simple spectator, and not to silence the facts just to please the powers that be.

You can rest assured that was the difficult path I chose to follow in the Council when I took the seat reserved for Venezuela. For those reasons, I could not remain blind and deaf to the evidence of aggression that piled up on our desks. Today, everybody knows that the accused´s version of the events in Bosnia, starting with the genocide in Srebrenica, was totally denied by the report presented in November 1999 by Kofi Annan, currently UN Secretary General. In his report, Annan valiantly denounces the cover up by important sectors of the international community, including himself as Head of UN Peace Operations, of what truly happened in Bosnia. In this context, I must refer the Honorable judges to the many denunciations I made in the Council, in particular after having personally witnessed what the policy of ethnic cleansing practiced by the accused´s subordinates meant.

Judge Robinson then addressed himself to me.

—Thank you very much, Ambassador Arria. This brings your testimony in this trial to an end. You are free to go.

— Thank you very much, your Honors.

Satisfied to have done my duty, I followed the usher into the same small room where six hours before I had waited my turn as a witness for the prosecution. Carla Del Ponte, Chief Prosecutor, and Prosecutor Geoffrey Nice came to say their goodbyes.

The Verdict

Back in New York I gave much thought to what might have been my testimony´s impact on the trial. Of course, the moment I left the Court building in The Hague, I also left behind the enormous weight I had carried since the first call by Carla Del Ponte. I believed that my written deposition and my oral testimony before the Court had surely contributed somewhat to avoid the recurrence of such crimes. It was what had fueled the struggle of the governments of Cape Verde, Djibouti, Morocco, Pakistan, and my own, Venezuela, in the Security Council. For us, the conflict in the Balkans, more than a military crisis, was a moral issue. Even if Judge Robinson had dismissed me as a witness in the judicial proceedings, I would never be able to dismiss that experience from my conscience, probably the most hurtful experience in my international public life.

It was on June 16, 2004, that I first received direct news about the Milosevic trial. It came in a letter signed by Prosecutor Nice, who informed me that Steven Kay had presented a motion requesting the Court to withdraw the accusation against Slobodan Milosevic as a party to the crime of genocide committed in Srebrenica "In view that the prosecution had not presented sufficient evidence of his responsibility in that crime against humanity."

Nice went on to tell me he had forcefully opposed the motion and had appealed to testimonies similar to mine to deny it, enclosing a copy of the letter he had addressed to the judges. In it, he states: "In keeping with the evidence presented by Ambassador Diego Arria, head of the Security Council ambassadorial-level mission sent to Srebrenica in April 1993 to ascertain the situation on the ground and report thereon to the Council, the Srebrenica enclave remained encircled by Serbian forces from 1993 to 1995. During that time, dozens of thousands of Bosnian Muslim refugees survived in an overpopulated city in miserable and inhuman conditions. Consequently, the crimes committed during that time in that place allow us to reach the conclusion that the accused, Slobodan Milosevic, was fully cognizant of the intentions of his subordinates acting in Srebrenica and prove that the genocide that took place in July 1995, was time before clearly foreseeable."

To conclude, Nice informed me that the Court plenary had "Denied the motion raised by the *Amicus Curiae* and determined that the testimony given by Diego Arria had contributed to clarify the nature of the accused's responsibilities in the commission of the crime of genocide in Srebrenica."

Mission accomplished, I told myself after reading Nice's letter. And that night, I confess I slept like I had not for months.

Six years after my participation in the Milosevic trial, Judith Armatta, a lawyer who had followed all the proceedings as a representative of the Coalition for International Justice, presented her book *The Twilight of Impunity*, published in 2010 by Duke University. It is a true and fascinating guide to those proceedings and in one of its pages she recalls that it was I, in my condition as Ambassador of Venezuela to the United Nations, who called the attention of the Council to what was really happening in Bosnia, even if its more powerful members, as well as the highest UN officials, systematically covered it up. "The report Ambassador Arria presented to the Security Council as coordinator of the ambassadors' inspection mission to Bosnia in April 1993 led the United Nations to pass a resolution acknowledging that in Srebrenica a genocide was taking place and – Armatta goes on to say – widely quoted by the media helped to place Milosevic under the spotlight of international public opinion."

In her book, Armatta notes that "By answering Milosevic's questions during his trial at The Hague, Arria proved that since 1993 Milosevic was aware of the tragedy brewing in Srebrenica, and his testimony helped to strengthen the accusation against him and to raise awareness about the maneuvers made within the United Nations to cover up the truth about developments in Bosnia."

On her part, Florence Hartmann, a journalist at the French daily *Le Monde*, later on spokesperson for the Tribunal and advisor to Chief Prosecutor Del Ponte, in her book *Le Sang de la realpolitik, l'affaire Srebrenica*, notes: "Diego Arria, at the time Venezuela's Ambassador to the Security Council, and now Special Advisor to Kofi Annan in New York, took part in the Milosevic trial and highlighted that since 1992 very clear alarm signals were being sent about what finally came to happen in Srebrenica in July 1995. His testimony marked an inflexion point in the proceedings."

Postmortem

Back in New York, I resumed my work as Special Advisor to the UN Secretary General Kofi Annan. The Milosevic trial had made an impression on me. However, it never crossed my mind that less than a year after I would once more be at The Hague tribunal as a witness, only this time not for the prosecution but for the defense in the trial of the chief Bosnian defender of Srebrenica.

I received the "invitation" by an e-mail dated February 30, 2004, signed by the Bosnian attorney and writer Edina Becirevic, whom I had met somedays before at an international conference held in Stockholm on the sovereignty of nations. On that occasion she had mentioned that she was a member of the legal defense team of a Bosnian Muslim commander named Naser Oric, accused of war crimes committed in areas close to Srebrenica, adding that the prosecution had not been able to present evidence of his presumed responsibility in such crimes.

During the Milosevic trial, Steven Kay – the supposedly impartial Friend of the Court – had asked me whether I knew of crimes committed by Bosnians aggressors against Serb civilians in Srebrenica. Only later would I learn that he was referring to Oric, a Bosnian resident of Potocari, who had served in the police unit charged with Milosevic's security, and who in 1992 had been named commander of the Territorial Defense of Srebrenica by the Bosnian government.

During the tumultuous summer of 1992, after crossing the Bosnian border, a brutal ethnic cleansing campaign was conducted by Serbian military and paramilitary forces in the recently occupied territories. Muslim civilians were forcefully thrown out of their homes and an unending stream of refugees began. In search of protection, they headed towards Srebrenica. At the time, twenty-four years old Oric was at the head of a force of some two to three thousand men. Even though poorly equipped, the force kept the Serb invasion at bay for three years. For Beciveric, to have resisted this onslaught by well-equipped armed forces was truly a feat. She went on to ask me to return to The Hague as a "high-level" witness for the defense in the trial against Oric. The legal team was headed by Vasvja Vidovic, a former judge in a Sarajevo court, and the British criminal lawyer John Jones. She also included a December 2003 summary of the case against Oric, who was in detention in The Hague since April 2003, by the American journalist Stacy Sullivan, of the Institute for War and Peace Reporting.

I had absolutely no knowledge of the accused, so I answered Bericevic's invitation by requesting more time to gather impartial information about the case. I didn't mention it, but I also needed to inform myself about her. A few days later I replied declining the invitation. I could not be a witness for the defense of an individual about whom I knew practically nothing.

Becirevic was not surprised. "I understand your position -she said when she received my reply – and I want to clarify that we do not want you to come to The Hague to speak on behalf of Commander Oric. All we want is for you to tell the Court what you saw during your mission to Srebrenica in April 1993 on behalf of the Security Council." She then added that they were basing their client's defense on my thesis that a slow-motion genocide was taking place in Srebrenica at the time of my visit. "That will be the crucial point of our defense. You can state at the beginning of your deposition that you do not have any knowledge of Commander Oric, so your statement will not be to defend him from the imputed crimes but only to give the tribunal an objective vision about what life was like in Srebrenica when you visited."

I still had my doubts, so I decided to consult my friend, Judge Richard Goldstone, who had been the Tribunal's first Chief Prosecutor. He found no objection to my return to The Hague if that was the scope of my intervention. To the contrary, he said: "It will give more weight to your thesis about the slow-motion genocide." I then called Becirevic to inform her that I accepted the invitation under that condition.

Two weeks later, I met the Bosnian Muslim commander's legal team in Geneva. We spent the day together. They explained their strategy and the role I was to play. A month later, we met again in Sarajevo. This time, I had the opportunity to study for the first time some critical documents about the Serbian siege of Srebrenica.

The accusation against Oric was that his men had attacked some mostly Serbian villages in the neighborhood of Srebrenica to steal food and farm animals. The defense argued that Oric's troops in the area had always "Taken defensive actions and made desperate efforts to secure food, given that Srebrenica was blocked by Serbian forces and international humanitarian assistance could not get in," as I had verified in 1993.

The prosecution did not mention the fact that in reality those properties belonged to forcefully displaced Bosnian Muslims who had had to seek shelter in Srebrenica. And here were the Bosnian defenders accused of the atrocities committed by the Serbian aggressors! Oric was prosecuted for not having stopped his men from committing those abuses. The defense did not deny that some Bosnian defenders might have indeed committed crimes but insisted that the weight of the law should fall directly on those individuals. It also appealed to some of Jake Sullivan's reports to stress that it was "Thanks to the initiatives taken by Oric that Srebrenica was able to survive the Serbian assault for almost four terrible years."

The Trial of the Bosnian Defender of Srebrenica

I arrived at The Hague for the third time on December 2, 2004, now as an enthusiastic witness for the defense of the "Defender of Srebrenica". Informed about what had happened during those years in Srebrenica, I welcomed the opportunity to express my solidarity with the families of the Bosnian victims. I had no inkling of what the Chief Prosecutor, who had compiled an almost three-hundred pages file of infamous lies, had in store for me. Once again, following the same path I had taken ten months before during the Milosevic trial, I went to the Court building. And, as had been the case then, upon entering the courtroom by the lateral entrance reserved for witnesses, I saw Commander Naser Oric for the first time in my life.

The presiding judge was Carmel Agius, of Malta, joined by Judge Hans-Henrik Brydensholt, of Denmark, and Judge Albin Eser, of Germany. The Prosecutor was Patricia Viseur Sellers, of the United States. Judge Agius started the proceedings by saying that it was customary to address ambassadors as "Excellencies," and then asked:

— So, Excellency, would you mind being so addressed.

I answered, with a smile.

— Your Honor, please abstain from doing so.

He smiled back and immediately gave the floor to John Jones, one of the lawyers for the defense, indicating that copies of my written testimony at the time of the Milosevic trial had been made available to the judges, the prosecution and the defense. Jones' first question was whether I had been a witness for the prosecution in the trial against Milosevic in February 2004. My answer was affirmative, so Jones went ahead following the same line of questioning.

— Did you prepare your seventy-eight pages, four hundred and ninety-five paragraphs deposition with the Prosecution's assistance? In the last few days, have you been able to review your testimony from that time? Do you now confirm its veracity?

I, of course, answered affirmatively to all the questions. Then Judge Agius intervened to warn that my written testimony, although admitted in the Milosevic trial, could not be used to replace evidence in the current trial. It was then Prosecutor Sellers´ turn to ask questions. As she got increasingly engaged in the tense confrontation between the defense and the prosecution, she made evident, to put it mildly, her total ignorance about what had truly happened in Srebrenica.

— During your visit to Srebrenica, did you visit the Bosnian Police barracks?

— There were no police barracks.

— And the Hospital?

— Neither was there a hospital in Srebrenica. On the other hand, I did visit the school where the remains of twelve children were scattered throughout the schoolyard, killed by mortar shells fired by Serbians besieging the enclave; something you have not asked me about.

Sellers changed her line of questioning and asked me:

— On many occasions you have described the living conditions prevailing in Srebrenica; so, I ask you if to your understanding the people of Srebrenica did not live under normal conditions? That is what you have stated, is it not?

— Yes. As I have said before, the only thing I saw in Srebrenica was people suffering under the weight of miserable living conditions, particularly, women, children, and the elderly.

To counter my testimony, the prosecutor then showed a poor-quality video, filmed, according to her, by some peacekeeper in September 1993. It showed a group of people taking part in what appeared to be a folk dance. Sellers then cynically asked: "Mr. Ambassador. Do you think that the video shows that not long after your visit to the enclave its inhabitants lived a normal life once again?"

I was aghast at the prosecutor´s gall.

– Your Honors, I could never have imagined that I would hear such statements, more so in a United Nations tribunal. It makes unspeakable mockery of the traumatized people of Srebrenica. First of all, the video´s lighting is low, so the physical destruction of the city is not evident. What it does show is a small group of people dancing, five months after Srebrenica was declared a Safe Area in April 1993. What Prosecutor Sellers dares to call a celebration is most probably the honoring of life by a few, even if not a normal life. I find it admirable, and I believe it shows a greatness of spirit in the face of adversity.

At that point Judge Agius felt it necessary to intervene.

– Prosecutor Sellers, this looks like a place where there is poverty all around. A distinctly different group seems to be enjoying a banquet and drinking champagne, although it is not precisely that what the video shows among so much devastation.

The prosecution was undaunted, even after the call to attention by the judge. Untroubled, she stuck to her guidelines. It reminded me of Milosevic´s steering of his own trial. She did not waiver and kept to the same strategy of accusing the accusers as her only line of defense. She went on to ask me if I had not seen groups of Serbian refugees in Srebrenica, to which I replied that I had not asked the suffering people whether they were Serbians, Croats or Bosnians. They were people in pain, and that´s all.

John Jones took the floor and asked me why was it that I had stated that Srebrenica was a thorn in UNPROFOR´s body.

– Let me give you a few examples – I replied – Mr. Yasushi Akashi, the UN Secretary General Personal Representative in Bosnia, went so far as to declare that most of the inhabitants of Srebrenica were smugglers. I ask myself, what did Mr. Akashi think might have been smuggled out of Srebrenica, a besieged and closed-off city? Even worse, Major Peter Tucker, a British officer serving as Adjutant to General Philippe Morillon, writes in his diary that in a meeting with the Bosnian Serb

General Zdravko Tolimir, second in command to Ratko Mladic, Morillon said: "I know you want to wipe clean the nest of terrorists in Srebrenica. I can do it for you, and it will save you many, many lives." I was obviously scandalized by Morillon's proposal and even more so when, as it became public knowledge, he argued that that was the way to talk to the Serbs. "The way they best understood." If that was what those high officials thought about the people of Srebrenica it didn´t take much to imagine they would do little or nothing to protect them. To add insult to injury, General Vere Hayes, the Chief of Staff to General Morillon in UNPROFOR, in declarations to New York´s daily *Newsday*, praised Ratko Mladic, the very same criminal indicted by this tribunal for genocide, for his good will in withdrawing his troops from Mount Igman. Hayes dared to state something even more reprehensible: "Sarajevo might still be under siege; but in humanitarian terms, it has never been strangled." For this general, eleven thousand dead and thousands of wounded did not mean the capital was being strangled. Obviously not, for during quite some time, Hayes and other officers were busy searching for the tunnel built by the Bosnian government under the Sarajevo Airport, claiming that it endangered UNPROFOR troops stationed there, exposing them to Serbian attacks. So, please forgive me, your Honors, if I turn once more to the video presented by Prosecutor Sellers, for I believe it is a cover up. It amounts to another attempt to bury the Srebrenica people´s tragedy. Memory of its existence had to be erased in order to accommodate an international community highly responsible for the genocide that took place in an area declared a Safe Area by the United Nations. That the United Nations – an organization I was proud to serve – should have lent itself to something so vile and odious, makes me truly ashamed. And that a tribunal in the creation of which I played a role as my country´s representative should lend itself to show this video, hurts me even more. I find it truly damnable that the United Nations should have made a video of a group of people celebrating life in order to hide the suffering and generalized misery prevailing in that same community.

At that point, Judge Agius asked me whether the prosecution had shown me that video during the Milosevic trial. I answered that it had never done so. Agius must have believed that the prosecution avoided using the video when its interest was to strengthen the accusation, as was the case with Milosevic, whereas now it did fit its purposes.

I was tempted to add that if Sellers had been in charge of the prosecution in the Milosevic trial and appealed to the same false arguments she was now using, Milosevic would have been exonerated, since Srebrenica lived under normal conditions. Out of respect for the judges, I refrained from doing so.

Edina Beciveric, in her book *Genocide on the Drina River*, published by Yale University in December 2013, recalls my court appearance during the Oric trial:

> "In the International Criminal Tribunal for the Former Yugoslavia, the Prosecution tried to prove the crime of genocide committed against the Bosnian Muslims, while in the trial against the Bosnian Muslim Commander, Naser Oric, it denied it had happened. The Venezuelan Ambassador Diego Arria summed up the paradox in his testimony during the Oric trial by highlighting that the same Prosecution was of one position during the Milosevic trial and of the opposite to accuse Oric.
>
> During her counter examination, Prosecutor Patricia Viseur Sellers insistently tried to prove that Ambassador Arria exaggerated about the terrible living conditions in Srebrenica, arguing he had not been there sufficient time to verify them. To this, the Venezuelan Ambassador replied, directly challenging the prosecutor: "I find it remarkably interesting that your question is exactly the same Mr. Milosevic made when I was a witness for the same Prosecutor's Office you represent, although I cannot imagine that your question has the same implications. Milosevic told me I had been in Srebrenica only a few hours, not enough to have an expert opinion. I replied that it does not take much time to be in a position to give what he called an expert opinion, and that a few hours were more than enough to become aware of the inhuman living conditions in the city."

Contrary to what I had thought when I heard them, the opening questions by the defense lawyer John Jones proved to be far from innocent or superfluous. They went to prove that the Prosecution that assisted in the preparation of my written testimony in the Milosevic trial, in the Oric trial used the same arguments as Milosevic to deny that Srebrenica was living under a slow-motion process of genocide.

To witness the same Prosecution who in the Milosevic trial used my testimony to accuse Milosevic of genocide, allege a year later exactly the opposite was enough to sicken me. It was as though the court now needed to prove its impartiality by condemning a Muslim Bosnian commander no matter what.

Two days later, the tribunal acquitted Naser Oric. It upheld justice and, I would add, contributed to a redress of history to which I contributed by solemnly swearing to "tell the truth, all the truth, and nothing but the truth."

The Death of Milosevic

Contrary to what its title may suggest, this chapter is not a postmortem to the war in Bosnia. My concern continued to be how to contribute to clear the truth about what happened in the Balkans. There was still no independent and exhaustive investigation of the thousands of victims caused by the invasion and control of Bosnian territory by order of Milosevic. How could I contribute to make sure such events never took place again? Then, at around 10 am of March 11, 2006, I heard the news that Slobodan Milosevic had been found dead in his jail at the Scheveningen Prison in The Hague, where he had been held for the last five years, waiting for the tribunal to pass sentence on his case.

Only two years had passed since I had faced Milosevic in the courtroom of the International Criminal Court for the Former Yugoslavia as a witness for the prosecution. The six hours-long interrogation I endured had been an experience I retained in my memory in all its details and could not put behind me. As such, the news that this man, who for many years had made fun of almost everybody, now, by his unexpected death, had once again made fun of the tribunal and of justice, saddened me.

Soon after the news, Vojislav Kostunica, Prime Minister of Serbia, requested that the International Tribunal conduct a full investigation into the causes of Milosevic's death. He was sixty-six years old and suffered from chronic and severe hypertension. His widow, who lived in Moscow, asked that no autopsy be practiced on his body, alleging that "For his family, such a procedure amounts to a profanation." The Dutch authorities disregarded the request and the autopsy, including a toxicology analysis to discard the possibility of poisoning, was conducted at The Hague's Legal Medicine Institute.

Speaking from Switzerland where she was vacationing, Carla Del Ponte, declared that: "Milosevic had nothing to gain and everything to lose by living longer. By his death, he managed to escape justice. He went to the grave knowing that the Trial Chamber had confirmed the charges of genocide against him. Now, I hope that the Serbia and Montenegro authorities as soon as possible place under arrest and deliver to The Hague Ratko Mladic and Radovan Karadzic, Milosevic's two main associates in Bosnia, who are still fugitives of justice."

One week later, on Saturday, March 18, the former strongman of Serbia was buried in a private ceremony at Pozaverac cemetery, in his native city, less than a hundred kilometers from Belgrade. The President of Serbia, Boris Tadic, refused the family's request to have him buried "with State Honors" at the Alley of the Great, in Belgrade. Three days later, on March 14, the tribunal closed the case against Milosevic without a sentence. Judge Robinson would deeply regret this situation since it deprived him and all the interested parties of the natural outcome of an exceptional process since it was the first time that a Head of State had been brought to trial under international law for multiple war crimes and crimes against humanity. Without any doubt, Milosevic would have been sentenced to life imprisonment.

Radovan Karadzic is Apprehended

Several years would go by before the Serbian police would apprehend Radovan Karadzic on July 21, 2008, in a small village at the outskirts of Belgrade. He was the main executor of Milosevic's policies in Bosnia and the former president of the so-called Srpska Republic. Karadzic had been in hiding for eleven years. In the photographs disclosed by the Serbian government, he now appeared as an old man, even though he was only sixty-three years old. He looked extremely thin, sported a long white beard, a ponytail and huge black glasses. Under the name of Dragan Dabic, he had dedicated himself to alternative medicine treatments.

No matter his long criminal record, ten thousand Serbs took to the streets of Belgrade to express their solidarity with Karadzic and to accuse of treason the Serbian President, Boris Tadic, for his arrest, his immediate extradition and handing over to the International Criminal Court in The Hague. The popular reaction in Sarajevo was exactly the opposite. There too, people took to the streets but, in this case, to celebrate. Karadzic was responsible for forty-three never ending months of shelling and for the murder, committed by Serbian sharpshooters, of those who dared transit the streets of the Bosnian capital, particularly along the so-called "Sharpshooters' Alley." All such criminal activities had caused the death of more than eleven thousand civilians.

It is simply impossible to explain how Karadzic and other fugitives of justice had managed to elude their "chasers" for so long. Particularly so given that the search was undertaken by Interpol, NATO, CIA, and other European intelligence services. We now know that all these institutions considered those arrests to be inconvenient since many of those individuals were perceived as heroes by wide sectors of the population and benefitted from the complicity of the police and intelligence services of Bosnia, Serbia and Montenegro and, most likely, of the Serbian Orthodox Church as well.

Faced with this reality, the Tribunal´s complaints served little purpose. In the course of my visits to The Hague, Chief Prosecutor Del Ponte had confided that "The fact that Karadzic and other fugitive criminals have not been handed over is a monumental disgrace for Serbia and for the international community." The situation changed when the Serbian authorities, realizing that their country would not be admitted into the European Union unless this obstacle was first removed, finally undertook to arrest the international justice fugitives. Nine days after Karadzic´s capture, on June 30, the Serbian Minister of Justice, Snezana Malovic, approved the extradition and ordered his immediate transfer to The Hague. Notwithstanding this "gesture" by the Serbian government of the time, the country is still not a member of the EU.

At the time, Serge Brammertz, who had replaced Del Ponte as Chief Prosecutor, declared that "All the merit for the capture of Radovan Karadzic and his handover to the Tribunal, belongs to Belgrade." The Prosecution held Karadzic responsible for the shelling of Sarajevo and other Bosnian cities, as well as the murder of civilians by his sharpshooters in many other Bosnian towns. He was also accused of setting up more than twenty concentration camps, in Omarska, Prijedor, Trnoploje, and other areas of Northern Bosnia. The occupying Serbian military and paramilitary forces systematically carried out torture and sexual assault and murdered many of the more than thirty thousand men and women that went through those camps.

When he arrived at The Hague, Karadzic announced, as Milosevic had done, that he would be his own defense attorney. In his first statement as such, with great impudence, he declared to the press that he knew nothing about the Srebrenica genocide and that he was appraised of it "Only now, upon arrival at The Hague." He also claimed that he knew nothing about the shelling or the sharpshooters in Sarajevo "A town very dear to me." "Those murders were committed by the Muslim Bosnians not by the Serbs."

Six years after these and many other similar statements, on March 26, 2016, the tribunal declared Karadzic guilty and condemned him to forty years imprisonment for war crimes committed to achieve the "Extermination of all the members of the Muslim community of Bosnia". Karadzic remained in jail at The Hague during the next five years and was transferred to a prison in the United Kingdom in 2021, where he will serve the rest of his sentence. He opposed the "change of domicile" on security grounds since it was in Wakefield Prison, in West Yorkshire, that Islamic extremists had stabbed to death the Serbian General Radislav Krstic, who was serving a thirty-five-year sentence for his role in the Srebrenica genocide.

Karadzic's transfer brought back to me a poem of his, written before the start of the war, titled "Sarajevo." In it, he predicted the destruction of the Bosnian capital and glorified the death and destruction that Milosevic, General Mladic and himself, planned and conducted throughout many years with overwhelming cruelty:

"Enveloped in smoke,
Amid armed groups,
Sheltered by armed trees,
Our conscience flies high.
Everything in sight is armed,
All is men in arms, combat, war."

General Mladic, the Most Wanted, Goes Down

After sixteen years on the run, on May 16, 2001, General Ratko Mladic, known as the Butcher of the Balkans by millions of Bosnians, the other most wanted man on earth, was finally captured in the small town of Lazare, in Northern Serbia. The media reported that at the time of his detention by Serbian police agents Mladic was in possession of two high caliber pistols but made no attempt at resistance. President Tadic gave very few details about the police operation, only stating that his government had taken the decision to extradite Mladic for trial by the International Criminal Court for the Former Yugoslavia in The Hague.

— "Today, with Mladic's capture, a very difficult and somber period of our recent history comes to an end," President Tadic declared to the press.

For the Bosnian Serbs, Mladic was a war hero who had devoted the best years of his life to the safeguard of his people. For the Muslim majority, he was a criminal, responsible for their suffering and their losses during a pitiless war of ethnic extermination. With international public opinion in mind, Serbian propaganda had shown pictures and videos of Mladic handing sweets to Muslim children in Srebrenica's main square in July 1995, only hours before the beginning of the cold-blooded massacre conducted under his direct orders. However, chilling images of the horrors that took place in that enclave in that month of July are still available. In one of those videos, one can see and hear General Mladic harangue his soldiers using words that will not be forgotten by whoever hears them: "When I give an order, it is as if it came from God himself!" David Harland, a UN official, told me that in a meeting with UN civilian and military officials, General Mladic informed them that his instructions were to kill everybody in the Zepa, Gorazde and Srebrenica enclaves. When an overwhelmed Harland asked him: "Everybody, General?" Mladic gave it a little thought and replied: "Yes, everybody except the women and children."

When she heard about Mladic's arrest, Munira Subasic, Director of the organization Mothers of Srebrenica, a grouping of family members of the victims established in 1995 to keep the pressure on the investigators of war crimes, regretted that "Those who were murdered cannot witness his arrest". Her husband Hilmo, her sixteen years old son Nermin and twenty-two other members of her family had perished in the carnage at Srebrenica.

Mladic's arrest came at a crucial time for Serbia. Brammertz, the Tribunal's Prosecutor was on the verge of accusing the Serbian government of non-cooperation in the long-standing search for Mladic. His intentions were known in Belgrade and the arrest of one of the worst criminals in European history since World War II could not be postponed any longer.

Mladic´s arrest impacted Europe´s conscience just as Obama Bin Laden´s death impacted the United States'. It also represented a remarkable diplomatic victory for Europe.

Mladic asked for permission to visit his daughter Ana´s grave before boarding his plane at Belgrade airport. Ana had been a brilliant twenty-three years-old medicine student. She shot herself in the head in March 1994, when she heard her father had committed atrocities and other terrible crimes in Bosnia. Late that afternoon, Mladic entered prison. On November 23, 2017, he would be sentenced to life imprisonment. His lawyers appealed but the tribunal would confirm his sentence on June 8, 2021.

Mladic´s conduct during the trial leading to his conviction had been rude. He jumped and threw insults and obscenities at the judges and the prosecutors, as well as at many of his victims' family members who were sitting on the other side of the armored glass wall. When the time came, in 2021, he listened to his sentence revealing no emotion.

— I remain a NATO target – he simply said – This tribunal is a creature of the Western Powers.

The Legacy of the Criminals

The poisoned legacy left by Milosevic, Karadzic and Mladic continues to divide Bosnia. It is a malaise that lingers above its people, not as heavily though, as that produced by the international community´s betrayal which abandoned it to its fate.

The finger points at the United Nations, particularly for the pitiful performance of its high officials, and at the world powers that chose to put their national interests and those of their allies above the people of Bosnia and the defense of their basic human rights.

In 1993, the Government of Bosnia and Herzegovina instituted proceedings in the International Court of Justice against the Federal Republic of Yugoslavia for non-compliance with the 1948 Convention on Genocide. That same year, in my condition as Permanent Representative of Venezuela to the

Security Council, I was able to verify that the Court had formally notified the UN Secretary General, at the time Boutros Boutros-Ghali, that it had accepted the Bosnian government´s request. It was the first time a government was indicted by an international tribunal.

The Court ordered the Federal Republic of Yugoslavia (Serbia and Montenegro) to immediately take measures to ensure that no military or paramilitary units received official endorsement to attack, or to abet or commit acts of genocide against the Muslim population of Bosnia-Herzegovina, including murder, summary executions, torture, rape, ethnic cleansing, the siege and destruction of cities and the starving of its people, and to stop the bombing and shelling of its towns and villages and the internment of its citizens in concentration camps.

There can be little doubt that the Court's warning was also addressed to the UN Security Council, and that the Council should not have ignored it. But it did, because the governments of the most powerful nations in the world, that is to say, those that then and now exercise control over the Security Council, view genocide with the most absolute distaste and prefer not to even mention it. It was to counter this reality that the five Non-Aligned countries who were members of the Council – Pakistan, Djibouti, Morocco, Cape Verde and Venezuela – had to strenuously insist that the Court´s mandate be included in a Security Council Resolution. It was the first time in all the years of the Bosnian war that the term genocide had come up in a decision by that fundamental body of the United Nations. However, the Permanent Members managed to ensure that the crimes against humanity committed against the Muslim Bosnian population be defined as "ethnic cleansing," a term without legal implications under the UN Genocide Convention, thus exonerating the United Nations from taking action.

The Verdict by the International Court of Justice

Fourteen years had passed from the moment Bosnia instituted proceedings against Serbia in 1993 up to February 26, 2007, when the ICJ's President, Judge Rosalyn Higgins, announced its decision. The Court's sentence filled the people of Bosnia-Herzegovina with indignation and gave Serbia unexpected satisfactions. Although the Court acknowledged that Serbia had not "Fulfilled its obligation under the Convention to prevent the crime of genocide" committed in Srebrenica in 1995, nor its obligation to punish those responsible, and although it did not cooperate with the International Criminal Tribunal for the Former Yugoslavia by arresting Ratko Mladic, it went on to assert that "Serbia had not committed, conspired or been an accomplice to organs or individuals at its service in the commission of the crime of genocide as alleged by the plaintiff."

In other words, the Court conceded that a crime of genocide had been committed but it did not place responsibility for it on anyone.

The sentence went on to dismiss the idea of a "financial compensation," alleging it was not the "Appropriate way to redress a non-compliance with the duty to prevent the genocide." That is to say, even though the government of Bosnia-Herzegovina had a right to reparations, it had no right to demand them from Serbia, even though Serbia had not fulfilled its obligation to abide by the Court's mandate of April 8, 1993.

Notwithstanding all the well-known and widely broadcasted evidence, the Court went as far as sentencing that it had not been proven "That the Serbian State had the manifest intention to exterminate all or a part of the Muslim population of Bosnia", and that it could not be proved beyond any reasonable doubt that the government of the Republic of Serbia-Montenegro "Had been clearly aware that a genocide had been committed or was in the process of being committed."

The ICJ reached this absurd conclusion without even considering Kofi Annan's November 1999 report to the UN General Assembly, in which the UN Secretary General denounced that "The Serbian militia murdered in Srebrenica and surrounding areas about twenty thousand Bosnian civilians", a staggering number that includes twelve thousand assassinations committed before the July 1995 massacre. The Court not only ignored what happened during those three terrible days, it also incurred in the serious mistake of taking for granted that the Srebrenica genocide was the only mass murder committed by the Serbian military and paramilitary forces.

Moreover, the judgment passed by the Court inexplicably considered that the loss of at least two hundred thousand human lives and the forced displacement of two million people did not reveal a policy of extermination by the Serbian government against the Muslim population of Bosnia, in every way similar to the one applied by the Nazi regime against European Jews. The judgment not only trampled on the victims′ inalienable human rights, but it also contradicted itself by exonerating Serbia of the crime of genocide while at the same time making her responsible for not having prevented the Srebrenica massacre. It is beyond understanding how the Court could have passed a judgment denying Bosnia and its people a just financial compensation for the enormous damages it had suffered. In real terms, it amounted to a denial of justice.

After the verdict it was revealed that the ICJ had acted without considering all the information available in the Serbian public archives, relying basically on documents provided by the Serbian government itself, most of them heavily edited. As this was the first time a State was indicted under the 1948 Genocide Convention, it is truly alarming to note how the Court chose to adopt a complicit or accommodating silence in a case of such importance.

The British lawyer Geoffrey Nice, who had served as Chief Prosecutor in the Milosevic trial, issued a public letter to recall that he had opposed the infamous agreement between the tribunal and its Chief Prosecutor Carla Del Ponte and the Serbian authorities, "Allowing to cross out information from the documents and to not send files in its possession." This agreement allowed the Serbian government to filter the information it provided the Court and suppress any evidence linking the Serbian State or its authorities to the genocide in Bosnia. As Nice said, in its deliberations the ICJ considered only documents that did not have a bearing on "The Serbian national interest" and, I would add, that did not touch upon the interests of other governments closely linked to the process, such as those of the United Kingdom, France, Russia and the United States. Without any doubt, neither the judges nor Prosecutor Del Ponte came out unscathed, given their cooperation in the exclusion of documents potentially incriminating for the governments of all those nations.

Although I cannot prove it, I have always believed that the Serbian government might have offered Prosecutor Del Ponte to deliver the still fugitive Ratko Mladic in exchange for handing over censored documents.

The Perfect Crime

In May 2007 I took part in an event organized in New York by the World Federalist Movement-Institute for Global Policy on the implications of the ICJ verdict and took the opportunity to voice my particularly harsh criticism of the Court's deliberations. I still wonder whether the Court would have made a different decision if the edited parts of the documents had become known. It had happened before, in the Adolph Eichmann trial, when his notes at the Wannsee Conference, where the extermination of the European Jewry had been decided, had been used as evidence.

I also wonder what might have happened if the governments of the United Kingdom, Russia, France and the United States had cooperated with the Court and given it access to all the information gathered by their Intelligence Services during those troubled years. At the event, I expressed my absolute certainty that all the censored and not shared information would have proven beyond any doubt that Serbia had direct responsibility in the crimes against humanity committed in Bosnia and the Srebrenica genocide. I concluded stating that, in my opinion, the distorted presentation of true events was done to conceal the inappropriate conduct of the Permanent Members of the UN Security Council and of UN Secretariat´s officials, accomplices in silencing the scope of crimes that undoubtedly amounted to terrorist acts in the very heart of Europe.

All of this raises even more questions. What kind of conclusions might the Muslim world have drawn from all the manipulation by the powers-that-be – political and judiciary - of the truth about Bosnia? Alien to the monstrous racist apparatus raised by Milosevic, Karadzic and Mladic, what did the vast majority of the Serbian people think? The world deserves that the United Nations and its judicial bodies serve the purpose for which they were created.

The case before the Court was an extremely lengthy process. It lasted almost fifteen years and when the verdict finally came, it allowed the Serbian state to deny its responsibility about the events that devastated Bosnia as a nation and a significant part of its population. The Court missed an historical opportunity to condemn a state for its criminal conduct. It sacrificed fundamental principles and thereby left the international community and its judicial bodies bereft of the moral standing and dissuasive strength needed to prevent future repetitions of similar crimes in other parts of the world.

Although the Bosnian citizens are European, Europe did not treat them as one of their own, but as Muslims, an odious approach that will no doubt continue to have grave consequences. In this context, it might be appropriate to quote the dissenting opinion of Judge Al-Khasawneh, of Jordan, Vice-President of the ICJ, who stated his disagreement with the Court's "assumptions and methodology" to reach a decision and with its "extraordinary feat of absolving Serbia of its responsibility for genocide in Bosnia and Herzegovina." He complained that the Court had not demanded to have access to all the Serbia Defense Council documents and had raised no objections to Serbia's refusal to hand over the totality of those files, even after admitting the case against the Serbian government for war crimes. Some videos and photographs showing the extrajudicial execution of Muslim prisoners in Srebrenica by members of the Serbian extermination groups called "Scorpions" were considered to be only expressions of political nature and therefore were not accepted as evidence by the Court. Judge Al-Khasawneh concludes: "The involvement of Serbia, as a principal actor or as an accomplice, in the genocide that took place in Bosnia and Herzegovina is supported by massive and compelling evidence and, therefore, Serbia incurred in international responsibility for the crime of genocide."

The Court´s manifestly manipulated judgment did not reflect the impartial position of its fifteen magistrates but, rather, the interests of the governments involved in the case, which are, after all, the same that nominate them. When one is confronted by realities such as this, the Preamble to the United Nations Charter comes to mind. It is governments rather than "We the Peoples…" who are entrusted with upholding and enforcing the maintenance of international peace and security, and for this basic reason, the call for "never again" was once again silenced by the two tribunals entrusted with that mandate´s judicial implementation.

I have always held that in Bosnia-Herzegovina and, more specifically, in Srebrenica, a perfect crime was committed. Noel Malcolm, a British historian and academician, in his extraordinary book *Bosnia. A Short History*, published by New York University in 1994 and the best among the dozens I have read about that nation, comments how between 1992 and 1995 Bosnia was known only for the war that destroyed it, and not for being a unique country, with a culture and political traditions as no other country in Europe, and the place where Roman Catholics, Orthodox Christians, Jews and Muslims converged. Great empires came and went in those lands: Roman, Carolingian, Ottoman, Austro-Hungarian. Such an extraordinary and rich past was buried by a war that did not obey to ancestral racial hatreds but to a sordid combination of ignorance, prejudice and interests, all perversely fueled by the blind expansionist fanaticism of Slobodan Milosevic in Belgrade. Far from considering such a rich legacy as an advantage, Europe's political leadership considered Bosnia's fragmentation and the implementation of an abhorrent apartheid as appropriate ways to stop what they absurdly and unjustifiably considered to be the surge of an Islamic threat in the heart of Europe.

It was not by accident, and not just another act of war, that the Sarajevo Library was destroyed by the Serbian aggressors in August 1992. Incendiary bombs, not normal ones, were used for that attack. The same happened to the Oriental Institute, a study and research center holding an impressive number of documents and manuscripts from the Ottoman era in Bosnia. Those attacks were the deliberate attempt to erase forever the rich history and cultural heritage of a nation that was known for its ecumenic past.

Within the Security Council, ignorance prevailed about what Bosnia stood for. It was such a serious situation that my colleague, Ambassador André Erdos, of Hungary, had to explain to a member of the P5 that "Bosnia was not an invention of Marshall Tito". When I asked him whether he was addressing the British or the French ambassadors, he preferred not to answer. He did say, however, that ignorance about what the Balkan states were and had been had a decisive influence in the policy adopted by the Council to deal with the so-called Balkan wars. How differently might all those situations have developed if the protagonists had been better known and understood!

Be it as it may, the Council's lack of knowledge made a powerful contribution to the perfect crime into which the situation in Bosnia turned. There is no other way to understand the ICJ's evident denial of justice regarding Bosnia's legitimate claims. Or the fact that the very same nations that approved its UN membership as a sovereign and independent nation in May 1992, shortly after went on to propose its territorial fragmentation to effectively separate its population along ethnic lines. The very same countries that had managed to put an end to the shameful social and political policies that burdened the black population of South Africa, now fostered an apartheid regime for Bosnia in the name of peace.

When the Security Council left Srebrenica, Zepa, Gorazde Tuzla, Bihac and Sarajevo at the mercy of their executioners, after it had declared them safe areas under UN protection, it committed the worst crime in its history. The leaders that fostered the partition of the Republic of Bosnia and Herzegovina, the legalization of apartheid, and the legitimacy of the so-called Srpska Republic, were never indicted. Neither were the UN Secretariat officials who promoted and gave legitimacy to the spoliation of two-thirds of the Bosnian territory, nor the magistrates of the International Court of Justice who by their inexcusable verdict denied Bosnia and its people the reparations they deserved.

I have always been under the impression that some European leaders believed their decisions were taken in the same medieval Christian spirit that made the Crusades possible, as if Bosnia and Herzegovina were some sort of modern "Holy Land," and the West duty-bound to liberate it from Muslim infidels. It has allowed them to get away with the perfect crime, perfect because there are no guilty parties.

A TRAGEDY WITHOUT AN END

On October 7, 2021, the municipal authorities of Sarajevo awarded me the status of Honorary Citizen.

I first visited the capital city of Bosnia in April 1993, when Sarajevo was not even a shadow of its past and no longer the showcase of European political, religious, ethnic and cultural harmony. It was a city in ruins, devastated by a ruthless war. I had never been in a battle front, so those initial and atrocious images of the city - besieged during two years by its Serbian aggressors, bombed almost daily by the heavy artillery they had placed on the slopes of the hills surrounding Sarajevo, and the heroic defense its inhabitants were putting up, are forever etched in my memory, as is my admiration for its people. Therefore, the distinction moved me deeply.

My solidarity with the Bosnian population was further acknowledged the following day in Mostar, where I was awarded the Peace Connection 2021 Prize, bestowed annually by the Mostar Center for Peace and Multiethnic Cooperation to individuals for their outstanding efforts in favor of peace. It was an honor previously awarded to such distinguished personalities as Nelson Mandela, Václav Havel and the Secretary General of the United Nations, Antonio Guterres.

Following such significant gesture by my Bosnian friends, I traveled in the early afternoon to Srebrenica, two hours away from Sarajevo. I had been there for the first time in April 1993, as head of the mission the United Nations Security Council had entrusted to the representatives of New Zealand, France, Hungary, Pakistan, Russia and Venezuela with the purpose of verifying on the ground the realities of the war initiated by the

Serbian government with the perverse purpose of carrying out a policy of "ethnic cleansing", that is to say, of extermination of the non-Serbian population of Bosnia and Herzegovina. I was now returning for the third time to Srebrenica. I travelled in the company of my daughter Manuela and of Emir Zlater, a very dear Bosnian friend. Together, we visited the monument erected in the village of Potocari, at the outskirts of the city, in remembrance and tribute to the more than eight-thousand Bosnian civilians massacred in cold blood during a three-days orgy of blood and death in July 1995, an event since then known as ¨the Srebrenica genocide¨.

It was amidst the monument´s overpowering surroundings, a beautiful meadow strewn with thousands of white-painted monoliths at the foot of a hill, that I had a brief but unforgettable conversation with Munira Subasic, president of Mothers of the Srebrenica and Zepa Enclaves organization. She was in the company of other women, also members of the organization, and of the lady director of the Memorial. After exchanging polite greetings, they informed me that, two days before, an exhibit had opened of the shoes recovered from the pits where both adult men and teenagers had been buried, murdered in that very same place. The Dutch Blue Helmets battalion deployed in the area had made no effort to save their lives.

I had met Munira Subasic in 2005, on the tenth anniversary of the genocide, and we were to meet again once more, ten years afterwards, on the twentieth. On both occasions I felt a knot in my throat but none so tight as the one I felt that afternoon when she asked me why, in April 1993, I had declared to the international media, standing by what was left of the city´s Town Hall, that a slow-motion genocide was taking place right there and then.

"And how was it – she asked me – that you anticipated what was going to happen two years after?" The same question had been put to me the day before in Sarajevo by the Great Mufti of Bosnia and Herzegovina.

My answer to both was dictated by my recollection of the horrors I witnessed in the streets of that city on that terrible day of April 1993, a reality much more despicable and terrorizing than the worse nightmare.

"You had to be blind – I told them - not to see what would soon happen if nothing was immediately done to prevent it. To have witnessed such horrors made me realize that what was then happening in the very heart of Europe represented an extraordinary challenge to the fundamental values of the United Nations, which we were sworn to uphold. That was the reason why, speaking from this very same place, I had declared that, as representatives of the United Nations Security Council, the world's preeminent political body, we were in Srebrenica to reiterate our commitment to protect them, and that we would do so. It was a promise that, to my shame, we unfortunately were unable to keep and that I have since found impossible to forget."

I understood that afternoon that it was shame that drove me to get involved much more actively and militantly in the conflicts that were debated in the world and deepened the moral obligation that has driven me since then, not to fall into the comfortable temptation to cover up by silence the truth about the Bosnian tragedy and about so many other unpalatable realities. I also understood that in shame lays the reason for authoring this book. By this, at least, I hope to settle accounts with history.

Ingram Content Group UK Ltd.
Milton Keynes UK
UKHW041553010623
422714UK00001B/89